The Struggle for
Black Political Empowerment
in Three Georgia Counties

The Struggle for
BLACK POLITICAL EMPOWERMENT
in Three Georgia Counties

LAWRENCE J. HANKS

The University of Tennessee Press

Library of Congress Cataloging-in-Publication Data

Hanks, Lawrence J., 1954–
    The struggle for Black political empowerment in three Georgia
counties.

    Bibliography: p.
    Includes index.
    1. Afro-Americans—Georgia—Suffrage. 2. Afro-
Americans—Georgia—Politics and government. I. Title.
JK1929.G4H36 1987   324.6'2'089960730758   86-24987
ISBN 0-87049-521-6 (alk. paper)

To my Wife, Daughter, and Son—
Diane, Shonda, and Julius
Because of their understanding, patience,
support, sacrifice, and unconditional love. More
than anyone, they have gone through the valleys
and over the mountains—not always in the best
of moods but always supportive, loving, and
willing to see what the next day would bring. I
thank God for each of them. I will love them
always—and two days after.

Contents

Tables

Preface: The Quest for Black Political Empowerment

The Voting Rights Act of 1965 removed the last legal barriers to black voting in the South. After over ninety-five years of pursuing access to the ballot following passage of the Fifteenth Amendment, the theorists of black political empowerment were no longer hindered from becoming practitioners. Given the realistic expectation that efforts towards black political empowerment would not receive substantial support from the white community, their goal was to gain proportional representation, i.e., if blacks constituted 50 percent of a population, they hoped to see them holding 50 percent of the elected offices in that particular political jurisdiction.

The theorists of black political empowerment argued that once blacks gained access to the ballot in predominantly black areas, they would elect other blacks to political offices. These newly elected officials would enact public policies favorable to the black community, and the socioeconomic status of the black community would rise. Thus, black political empowerment called for more than just having black faces in office—these officials were supposed to have an impact on the status of black life.[1]

The black political empowerment process, then, has, in theory, three measurable phases: (1) blacks holding offices in proportion to their numbers in the population; (2) the enactment of public policies favorable to the black community; and (3) the rise in the socioeconomic status of the black community. In most political jurisdictions across the black belt South, this process has not even reached phase one. The political transformation, i.e., the change from all white elected officials to black proportional representation, which was supposed to have been facilitated by the Voting Rights Act of 1965, is still a dream—not a reality. This book seeks to explain why this transformation has not materialized and also to explore how such a goal can still be reached in the future.

To fully appreciate the gravity of the failure to reach the first phase in the political empowerment process, one must understand that a tremendous amount of resources was directed toward gaining access to the ballot. Black access to the ballot was considered to be crucial by those who took the instrumentalist view of the black political empowerment process. To have gained that access and still not to have realized phase one—blacks' holding office in proportion to their numbers—has been a severe disappointment for those who argued for the validity of the black political empowerment theory.

The instrumentalist approach to politics had at its core the thesis that black political participation could be used as a tool for improving the socioeconomic status of blacks. The rationale for this approach rested largely on the powerful case that can be made for the government's having traditionally played either a facilitative or repressive role with regard to black efforts toward political, social, and economic equality. Chapter 1, while tracing the development of the instrumentalist strategy from its inception to its contemporary form, examines the contradictory roles the government has assumed—from the legitimation and codification of slavery through the legislation of the Second Reconstruction which made the modern quest for black political empowerment possible.

Chapter 2 reviews the literature that addresses the problem of black political participation since the passage of the Voting Rights Act of 1965. This is the appropriate literature to consider because the overwhelming majority of black politicians is elected primarily by black voters. In other words, if one is interested in accounting for the presence or absence of black elected officials, one would have to study the political behavior of those who place them in office.

The literature on black political behavior can be divided into two major categories: (1) the micro-behavioral literature focusing on individual aspects of participation and (2) the macrostructural literature that focuses on the contextual aspects of participation. This literature does not explain the various levels of black proportional representation in black belt Georgia, a state with twenty black majority counties. It will be postulated that the literature on collective action explains more about black proportional representation than the forestated literature. The collective action literature suggests that the interrelationship between leadership, organization, and resources will provide the best explanation for the various levels of black proportional representation. Three case studies are offered in support of this thesis.

Chapters 3, 4, and 5 are case studies of three black belt Georgia counties: Hancock, Peach, and Clay, during the period 1960 to 1982. The areas examined provide examples of black belt counties with three different rates of black proportional representation from 1972–82. Hancock averaged fourteen black elected officials per year; Peach averaged six, and Clay had zero. The case studies of Hancock, Peach, and Clay reveal the ways in which leadership, organization, and resources were pivotal in the black political empowerment process.

Chapter 6, a comparative analysis of the empowerment processes in Hancock, Peach, and Clay, serves as a summary of the salient characteristics of each county and further illustrates the important differences and similarities of the key organizational features of each county.

The epilogue offers some brief concluding remarks. Whereas the primary attention of this entire book is on the disempowered black community, the epilogue focuses on the debate concerning the effectiveness of black elected officials as a means of facilitating black socioeconomic advancement.

Acknowledgments

This book actually began during the summer of 1964 as I diligently drilled my father with questions from the Georgia literacy test. When I learned that blacks had to take this test while whites did not, I began asking questions about politics and its impact on race relations. I have been asking them ever since. A number of people have nurtured and sustained me from that hot, muggy day in southwest Georgia to the present time. Without these people, my life would be far less meaningful, and I could not possibly miss this opportunity to acknowledge their help.

My teachers at the Asbury Speight Elementary and High School had a significant impact on my career ambitions: the late Gazzie Thornton Bankston encouraged me to question; the late Frankie J. Bradley, my eighth-grade history teacher, was a living example of triumph in the face of racial oppression; and Linda Smith, Katherine Lewis, and the late T. I. Johnson convinced me that I could become a "Morehouse Man."

"The Morehouse Years" were the salad days—days of fun, pain, and growth. Gabrielle Hubert, Paul Guynes, Abraham Davis, and Robert Brisbane encouraged me to pursue graduate education. For their continuous encouragement, I will always be grateful. Adverse Ponder, Vincent Stovall, Reginald Capers, Oliver Robinson, Derrick Dunn, Larry Calhoun, Horace Allen, Dwayne Reed, better known as "The Graves Hall Rat Patrol," became my brothers—they set a standard for friendship that few have been able to meet. Our adopted dorm mother, Mrs. Estelle Stovall, helped us to understand that the positive attributes of family had little to do with family trees and bloodlines—these attributes are largely functions of trust and experience.

The Harvard years were years of re-examination. The objective goal of those years was to obtain the Ph.D. in political science, and I feel a sense of tender affection and thankfulness to those who helped me along the way. After I literally fell through her office door one cold January day in 1980, Ethel Klein and I began discussing my research interest. She agreed to advise me, and, from that day forward, she was an invaluable counselor. Moreover, she made me appreciate the difficult task of balancing teaching, scholarship, family, and friendship.

There are other individuals who helped me directly with my dissertation: Martin L. Kilson provided a tremendous amount of support—he was always there when it counted. Donnie Bellamy made life quite comfortable for me in Peach County; my Kappa Alpha Psi brothers in Hancock County were truly brotherly in the PHI NU PI sense of the word (PHI NU PI is Kappa jargon for something that we don't want you non-Kappas to know about); the Southern Regional Council and The Voter Education Project provided the experience which led to my research choice; and the Whitney Young Foundation subsidized my endeavors.

My graduate school experience made me constantly examine why I was pursuing such a seemingly elusive goal. I inherited the perseverance to continue from my family, who, in many ways, were responsible for my academic career.

My parents, James and Kathleen Hanks, by example as opposed to theory, showed me and the rest of my sisters and brothers what their expectations and values were. For both of them, I am thankful.

My mother encouraged me to critically analyze current events from an early age. Her perception of me as a bright, precocious political analyst at the age of eight is perhaps the major reason for my choice of political science as a field of study.

My father, an unlettered man with an intuitive intelligence often missing in many trained minds, always encouraged his kids to pursue education. Despite the fact that he would have loved for one of his three sons to take over the farm one day, he never actively dissuaded any of us from following our own dreams. For this, Dad, I thank you.

My sister Frances was an ideal academic role model. When she graduated from Tuskegee University, I was about nine years old, but impressed by the pomp and circumstance nonetheless. When she received her M.A. from New York University, she made sure that I was there. She has always been there to encourage and to aid wherever possible. This is simply to thank you, Sis, for the encouragement, the SAT studying manual, the trip to the United Nations building, the typewriter that got me through college, and most of all, your faith in me.

My other sister, Carolyn, was my first teacher. Disobeying all the rules about what kids could learn at certain ages, she would teach as long as I would ask. She would bend twigs from shrubs to form alphabets and write big alphabets on the dirt road in front of our house to make learning fun. Thank you, Sis, for believing in me so soon.

My brother Paul was born with a Ph.D. in electronics. If it can be put together or torn apart, he is capable of doing both well. He was one of my biggest fans while I was in graduate school. In fact, we have somewhat of a mutual fan club: he admires my patience and persistence while I admire his valuable practical skills—he was in my corner all the way.

My other brother, Hasan, always encouraged me to seek truth for myself. He often said, "The world is so vast with so many cultures and belief systems, how can someone else tell you what is right for you." For this sound advice, I will always be grateful.

My graduate school experience would have been far less meaningful without the friendship of the following people: Brenda Hunter, Cathy Hunter, Oliver Hunter, Livia Sapp, Walter Dogan, Mark Hamilton, Willie Woodruff, and Adlai Pappy. It would take volumes to express what their friendship has meant to me—a mere mention will have to suffice.

The dissertation could not have been transformed into a book without the help of Diane and Shonda Hanks, my wife and daughter respectively. Additional support came from the administrators, faculty, staff, and students of Tuskegee University. Chief among them are: Benjamin Payton, Ollie Williamson, William O. Jones, Mary A. Jones, Avery Webber, Lorraine Freeman, Debbie Morris, Carl Morris, Jill Hill, Walter Hill, Frederick Patrick, Roderick Van Royal, John Steele, Lynda Murray, Stuart Chavis and Kevin Sears.

I have experienced much since that hot, muggy day in southwest Georgia. To those, named and unnamed, who have helped me along the way, I am eternally grateful.

Lawrence J. Hanks
July 1986

1. Historical Background: The Development of the Instrumentalist Strategy

The strategists of the post–World War II civil rights movement found the rationale for their instrumentalist strategy in the promise of democratic theory and in the practice of the United States government. From the time that black Americans arrived in this country, the government had acted either as a facilitator, a repressor, or both, with respect to the quest of blacks for political, social, and economic parity. Hence, the proponents of instrumentalist politics viewed black political empowerment as a way of increasing the odds that the government would act as a facilitator.

The instrumentalist approach to politics that gained widespread legitimacy during the postwar civil rights movement was not a new strategy. The roots of instrumentalist black political participation lie deep in the history of the relationship between black Americans and our democratic political system. Focusing on the historical periods between the founding of the nation and the massive southern resistance movement, Piven and Cloward provide a vivid description of that relationship:

In each period ascendant elites employed the powers of the national and local governments to enforce the subjugation of blacks. The entire apparatus of government—its legislatures, its judiciaries, its executive branches—has been mobilized to perpetuate caste arrangements in the South and segregation and discrimination in the North. Legislatures enacted laws to deprive blacks of political rights and refused to prevent institutions from depriving blacks of economic and social rights; the courts wove a net of opinions which legitimized the actions of other branches of government and of private institutions; and the executive levels of government employed their powers, especially police powers, to enforce the interests of private elites in exploiting the black labor force.[1]

The history of black Americans may be divided into five major periods preceding the post-WWII Civil Rights Era (1955–68). The periods are as follows: (1) The Pre-Slavery Era (1619–41); (2) The Era of Slavery and the Civil War (1642–1865); (3) Reconstruction (1865–77); (4) The Nadir (1877–1909); and (5) The Era of the NAACP (1910–54).

This chapter examines the degree to which the United States government played a facilitative or repressive role during each of these periods. It further examines the development of the theory of black political empowerment as the government began to facilitate social change after the *Brown Decision* of 1954.

The Pre-Slavery Era (1619–41): Blacks as Indentured Servants

The first blacks in American colonies were not slaves–they were indentured servants. Since there was no precedent in English law for slavery, the first twenty blacks brought to Jamestown in August of 1619 were accorded the same status as white indentured servants.[2] These pioneer black colonists interacted on a basis of equality. Although blacks were also objects of curiosity because of their different racial features, this curiosity was initially benign—it did not manifest itself in the form of discriminatory laws. Blacks and whites lived, worked, and socialized together on an equal basis.[3]

These first black colonists were making their strides towards the American Dream. As they completed their indentured servantships, many of them began to accumulate money, property, and their own indentured servants. Blacks voted in eleven of the thirteen original colonies and held minor political offices. However, this upward climb was not to continue unchecked. Between 1619 and 1664, slavery was made legal in six colonies, and the colonial courts facilitated and legitimated the status of blacks as "slaves." Thus, it became apparent that those who held political offices had the power to make changes.

The popular colonial perception of blacks as "different" and "exotic" laid the foundation for the eventual legal codification of slavery. The first black "settlers" were from an entirely different continent than the white settlers; their language and customs were different; and their darker pigmentation set them apart. These differences were eventually translated by their fellow settlers to mean inferior. When the white settlers began to experience labor shortages, the notion of black inferiority became a convenient rationale for black enslavement. Moreover, blacks as slaves offered advantages that white indentured servants and Indians did not: (1) they were a highly visible group that could not hide in the general population; (2) although they had a history of agricultural life in Africa, they knew little of the surrounding countryside (this served as a disincentive for running away); and (3) as they had no country to appeal to, blacks could be treated in any fashion without danger of there being repercussions.[4] Thus, blacks were consummate slave material. Beginning with the *Hugh Davis Case* (1630), the courts began to give the popular notion of black inferiority legal sanction.[5]

Hugh Davis was a white male Virginian. He was brought to court for having had sexual relations with a black woman. The court ordered that he would be whipped for "defiling his body in lying with a negro."[6] Thus, the Virginia courts began to lay the basis for the legal legitimation of the notion of black inferiority.

One manifestation of the deteriorating status of blacks after 1619 was their extended terms of indentured servantship. Fabricated infractions of contracts were commonplace as reasons for extending the term of the contract. The *John Punch Case* (1640) is illustrative of this phenomenon. John Punch, a black indentured servant, ran away with two white indentured servants. The three servants were apprehended and taken to court. The two white indentured servants were sentenced to four additional years of labor beyond their initial seven-year contract. John Punch was sentenced to "serve his master or his assigns for the time of his natural life." In other words, Punch was a slave for life.[7]

After 1640, blacks could not be indentured servants. When they came to the colonies, they came as slaves. The *Manuel Case* (1644) illustrated the continual pattern toward codification of this trend. Manuel, a mulatto, had been purchased as a "slave" by a Thomas Bushrod. Manuel sued for relief, and the case was presented to the Virginia Assembly. They ruled that he was not a slave. Nonetheless, they required him to continue to serve Bushrod for twenty-one years, an unusually long term of service.[8]

The Era of Slavery and the Civil War (1642–1865)

Beginning in 1630 with the *Hugh Davis Case,* the colonial courts laid the foundation for the statutory recognition of slavery. Massachusetts was the first colony to give such recognition to slavery in 1641. Other colonies followed: Connecticut, 1650; Virginia, 1661; Maryland, 1663; New York and New Jersey, 1664; South Carolina, 1682; Rhode Island and Pennsylvania, 1700; North Carolina, 1715; Georgia, 1750.[10] The passing of such statutes later provided the rationale for the instrumentalist approach to understanding politics: because black subordination was facilitated and legitimated by the government, it followed that overcoming this subordination would require political participation by those who opposed the subordination. Thus, as the groundwork for black subordination was being laid, so was the intellectual foundation for overcoming this subordination.

As the colonists approached the Revolutionary War, slavery was accepted as an integral part of the colonial economic system. Save for the Quakers who formed the Society of Friends in 1688 and became a pioneer group in opposing slavery, there was little organized white opposition to slavery. Although black resistance was not rare, popular rationalizations held that blacks were happy with their condition. However, the colonists' struggle to be free brought out the irony of their having slaves. It was not difficult to see the contradiction between the protests and the practices of the white colonists. They delegitimated their own claims to freedom as long as they denied freedom to others. This persuasive logic gave the abolitionist movement momentum and enabled it to attract new members to its cause.

In addition to such philosophical arguments, actual events, like the martyrdom of Crispus Attucks, had a galvanizing effect on the abolitionist movement: a black man had been the first to die for America's freedom when, in actuality, he himself was not free—he was a fugitive slave. Moreover, some five thousand blacks fought in the Continental forces.[11] This created a great embarrassment for the colonists. Would they continue to hold men in bondage who had fought for their independence? Despite the irony of the situation, the answer was yes.

When the colonists gained their freedom and independence from the British in 1776, slavery was legal in all of the independent states that would eventually become united. With the black population of 570,000, out of a total population of 2,500,000, approximately 20 percent of the people of this soon-to-be-united nation were slaves in a nation founded on democratic principles: 40,000 of the blacks were "free persons of color."[12]

The Declaration of Independence was the philosophical expression of the democratic ethos on which the Revolution was fought, and it expressed the idealized values of a democratic republic. The following famous passage is rich in its explication of democratic principles: " . . . We hold these truths to be self-evident, that all men are created equal, that they are endowed by their Creator with certain unalienable Rights, that among these, are Life, Liberty, and the pursuit of Happiness. That, to secure these rights, Governments are instituted among Men, deriving their just powers from the consent of the governed . . . "[13] Thus, the notion of equality, unalienable rights, and government by consent of the governed became cornerstones of American democratic philosophy.

Nonetheless, the gap between the ideal and the real was obvious. This basic belief in human equality was contradicted by the existence of a 20 percent slave population, who had no social status, no respect as legitimate human beings, and no political rights. Slave life varied tremendously according to plantation, locale, and era. However, the general rule was that slaves had no civil rights. There were slave codes which protected them from excessive cruelty and required them to be supplied with the necessities for health; but, for all practical purposes, these codes were more beneficial to the masters than the slaves. Richard Bardolph offers us a standard depiction of black civil rights during slavery:

Blacks could not testify against whites in court; they could be put to death for offenses against whites which, if committed by whites against blacks, commonly drew little more than a reprimand, if indeed the courts took notice of them at all. Slaves and free Negroes were commonly required to step aside at a white man's approach, and when a slaveowner's property rights in his servant collided with the latter's slender legal rights as a person, property rights usually prevailed. Blacks were forbidden to carry firearms, to hunt, to possess liquor, to assemble in groups of more than four or five except for certain specified purposes, to own horns, whistles, drums, or any other devices which could be used as signals. They were forbidden to leave their owner's plantation without a written pass, and were subject to early curfews. Even their marriages had no status in law, and could be arranged, dissolved, or rearranged with new partners, at their owners' pleasure.[14]

Free southern blacks were not much better off than the blacks in slavery. Newly freed slaves were required to leave many southern states and many free blacks were re-enslaved due to legal maneuvering and their lack of legal rights. There were vocational limitations concomitant with their inability to receive any type of formal education. Blacks in the antebellum South were certainly not considered equal to other citizens; free blacks had few, if any, more rights than their enslaved counterparts; and blacks in the North were not treated as equal citizens. Thus, at the time of the writing of the Declaration of Independence, the theoretical notion of human equality was not supported by any popular notion that blacks were equal to whites in the American democracy.

The unequal status of blacks in the social, economic, and especially, the political arena led to a denial of their unalienable rights to "life, liberty, and the pursuit of happiness." Slavery, unequal treatment under the law, the unpunished destruction of black lives, and Jim Crow legislation represented the failure of the American government's ability to secure the unalienable rights of life and liberty for black Americans. Without the assurance of being free and reasonably confident that one's life is not threatened, the pursuit of happiness becomes difficult—if not impossible.

The idea of governmental legitimacy being based on the consent of the governed was developed by John Locke. In his *Of Civil Government*, Locke states that "the liberty of man in society is to be under no other legislative power but that established by consent in the commonwealth . . . nor under the dominion of any will, or restraint of any law, but what the legislature shall enact according to the truth put in it."[15]

This idea was incorporated into the Declaration of Independence when Jefferson stated that "governments are instituted among Men, deriving their just powers from the consent of the governed." Since the denial of the black franchise constituted a lack of consent, the American government was illegitimate by its own philosophical standards.

The presence of blacks in the American polity produced a strong tension between the democratic principles espoused by the Declaration of Independence and the actual status of blacks within this democracy. These tensions would proliferate with the drafting of the Constitution of the United States. Robert Dahl asserts that " . . . the tension between the effort to maintain a democratic republic and yet deny political equality to Afro-Americans has dominated political life in the country from the Constitutional Convention to the present day."[16]

Whereas the Declaration of Independence is a philosophical statement of the American democratic political philosophy with no legal bearing, the U.S. Constitution is the legal document that embodies the laws of the land. And although the United States Constitution is the constitution of a nation built on democratic principles, slavery—that least democratic of institutions—though not named explicitly, is referred to on several occasions: Article 1, Section 2 contains the "three-fifths compromise," under which slaves would be counted as three-fifths of a person for purposes of representation and taxation; Article 1, Section 9, prohibited a ban on the slave trade until 1808; and Article 4, Section 4—the Fugitive Slave Clause—required that all runaway slaves be returned to their masters upon request. Moreover, several other portions of the Constitution were instituted with the notion of slavery in mind.[17]

A national constitution of a democratic nation that acknowledges the institution of slavery is an apparent contradiction. The contradiction can be reconciled, however, when one considers that, according to the prevailing ideology of the age, blacks were viewed as less than human—inferior creatures incapable of handling the responsibility of citizenship.

Thomas Jefferson was confused, at best, about the black race's potential for development. While he was sure that blacks were inferior in their present state, he was unsure as to whether this inferiority was natural or a consequence of slavery. On different occasions, he expressed dissimilar ideas. Two years before the writing of the Constitution he said the following:

> Some have been liberally educated, and all have lived in countries where the arts and sciences are cultivated to a considerable degree . . . But never yet could I find that a black uttered a thought above the level of narration, never see even an elementary trait of painting or sculpture. . . . The improvement of the blacks in body and mind, in the first instances of their mixture with whites . . . prove that their inferiority is not the effect merely of their condition of life.[18]

Jefferson revealed his uncertainty regarding this argument when he wrote to a friend during the same year, "I suppose the black man, in his present state, might not be [equal in body and mind to the white man]. But it would be hazardous to affirm that, equally cultivated for a few generations, he would not become so." [19]

Eighty years later, Abraham Lincoln did not subscribe to the argument that blacks' inferiority justified the denial of their civil rights. While he stood firmly with those who professed white supremacy, he saw no need to withhold from blacks the inalienable rights guaranteed by the Declaration of Independence. Lincoln expressed these sentiments in the first Lincoln-Douglas debates:

> I have no purpose directly or indirectly to interfere with the institution of slavery in the States where it exists. I believe I have no lawful right to do so, and I have no inclination to do so. I have no purpose to introduce political and social equality between the white and black races . . . But I hold that not withstanding all this, there is no reason in the world why the negro is not entitled to all the natural rights enumerated in the Declaration of Independence, the right to life, liberty, and the pursuit of happiness.[20]

Lincoln's speech provides a good example of the discontinuity between the ideal and the real. He failed, at least at this point, to address the fact that slavery and inalienable rights are mutually exclusive. Nonetheless, Lincoln's view was a relatively progressive one for the antebellum period.

Throughout the pre–Civil War era, a biblical defense of slavery was immensely popular with those who needed to believe that slavery was consistent with democracy and morality. This defense was based on an argument that blacks were descendants of Ham, who was cursed by Noah (Genesis 10:20-27). The alleged curse stipulated that the descendants of Ham would be black and servants throughout the course of history. With the strong fundamentalist Protestant tradition in the South, this argument was a strong and comfortable one—the status of blacks as slaves became an act of God not subject to critical inquiry.[21]

The general acceptance of black inferiority was so strong that it even permeated the ranks of the abolitionists. Though they fought for black emancipation, many of them felt that blacks were not capable of living on equal terms with whites. Blacks were to be treated humanely, but not necessarily as equals.

Thus, the period from the Constitutional Convention in 1787 until 1857 was marked by philosophical tensions originating from the paradox of a democratic republic that maintained slavery. Though there was diversity in beliefs about racial issues in the nation, the common ideology was one of blacks' inferiority, a notion that served to justify their lack of civil rights. However, the idea of the inferiority of blacks was merely a popular notion supported by social customs until 1857, when the *Dred Scott Decision* would give the notion the status of legal fact.

The *Dred Scott Decision* of 1857 provided another argument for the denial of civil rights to blacks. The argument was simply that the founding fathers were not referring to blacks when they used the words "men," "people of the United States," and "citizens." Moreover, Chief Justice Taney stated, the founding fathers intended to embody in our organic law the universally accepted opinion among civilized whites that Negroes had "no rights which the white man was bound to respect."[22] Thus, the inferiority of blacks in the popular mind and in the minds of the founding fathers were legally sanctioned by the Supreme Court of the United States.

The constitutional recognition of slavery and the Supreme Court's *Dred Scott Decision* further confirms, in retrospect, the rationality of the instrumentalist approach to politics. These pivotal life-altering decisions had been made under the rubric of legitimate government. In order to make changes, it was incumbent upon the opposition to place themselves in decision-making roles. Much of this opposition came from the Abolitionist Movement.

The Abolitionist Movement began to gain additional force after the Revolutionary War. Several factors facilitated this phenomenon: (1) many whites became sympathetic to the black quest for freedom after blacks participated in the war; (2) some people began to feel that slavery was neither efficient nor profitable; and (3) some were convinced that the natural-rights philosophy of the Revolution also applied to blacks. Vermont was the first state to abolish slavery. In its 1777 constitution, it stated that male slaves would receive freedom at age twenty-one, and women at age eighteen.[23] By 1804, slavery was outlawed in all the original states north of Maryland and Delaware.[24] But restrictions based on race were still plentiful: state statutes confined blacks to menial labor jobs; segregated education was widespread; blacks were disfranchised, and open housing did not exist; and the criminal justice system was biased against blacks. Moreover, Jim Crow was widespread in the North, and many public places had separate provisions for blacks.[25]

Nonetheless, the American Revolution had forced the anti-slavery movement to take a stand on the humanity of blacks. Heretofore, a heterogeneous group of abolitionists wanted to free blacks for moral as well as pragmatic reasons.

The history of the antislavery movement falls roughly into three periods: (1) the period of colonization; (2) the formation of the American Anti-Slavery Society between 1833 and 1839; (3) and the organization of the Liberty Party.[26]

The American Colonization Society was primarily concerned with sending free blacks to some colony outside the U.S. Thus, the major thrust was for conditional abolition, i.e., blacks should be freed if there were plans to remove them from the United States. Conditional abolition allowed for support from all sections of the country and from all classes of men because one could be a racist or an egalitarian and support this measure. The ACS began to falter when many of its members began to view blacks as citizens denied constitutional protections and the rights of the Constitution and the Declaration of Independence.[27]

The American Anti-Slavery Society, formed in 1833, was a

much more homogeneous group than the American Colonization Society. The members felt strongly that blacks were included in the Declaration of Independence and the Constitution. Thus, blacks had a right to remain in America and enjoy the rights and responsibilities of citizens in a democratic nation. The period from 1833 to 1839 can be basically viewed as an era of intensive efforts to affect public opinion concerning slavery: the philosophy of slavery was attacked and not allowed to completely dominate the country; the North was mobilized by the abolitionists, and a network of antislavery societies was established. Whereas the actions of the organization from 1833 to 1839 were primarily directed toward affecting public opinion, a need for direct political action was perceived as being crucial.[28]

Direct political action was seen as the most feasible approach to the abolition of slavery by some members of the American Anti-Slavery Society. They lost many of their members and supporters when William Lloyd Garrison injected women's rights into the movement.[29]

The Liberty party was a party without politicians and without a platform in the usual sense of the word. Its primary focus was hostility to slavery; and its primary interest was in forcing one of the old parties to adopt a firmer stand against slavery. The Free Soil party eventually took on the cause of abolition, and, when Lincoln became president in 1860, the cause of abolition would be in Republican hands. With the thirteenth Amendment in 1867, the abolitionist objective was finally achieved, but not without a civil war.[30]

The Civil War (1861–65)

The Civil War raged in America from 1861 to 1865. Historians differ with respect to what it should be called, as well as to which of its causes should be emphasized most. There are three major schools of thought on the issue of contributory causes: (1) the war was forced upon the South as the final act in a movement to abolish slavery; (2) the war was a struggle to check centralization of power in the federal government and to preserve the constitutional safeguards of minorities in the nation at large; and

(3) the dissimilar economic development of the two sections was the primary reason for the war. Regardless of one's arguments with regard to the most salient cause, all historians agree that there would not have been a civil war if there had not been slavery.[31]

When the American Anti-Slavery Society was formed in 1833 with the expressed purpose of gaining black freedom without expatriation, the South and the North were set on a course that would eventually make them collide. A strong sectionalism had developed that could not be reconciled: there were simply too many differences. The antislavery North and the proslavery South disagreed on the following issues: (1) the potential for black intellectual and moral development; (2) the consequences of complete emancipation without expatriation; (3) the true character and usefulness of the institution of slavery; (4) the status of slavery under the Constitution; and (5) the nature of the federal government, the limits of its powers, and the residuary authority of the states.

The proslavery South saw the handwriting on the wall with the election of Abraham Lincoln in 1860. The South seceded because they figured that . . . "once in control of the power and patronage of the federal government, the antislavery forces will introduce the debate into the South, build up the party there, set non-slaveholder against slaveholder, and bring about the abolition of slavery by the orderly process of state constitutional action."[32] Feeling defenseless against such a legitimate political attack, the Southern states felt that there was no choice but to secede. Secession led to war, the North won, and slavery had been defeated.

Reconstruction (1867–77)

When Lee surrendered in 1865, blacks living in five New England states—Massachusetts, Rhode Island, Maine, New Hampshire and Vermont—were eligible to vote freely. However, these blacks made up only 6 percent of the national black population. Blacks in New York could vote if they had an estate worth $250.00 (there was no such requirement for whites).[33]

Between 1865 and 1868, Northern white voters in Connecticut, Wisconsin, Kansas, Ohio, Michigan and New York rejected referenda that would have given blacks the right to vote. Thus, while southern black males were obtaining the right to vote, most blacks outside the South remained disfranchised. A quick view of the election returns reveals that all states with a relatively large black population continued to support elections for whites only.[34] After the war, the crucial business was to heal the nation. Lincoln favored a mild plan for readmitting the South to the Union, a plan which did not include universal suffrage—only black war veterans and other very intelligent blacks would be allowed to vote. Already leery of the "Lincoln Plan," the Radical Reconstructionists were displeasured with Johnson after the Lincoln assassination, and ended by implementing their own plan.

The disagreements between Congress and Johnson were the same basic disagreements that it had had with Lincoln concerning the best plan for Reconstruction, for, in fact, Johnson basically agreed with Lincoln. Thus, when Congress submitted a civil rights bill to him and attempted to strengthen and extend the Freedman's Bureau Act, Johnson vetoed the measures. Congress retaliated by eventually overriding both vetoes and took political control of Reconstruction.

The Radical Reconstructionists in Congress, between 1866 and 1875, enacted most of the progressive civil rights legislation that this nation had ever had: the Civil Rights Act of 1866, the Reconstruction Acts of 1867, the Fourteenth and Fifteenth Amendments, the Lodge Bill, and the Civil Rights Act of 1875 were all legislation designed to ensure civil rights for blacks.

The Civil Rights Act of 1866 made blacks citizens, with all of the rights and responsibilities thereof. The Reconstruction Act of 1867 stipulated that new constitutions should be drafted in the former confederate states by male citizens "of whatever race, color or previous condition." The constitution would give the right to vote to all who were eligible to vote for delegates to the conventions. To insure that the Civil Rights Act of 1866 would be permanent and unaffected by the president, Congress, or the Supreme Court, Congress drafted the Fourteenth and the Fifteenth Amendments to the Constitution, which were ratified in 1868 and 1870, respectively. These measures were enacted primarily for three reasons: (1) to insure loyal governments in the South; (2) to give blacks a political weapon by guaranteeing their political rights; and (3) to insure the supremacy of the Republican Party.[35] The Civil Rights Act of 1875 moved from the political arena to the social—it gave blacks access to all places of public accommodation.

Black delegates were elected to all of the state constitutional conventions which met in 1867–68. In states where the black population was low, the black representation was low. However in states with a high black population, the representation was considerable higher: in Alabama 18 of 108 were black; in Florida, 18 of 45; in Georgia, 33 of 170; in Mississippi, 17 of 100; in Louisiana, there was a racially balanced delegation; and South Carolina had the only black majority delegation, 76 of 124.[36]

Blacks were elected to all of the state legislatures after the new constitutions were approved. With many whites excluded from voting because of their participation in the Confederate rebellion, there were more black voters (703,400) in the Reconstruction South than white voters (600,000).[37] However, this black numerical majority was never translated into a state house majority: in no state did blacks ever constitute a majority in both houses of the legislature; and it was only in South Carolina that there was a majority in the lower house.[38]

Regardless of one's philosophical predilections concerning Reconstruction,[39] there is no disagreement that it was a period of unprecedented black political empowerment and participation. At the state level, six blacks served as lieutenant governors, although no black was ever elected governor. Many blacks held administrative positions at the state, county, and municipal levels. Between 1860 and 1880, a total of sixteen blacks served in Congress: two in the Senate, and fourteen in the House of Representatives.[40]

That blacks held office during this period would provide the strongest evidence to support the legitimacy of the instrumentalist approach to politics; their accomplishments—not their mere presence—proved that black elected officials could bring practical results. Goldston cites their accomplishments as follows:

> They provided for universal suffrage by removing property requirements for voting; abolished the medieval system of imprisoning people for debt; abolished such cruel and unusual punishment as whipping and

branding; reduced the number of crimes for which a man could be executed . . . and established statewide free public school systems (the first in Southern history). Although they did not redistribute the land, they did pass laws to protect the small farmer, and they attempted to institute a rational system of taxes. Nor were these benefits intended exclusively for Negroes. They were vital advantages also to the poor Southern whites. In effect, the Reconstruction state governments were attempting to bring about a peaceful *socio-economic revolution* in Southern society which would have benefited most Southern whites as well as Negroes . . . [Emphasis added].[41]

From 1886 to 1875, the radical Republicans tried to bring democracy to the South. After the passage of the Civil Rights Act of 1875, blacks in the South had all of the legal rights black Americans enjoy today: including the right to vote and access to places of public accommodation. Thus, rough political and social equality was a reality. Thaddeus Stevens, one of the most powerful politicians of his day, realized that an economic component was also important. He tried, without success, to pass a radical land-reform bill that would have given every black male forty acres and a mule.[42] Nonetheless, Reconstruction was the apex of black political success, and an instance in which the government was an instrument of social betterment for blacks, but not for long. However, the strides made by blacks during this period have always stood as a vivid example of the efficacy of instrumentalist politics. The effects of Reconstruction served as evidence that black office holding could play a pivotal role in leading the black community toward a better quality of life.

Reconstruction policies had always received a cold reception in the South. Dymnally asserts that "the refusal of the political leaders of America to ground political freedom on economic freedom doomed Reconstruction and paved the way to our present crisis."[43] However, a number of coinciding factors led to the demise of Radical Reconstructionist rule: (1) the Radicals suffered a crisis in leadership when Thaddeus Stevens and Charles Sumner died—their successors were more interested in the business potential in the South than in human rights; (2) many northerners had simply grown tired of the fight and wanted to return to normalcy; and (3) the Supreme Court became increasingly hostile to the legislation of Reconstruction.[44]

Steve Lawson explains the situation as follows:

These debilitating decisions of the Supreme Court and the subsequent retreat of the Justice Department reflected a pattern of thought that emerged in the North during the 1870's. If W. R. Brock is correct, and the "concept of Negro equality demanded interference with the process of local government on a scale never before contemplated in America or in any other nation," few northerners were willing to pay the price for drastically transforming the federal system. After fifteen years of civil war and reconstruction, northerners were content to let white southerners manage racial affairs without supervision. Some believed that southern blacks having received the ballot could protect themselves and did not require further assistance; others ceased caring, because they were disillusioned with the results of Radical Reconstruction. Appalled by the corruption of the period, they found a scapegoat in the Negro and came to regret having given the suffrage to the "uneducated" freedman in the first place. The protection of civil rights ceased to be an appealing issue for the Republican party, and a majority of its members turned their attention to development of the country's economic resources. Anxious to reunite the nation and to exploit industrial opportunities jointly with Southern whites, the GOP agreed to the compromise of 1877 . . .[45]

The Supreme Court, between 1873 and 1876, devitalized the Fourteenth and Fifteenth Amendments and declared portions of the Enforcement Act of 1870 unconstitutional. The dismantling started in 1873 with the *Slaughter House Cases* and was followed by *U.S. vs Reese* and *U.S. vs Cruishank* in 1876.[46]

The *Slaughter House Cases,* though they did not involve blacks, nullified the privileges and immunities clause with respect to black civil rights. The court ruled that "state and federal citizenships are separate and distinct"; that the amendment forbade *state* impairment of privileges and immunities that persons enjoyed as citizens of the U.S. Moreover, the court reasoned that most civil rights are attributes of *state* citizenship and therefore beyond the reach of the amendment. The Fourteenth Amendment, with this 1873 ruling, had been severely weakened.[47]

In *U.S. vs Reese,* the Supreme Court declared portions of the Enforcement Act of 1870 unconstitutional. It declared that the "fifteenth Amendment extends no positive guarantees of the franchise, and does not 'confer the right of suffrage upon anyone' but merely prohibits both the federal and state governments from excluding persons from voting by reason of race, color, or previous condition of servitude." Thus, there was no positive guarantee of the black person's right to vote.[48]

In *U.S. vs Cruishank*, the Court ruled that the "Fourteenth Amendment prohibits a State from depriving any person of life, liberty or property, without due process of law; but this adds nothing to the rights of one citizen against another one."[49] In other words, as long as the "state" was not a party to a deprivation of the right to vote, there was no infringement of the Fourteenth Amendment.

The Compromise of 1877

The legislation of the Radical Republicans never had a mass following in the white South, and their policies were always challenged if not completely undermined, despite the presence of Union troops and the enactment of federal enforcement legislation. Although black voting had been effectively mitigated throughout the Reconstruction period, the Compromise of 1877 officially withdrew the federal troops from the South and restored home rule. The details of the compromise are as follows: in return for southern support of the Union, an acceptance of national supremacy, and an agreement to allow Hayes to assume the presidency without a majority of the votes, the national government agreed to end military occupation of the South, to cease its efforts at arranging southern society, and to lend tacit approval to white supremacy in the South.[50]

The Nadir (1877–1909)

Though the practical impact of the Radical Republican legislation was unstable at best, the Compromise of 1877 gave official sanction to the segregationist policies of the South. The fierceness of the attack on the segregationist South had been lessening for quite some time. The Radical governments in the South did not take power until 1866; on average, they lasted four-and-a-half years. By 1877, all of the former Confederate states were firmly in the hands of the southern Democrats.[51] Nonetheless, Hayes's removal of the few remaining troops in the South marked the end of the official Reconstruction Era. For almost the next four decades, the state, local, and federal governments would serve as instruments of black subordination in the South.

Continuing its anti-civil rights crusade during the Nadir, the

Supreme Court cleared the way for segregation. This feat was accomplished primarily through three cases: *Hall vs De Cuir* (1878); the *Civil Rights Cases of 1883;* and *Plessy vs Ferguson* (1896).

Hall vs De Cuir declared that a Louisiana Reconstruction statute guaranteeing nonsegregated seating was an "unconstitutional invasion of a state on the federal government's exclusive jurisdiction over interstate commerce." The court held that a statute forbidding discrimination on public carriers was an undue burden on interstate commerce.[52]

The *Civil Rights Cases of 1883* declared the Civil Rights Act of 1875 unconstitutional. This act had forbidden segregated public accommodations. In this ruling, the court saw fit to explain congressional intent. They ruled that "The essence of the law is not to declare that all persons shall be entitled to the full and equal enjoyment of accommodation . . . but that such enjoyment shall not be subject to any conditions applicable only to citizens of a particular race, or color, or who have been in a previous condition of servitude."[53]

In 1896, the Supreme Court upheld state laws requiring segregation of the races in *Plessy vs Ferguson.* Although segregation laws involved state action, the Court held that segregating the races did not violate the equal protection clause of the Fourteenth Amendment as long as persons in each race were treated equally. Thus, schools and other public facilities that had a policy of segregation won constitutional approval, given that they were equal.[54]

The Supreme Court was echoing the philosophy elucidated by Booker T. Washington in his famous "Atlanta Exposition Address" in 1895.[55] Washington argued that blacks, in all things social, could be as distinct as the five fingers, while in all things good for mutual progress they could work together as the five separate fingers on the same hand work together. Washington felt that social and political thrusts should be postponed in favor of black self-improvement and industrial training. He felt that through economic independence and a high degree of industrial skills, blacks would eventually earn full freedom and equality because of their economic importance.[56] Thus, Booker T. Washington argued for economic independence as the instrument for black betterment. Political power was deprioritized; it could wait until a strong economic base was established. Since this view echoed what many of the white leaders wanted to hear, Washington received their financial and moral support. Though he was severely criticized by fellow blacks, Booker T. Washington was realistic in his assessment of what progress was possible. Moreover, the long-run implications of his policy are indeed important to black political development.[57] After the Compromise of 1877, the redeemed governments of the South resorted to a variety of measures—from laws aimed at illiterates to fraud and intimidation—to eliminate black voters. By 1892, the number of black electors had been reduced by half. However, the more resourceful blacks continued to participate, and white political leaders perceived a need to make their disenfranchising measures more intense.[58]

While the Republicans lost in their bid to pass the Lodge Bill, Mississippi was leading the South in developing legal devices to end black voting when it called for a constitutional convention in 1890. The Mississippi delegates utilized the same technique used by the founding fathers—they made references to problems without actually naming them. Thus, although the Mississippi constitution made no explicit reference to blacks, they were the chief objects of the measures adopted. The convention instituted residence requirements that would disenfranchise black sharecroppers and tenant farmers; certain crimes would be punishable by disenfranchisement (since blacks were allegedly predisposed to criminal behavior). Blacks, in general, were too poor to be reasonably expected to pay the poll tax, and the high black illiteracy rate would, it was hoped, keep them from passing the "literacy and understanding" test.[59]

The Mississippi state constitution won the approval of the U.S. Supreme Court in 1898. The court ruled in *William vs Mississippi* (1898) that the suffrage qualifications were not discriminatory "on their face." Thus, the Mississippi state constitution was used as a model for the other southern states. Between 1890 and 1910, all of the southern states rewrote their constitutions; Louisiana even enacted a grandfather clause to ensure that the literacy test would disqualify blacks exclusively. Moreover, the introduction of the direct primary in the South, which many states restricted to whites only, virtually guaranteed white supremacy.[60]

The voice of black protest was not completely eradicated during this period. The loudest voice was probably that of W. E. B. Du Bois, who vehemently opposed the gradualism of Booker T. Washington. In his *Souls of Black Folk,* Du Bois offers a powerful refutation of the Washington philosophy:

It has been claimed that the Negro can survive only through submission. Mr. Washington distinctly asks that black people give up, at least for the present, three things—First, political power; Second, insistence on Civil rights; Third, higher education of Negro youth; and concentrate all their energies on industrial education, the accumulation of wealth, and the conciliation of the South. This policy has been courageously and insistently advocated for over fifteen years, and has been triumphant for perhaps ten years. As a result of this tender of the palmbranch, what has been the return? In these years have occurred: (1) The disfranchisement of the Negro; (2) The legal creation of a distinct status of civil inferiority for the Negro; (3) The steady withdrawal of aid from institutions for the higher training of the Negro.

These movements are not, to be sure, direct results of Mr. Washington's teachings; but his propaganda has . . . helped their speedier accomplishment . . . And Mr. Washington thus faces the triple paradox of his career.

1. He is striving nobly to make Negro artisans, business, and property owners; but it is utterly impossible, under modern competitive methods, for workingmen, and property owners to defend their rights and exist without the right of suffrage.

2. He insists on thrift and self-respect, but at the same time counsels a silent submission to civil inferiority such as is bound to sap the manhood of any race in the long run.

3. He advocates common-school and industrial training, and depreciates institutions of higher learning; but neither the Negro common-schools, nor Tuskegee itself, could remain open a day were not for teachers trained in Negro colleges, or trained by their graduates.[61]

Du Bois founded the Niagra Movement in 1905. The movement, composed of a group of young black intellectuals, was dedicated to full citizenship for blacks. Compared to Washington, this group was considered militant since its "Declaration of Principles" was a sharp departure from the Washington school of thought. Although financial problems and internal squabbles led to its demise in 1910, it laid the philosophical foundation for the NAACP.

While the Niagra Movement was crumbling, Du Bois began to meet white liberals who believed in his ideas. The demise of black civil rights was creating a new breed of activist who felt that individuals had to be mobilized for the goal of racial justice and equality. Goaded by the Springfield, Illinois, race riot of 1908, many of this new breed convened at a conference in the spring of 1909. These representatives, including Du Bois and some of the members of the Niagra Movement, mandated the creation of a permanent organization "to promote the cause of racial equality and justice." Thus, the NAACP was founded in 1909—the Nadir was ending.[62]

Black Ballots and the
Changing Opportunity Structure

An "opportunity structure" is the interactions between outside support and societal events which may facilitate or repress successful collective action towards the realization of the interests of a particular social movement. Between 1909 and 1954, the opportunity structure became favorable to the goal of black instrumentalist politics. The use of black soldiers in two world wars caused many Americans to question the treatment of blacks in America; the migration of blacks to the industrial centers led to a windfall with respect to black political power; and the founding of the NAACP in 1910 began the major quest for enfranchisement and desegregation.

World Wars I and II, like the Revolutionary War, strained the already existent tensions between the ideals of the American creed and the actual condition of blacks in America. While blacks were fighting abroad to "make the world safe for democracy," they were being lynched at home. Equally ironic, while fighting racism in Europe, they were the objects of racism in their own country. Capitalizing on this potentially embarrassing situation, A. Phillip Randolph was able to win from President Roosevelt the first major civil rights concession since Reconstruction.

A. Phillip Randolph, the president of the Brotherhood of Sleeping Car Porters, was appalled by the irony of a segregated armed forces that was fighting racism. The discrimination blacks faced in the war industry added insult to injury. Thus, Randolph decided to call for a "March on Washington" to protest both evils.

This placed Roosevelt in a precarious situation: would he endorse an effort to end segregation in the armed forces and discrimination in the war industry and risk losing the political support of the southern delegation or would he offend Randolph and risk embarrassment as the leader of a nation proclaiming freedom abroad that had protestors calling for freedom at home? Roosevelt opted to save face abroad. He signed an executive order establishing a Federal Employment Practices Commission on June 25, 1941; the scheduled march was less than a week away. Although Randolph called the march off, desegregation of the armed forces would not come until seven years later.[63]

The effects of the world wars in facilitating northern migration of blacks cannot be overestimated. When the NAACP was founded in 1910, more than 90 percent of black Americans lived in the South, and 80 percent were employed in agriculture or domestic services. By the time of the post-WWII civil rights movement, approximately half of all blacks lived in the industrial North.[64] This population shift, which was also facilitated by southern economic modernization and racial hostility, would have an important impact on the quest for black empowerment.

During two periods of migration, 1910 to 1920 and 1940 to 1950, over 4 million blacks went to the industrial urban north in search of a better life. They were concentrated in the states with the most electoral college votes. Thus by the 1930s blacks in the North had gained enough political strength to be noticed in national elections. The black vote became the "balance of power" and was not to be discounted. By 1956, blacks were located in the ten most populated industrial states.

The Era of the NAACP (1910–54)

The NAACP's goal was to secure the franchise. The method would be litigation—constant and persistent litigation. Their strategy was to attack the weakest challenge first. Since the framers of the new state constitutions were especially careful not to mention race in their requirements for registration, the Supreme Court approved them. But the grandfather clauses were a bit more blatant than the other measures, and hence more easily attacked.[65]

Oklahoma amended its constitution to excuse anyone who was eligible to vote on January 1, 1866, or "anyone who was a lineal descendent of such persons," from having to take the literacy test. The clear intent of this measure was to single out blacks for unequal treatment. Since a very small number of blacks could vote before 1866, few blacks would benefit from this provision, whereas practically all whites were thereby exempted from the literacy test. After the Justice Department prosecuted several Oklahoma registrars for discrimination in congressional elections, the case eventually reached the Supreme Court in 1914. The NAACP filed an *amicus curiae* brief arguing that the standards for exemption had been ingeniously worded so as to disenfranchise blacks. The Supreme Court agreed in 1915. However, the victory was short lived.[66]

The state of Oklahoma would not be easily denied its "right" to disenfranchise its blacks. The legislature developed a new criteria in 1916. The new stipulation required "that all citizens qualified to vote in 1916 who failed to register between April 30 and May 11, 1916, should be perpetually disenfranchised, excepting those who voted in 1914." This revised grandfather clause went unchallenged for twenty years. Nonetheless, the high tribunal finally ruled against this measure in *Lane vs Wilson* (1939). The court ruled "that the Fifteenth Amendment nullifies sophisticated as well as simple-minded modes of discrimination. . . . The legislation of 1916 partakes too much of the infirmity of the grandfather clause to be able to survive."[67]

The grandfather clause was now a thing of the past. Nonetheless, the white primary, the poll tax, the literacy test, and the understanding clauses remained legal barriers. The period from the first grandfather clause defeat in 1915 to its last defeat in 1939 was an intense time for the NAACP. Their major effort during this period was an all-out attack on the southern white primary, specifically the Texas white primary.

Until 1923, the state of Texas gave each county the option of deciding whether or not they would allow blacks to vote in the Democratic primary. Bexar County allowed its blacks to vote; but after the black vote played a decisive role in defeating D. A. McAskill in his bid for district attorney in 1918, he led an effort to enact legislation barring blacks from voting in the Democratic primary. McAskill was no doubt spurred to action by two court decisions: The Texas Supreme Court ruled in 1916 that a political party was a private voluntary association; in the same decisions it ruled that party officials were not government officials and that a primary was not in the same category as an election. Also, the U.S. Supreme Court ruled in 1921 that the act of nomination was not a part of the electoral process. The Texas legislature passed legislation barring black participation in the Democratic primary in 1923, and the Democratic party obeyed the mandate on July 26, 1924, by adopting it as a party policy.[68]

The first case attacking the white primary, in what became known as the Texas White Primary Cases, was *Nixon vs Herndon* in 1927. Beginning in 1924 in the lower courts, it took three years before the Supreme Court ruled that the white primary violated the Fourteenth Amendment, i.e., the state had deprived Negroes of equal protection under the law, with color providing the basis of discrimination. The Supreme Court left open the question of whether the primary was part of an election, and, thus, the NAACP desire to win a victory based on the Fifteenth Amendment was not achieved. Without such a ruling, the states were free to find new methods of denying blacks the vote that would not violate the Fourteenth and Fifteenth Amendments.[69]

Nixon vs Herndon, filed in the lower courts in 1925, was the beginning of a long fight toward the death of the white primary. The white primary was eventually ruled unconstitutional in *Smith vs Allright* in 1944. There were a few legal challenges, like that of the "grandfather clause," but by 1952, the Supreme Court had made it clear that the white primary was a relic of the past. The death of the white primary brought forth a new era of black registration.[70]

The re-emergence of blacks in southern politics began with *Smith vs Allright* (1944). This decision created the first opportunity for black political mobilization in the South in the twentieth century. At the time of the ruling, black registration in the eleven southern states stood at approximately the levels obtained after the mass disenfranchisement during the 1890–1910 period. The fall of the white primary encouraged many blacks to register and vote. Despite the poll tax, understanding clauses, and literacy tests, black registration rolls continued to increase. Blacks began voting in record numbers, although the voting patterns were not even across the South: Georgia, Texas, and North Carolina had black turnouts of 85,000, 75,000 and 40,000, respectively, in the 1946 primaries, while Alabama, Louisiana, Mississippi, and South Carolina each had fewer than 5,000 black citizens voting.[71]

As it pursued the defeat of the white primary, the NAACP was simultaneously attacking the legality of segregation. And when the white primary was overthrown, all efforts were focused on the defeat of segregation. The first victory was *Missouri ex rel Gaines vs Canada* (1938). The court brought attention to the definition of equality by overruling a Missouri state law that required blacks to attend out-of-state schools and even provided them with financial aid to do so. This allowed Missouri to avoid integration of their own schools. Because blacks were not being provided education within the state, the court ruled that they were being denied equal treatment under the law. Nonetheless, this ruling did nothing to change the notion of "separate but equal." It would take sixteen more years and three more Supreme Court cases before the Supreme Court would rule in *Brown vs Board of Topeka* (1954) that the notion of "separate but equal" was null and void.[72]

Brown vs Board of Topeka was a landmark decision, for it changed a Supreme Court ruling that had stood for more than half a century. For the first time since Reconstruction, the law of the land was on the side of those who pushed for the end of segregation and of disenfranchisement. Although the Supreme Court ruled the following year that desegregation could proceed "with all deliberate speed"[73]—a phrase that was used to justify procrastination and delay—the die had been cast. The Supreme Court ruled that segregation in education was unconstitutional. The South was ready to oppose this ruling with a massive resistance movement.[74]

The two major goals of the civil rights movement were the desegregation of public facilities and the securing of voting rights in the South. This discussion will focus primarily, though not exclusively, on the quest for voting rights. Civil rights activists hypothesized that political power could eventually be translated into economic power. Although black power in the North had not transformed the lives of the black poor,[75] their numerical dominance in

the black belt South would enable blacks to be office holders themselves in an environment of predominantly black policy makers.
Thus, visions of a second Reconstruction were at hand.

The Post–World War II
Civil Rights Movement, 1955–68

Martin Luther King, Jr., came to national prominence as the
leader of the successful year-long Montgomery Bus Boycott,
which started December 5, 1955.[76] By the time the boycott was
over in 1956, the black vote was becoming a salient factor in the
politics of the Democratic Party.

Nineteen fifty-six was an important year for political participation in the northern black community. Ever since the New Deal,
blacks in the North had been strong supporters of the Democratic Party. This loyalty became more important politically as
more blacks began to move to the northeast. Thus, when the Dix-
iecrats revolted in 1949, the Democratic Party was free to try to
court the white South, since the black vote seemed to be stable
regardless of their public policy and the percentage of blacks
voting Democratic continued to increase. However, enraged at
the treatment of southern blacks and the defeat of the 1956 civil
rights bill at the hands of Democrats, blacks in the North and
South defected from the Democrats either by not voting or by
voting for Eisenhower. Black loyalty could not be taken for granted
any longer. This defection informed the Democrats that they
would have to decide who they wanted to hold on to: the northern urban black vote or the southern white vote—they could not
have both. Thus, for the first time since enfranchisement, blacks
were being courted.[77]

For example, it was Lyndon Johnson, who had voted no on
every piece of civil rights legislation since 1937, who actually en-
gineered the compromises necessary to pass the civil rights act
that he had worked so hard to defeat the previous year. Johnson
sensed that he would have to change his attitude toward black
constituents in order to fulfill his presidential ambitions. Thus,
the Civil Rights Act of 1957, the first piece of civil rights legislation in eighty-two years, was a reaction to the increasing strength
of the black vote.[78]

Martin Luther King, Jr., began to focus on the importance of the black vote, in particular the southern black vote. School desegregation was not enough if blacks were still out of political power. King articulated his dreams of what the ballot could achieve when he spoke in Washington, D.C., on May 17, 1957, as part of the "Prayer Pilgrimage for Peace":

> Give us the ballot and we will no longer have to worry the federal government about our basic rights. Give us the ballot and we will no longer plead to the federal government for passage of an anti-lynching law. We will by the power of our vote write the law on the books of the South and bring an end to the dastardly acts of the hooded perpetrators of the salient misdeeds of bloodthirsty mobs into the calculated deeds of orderly citizens. Give us the ballot and we will fill our legislative halls with men of good will and send to the sacred halls of congress men who will not sign a Southern Manifesto because of their devotion to the manifesto of justice. Give us the ballot and we will do justly and love mercy. And we will place at the head of the southern states governors who have felt not only the tang of the human but the glory of the divine. Give us the ballot and we will quietly and non-violently, without rancor or bitterness, implement the school decision of May 17, 1954. Give us the ballot and we will help bring this nation to a new society based on justice and dedicated to peace.[79]

Upon his return from the pilgrimage, he called together approximately fifty southern black ministers in Atlanta, Georgia. The meeting resulted in the formation of SCLC, the Southern Christian Leadership Conference. Their first major goal was to conduct a campaign to add 3 million blacks to the rolls in time for the 1958 election.[80] They failed in their effort, but the black vote was continuing to increase (see Table 1). All eyes were focused on the future.

The 1960s: The Politics
of Direct Action and Voter Registration
Direct action with the goal of desegregation of public facilities would dominate the first two years of the decade. The ballot would regain its prominence with the presidential initiative that led to the formation of the Voter Education Project. Victory was in sight and the civil rights activists would not be denied.

The sit-in movement began in Greensboro, North Carolina, at Woolworth's department store on February 1, 1960. After having been refused service at the bus terminal's lunch counter the previous day, Ezell Blair and Joseph McNeill decided to stage a protest. They were joined by two others on the second day. Within two weeks, the sit-in movement had spread to Virginia, Tennessee, and South Carolina. The first use of violence against the demonstrators was in Nashville on February 27, but the movement continued to spread. The sit-ins hit Atlanta on March 15, and the simple threat of sit-ins brought desegregation to variety stores in Houston and San Antonio, Texas. The students finally organized themselves at a conference at Shaw University on April 15, 1960. In a meeting the following month in Atlanta, the name "Temporary Student Nonviolent Coordinating Committee" was decided upon. At an October conference, the word "temporary" was dropped and the Student Nonviolent Coordinating Committee had its permanent name.[81]

The short, ten-month life of SNCC was extremely productive. By mid-August, the U.S. Attorney General issued a statement announcing the abolishment of discriminatory practices in sixty-nine southern communities.[82] Ironically, the victory had not been won in Atlanta, the city "too busy to hate" and the home of Martin Luther King, Jr.

In mid-October, King reluctantly became part of the Atlanta desegregation effort. He was reluctant because the Atlanta black elites wanted to handle desegregation in their own way, the way of the conservative coalition. After the students seized the desegregation leadership, King felt he could no longer remain neutral when he was asked to join. Thus, on October 19, 1960, King led students to desegregate Rich's restaurants and lunch counters. King was arrested immediately—an occurrence that would have national ramifications.[83]

Some months earlier, King, who had recently moved to Atlanta from Montgomery, was stopped in Dekalb County, a suburb of Atlanta. Many argue that he was stopped because he was with a white woman, the writer Lillian Smith. Whatever the motive, King was placed on probation for not having a Georgia driver's license. Then, at the time of Rich's sit-in, because of his involvement, King's probation was revoked. The Dekalb County judge sentenced him to four months of hard labor at the infamous Reidsville State Prison.

The King imprisonment immediately made national news, and the attempts of Mayor Hartsfield to avoid publicity at Atlanta's expense were going up in smoke.[84] Many supporters were outraged that such harsh punishment could be doled out to an American citizen for peacefully protesting. King's imprisonment presented a major challenge to Nixon and Kennedy. A favorable overture to King could possibly solidify the black vote for the candidate, but the white South would be offended. Nixon, lacking any substantial black support, feared losing the white South and so chose not to speak out in King's defense, although he was urged to do so by his advisers. However, both of the Kennedys, the presidential candidate and his brother, seized the opportunity. On the day following King's transfer, John Kennedy phoned Mrs. King to inform her that he was using his personal influence to try to aid in King's release. Bobby Kennedy called the county judge to see why King had been denied bail. King was released on October 27. The following Sunday at Ebenezer in Atlanta, "Daddy King," who had previously opposed Kennedy because of his Catholic faith, vowed to work for the Kennedy presidential campaign. The black community viewed Kennedy's action as support for the movement. To make sure that the point was not missed, two million copies of brochures praising Kennedy's actions were circulated in the ghettos of the nation's largest cities. Most political analysts credit this strategy with having delivered the black vote to Kennedy.[85] The analysts also agreed that these votes provided the margin of victory. Helen Fuller stated the analysis as follows:

> It had been Kennedy's strength in the great Northern cities to which southern negroes had migrated that produced hairline victories for the Democrats in the eight states experts consider crucial to success in any close election—New York, Illinois, Pennsylvania, Michigan, Maryland, Missouri, Minnesota, and New Jersey. All but one—Missouri—went to Eisenhower in 1956. All eight went for Kennedy in 1960, on the strength of the big-city vote. The Republican National Committee, using Philadelphia as a laboratory, made a precinct-by-precinct study of why this happened. The study revealed, among other things, that their candidate won only 18 percent of the Negro vote, leaving 82 percent for Kennedy.[86]

Blacks might reasonably expect positive civil rights policy from the Kennedy presidency: Kennedy had criticized Truman's lack of courage in refraining from using the power of executive action to further civil rights causes; he had campaigned openly for black support; and blacks had provided his margin of victory where it was needed most. However, civil rights turned out not to be Kennedy's top priority.[87] First on the president's agenda was his social and economic program, and to promote it he needed the votes of powerful southern legislators. Thus, conciliation toward the South was in order. This pragmatic conciliatory policy began with the appointment of three staunch segregationists to federal judgeships: J. Robert Elliot of Georgia, William H. Cox of Mississippi, and E. Gordon West of Louisiana. One could reasonably argue that this one act seriously undermines any attempt to portray Kennedy as a principled advocate of civil rights. These three judges would go on to rule consistently against the movement.[88]

Kennedy had referred to Eisenhower as being insincere when he refused to issue an executive order mandating the discontinuance of discrimination in federally aided housing stating that this could have been done by his predecessor with a stroke of a pen. However, after Kennedy had been in office over a year, he still had not signed the same order. Civil rights activists started a "Send a Pen" campaign; literally thousands of pens were sent to the president for that purpose.[89]

Nonetheless, the politically unsophisticated black masses were still enamoured of Kennedy, still infatuated by having actually been courted by a president. Moreover, Kennedy had appointed more blacks to top federal jobs than any president in history, and this impressed those who were relatively politically unsophisticated. What the black leadership hoped for from the administration were: (1) legislation to establish a permanent Fair Employment Practices Commission; (2) legislation mandating nationwide school desegregation; (3) a civil rights bill giving the attorney general the power to institute suits; (4) and executive orders striking down segregation in federally aided housing and enforcing existing orders mandating the end of discrimination by private companies handling government contracts. But Kennedy had his own ideas concerning the best way to achieve civil rights goals.[90]

The direct action of SNCC and other civil rights groups were proving to be a disruptive element for Kennedy. The Freedom Riders wanted federal intervention, which Kennedy was reluctant to provide because of the fear of endangering his chances of successfully courting the southern legislators. Kennedy soon decided that urging voters' registration in the South rather than direct action would best suit his purposes.[91] He could still champion civil rights, but through a more politically legitimate channel. Thus, he argued that civil rights groups should pursue the franchise. Lomax states the Kennedy argument as follows:

(1) Voter registration is the area where the Justice Department has the most power; it can move swiftly, and if need be, on its own motion. (This power was guaranteed by the civil rights bill passed in 1957.)

(2) Voter registration is the one civil rights item white supremacists cannot afford to oppose publicly, for the right to vote is basic to the American system of government.

(3) Negroes have the most difficulty in areas where their numerical strength poses a political threat. If these Negroes voted, they could help elect better officials. This, in the Administration view, would be the critical step toward general civil advancement.

(4) A major increase in the number of southern Negro voters would not only change things at home but would change the complexion of Congress: Southern reactionaries would either mend their ways or run the risk of being voted out of office. Then, and only then, could the Administration get its liberal legislation, including civil rights through Congress.[92]

The leaders of the major civil rights organizations were called to a meeting to discuss the idea. Although the activity of voter registration had been attractive to many of SCLC's members since its founding in 1957, direct action seemed to have been the dominant civil rights thrust since that time. Moreover, a shortage of funds dictated that money available would be used for their main activity. However, with administrative support and financial backing from the foundation-supported Voter Education Project (VEP), voter registration became a much more realistic goal. Initially viewing this benevolence as a ploy to stop the effectiveness of their disruptive tactics, SNCC eventually decided to take part in the effort. They took advantage of a subsidized opportunity to expand their repertoire of strategies.[93] In fact, Kennedy's plan of diverting energy from disruptive tactics was a failure, if this was his motive. Direct action escalated after the founding of VEP—Albany, Birmingham, and Selma were waiting in the wings.

The vigor with which the administration supported the registration effort led many of the activists to believe that the federal government would assure their safety; this was not the case. Although the increases in black registration were substantial between 1962 and 1964 (see Table 2), violence and constant harrassment was the price paid for this victory. The 1964 Mississippi Freedom Summer was a violent period: it produced thirty-five shooting incidents, with three persons injured, thirty homes and other buildings bombed, eighty persons beaten, and six murdered.[94]

The foot soldiers for the battles of Freedom Summer were provided by SNCC; they were an important force in the quest for the ballot. Although they were considered the most militant of the civil rights groups, they eventually embraced the notion of voter registration. In fact, SNCC workers took the notion to new heights and began to articulate the theory of black political empowerment. Stokely Carmichael was perhaps the most vocal proponent of this notion. In *Black Power: The Politics of Liberation in America,* Carmichael links black power and black political empowerment:

> In such areas of Lowndes, where black people have a majority, they will attempt to use power to exercise control. This is what they seek: control. When black people lack a majority, Black Power means proper representation and sharing control. It means the creation of power bases of strength, from which black people can press to change local or nationwide patterns of oppression—instead of from weakness. It does not mean merely putting black faces into offices.[95]

Motivated, among other things, by the notion of black political empowerment, SNCC and other civil rights organizations worked long, hard, and often fruitless hours in the black belt areas between 1962 to 1964. The time spent was considered the price that had to be paid for the envisioned fruits of enfranchisement. It was hypothesized that blacks in the black belt could take political control and, having done so, could enact public policy that would benefit the black community. Even in areas where blacks were a minority, enfranchisement would bring them some measure of influence.

Despite the enthusiasm of the workers, the VEP efforts across the South were largely failures. The barriers of fear, apathy, violence, and intimidation could not be overcome. Moreover, literacy tests were still being used to hamper the registration process. Referring to Mississippi's Freedom Summer, David Garrow writes that registration efforts produced almost as many acts of violence as they did voters.[96] The Civil Rights Bills of '57, '60, and '64, with their emphasis on individual litigation to protect voting rights, were not protecting COFO workers in Mississippi. Thus, it was obvious that a voting rights act with teeth in it was needed. King began to plan a protest at Selma to press for new federal legislation to protect black voting rights.

Throughout the Selma Movement, King continued to write and speak about the power of the ballot. "If Negroes could vote . . . there would be no more oppressive poverty directed against Negroes.[97] He wrote that "voting is the foundation stone for political action."[98] Thus, success at Selma was seen as a major challenge that had to be conquered. "SCLC went to Selma with one goal in mind: to win a strong federal voting rights law that would provide for executive branch enforcement of southern black's constitutionally guaranteed right to vote."[99]

Using the tactic of "nonviolent provocation," success was imminent when Selma law-enforcement authorities made Sunday March 7, 1965, "Bloody Sunday." The nation was outraged when the violent footage was broadcast across the nation. President Johnson called a special session of Congress and announced to the nation that Americans had to overcome the problem of black disenfranchisement. He pledged his unequivocal support for a strong voting rights bill.[100] When the bill was signed into law August 6, 1965, there was widespread jubilation in the civil rights community.

The passage of the 1965 Voting Rights Act by Congress in August of 1965 had been heralded as a milestone in civil rights legislation. For the first time in the history of this country, there were no legally sanctioned barriers that mitigated the ability of blacks to vote. Thus, the act has been called the most effective piece of civil rights legislation ever passed by Congress. The law stipulated the following: (1) any state or subdivision that maintained a test or device as a prerequisite to registration or voting as of November 1, 1964, and had a total voting age population of which less than 50 percent were registered or actually voted in the 1964 presidential election would be covered; (2) when a covered area sought to change its voting qualifications or procedures from those in effect on November 1, 1964, the area must either obtain the approval of the U.S. Attorney General or initiate a federal court suit; (3) literacy tests were banned permanently as a prerequisite to voting; and (4) federal examiners could be sent to covered areas if it was necessary to guarantee Fifteenth Amendment rights.[101]

The original act covered Alabama, Alaska, Georgia, Louisiana, Mississippi, South Carolina, Virginia and twenty-six counties in North Carolina. These states could not easily change their laws to circumvent the intent of the Voting Rights Act.[102] Thus, widespread voter registration was the order of the day (see Table 3). The stage had now been set for the long-predicted widespread black political participation that would lead, it was hoped, to black political empowerment.

2. The Review of the Literature: Explanations for the Lack of Black Political Empowerment

The Voting Rights Act of 1965 redefined the parameters for black political participation in the South—the effects would ripple across the nation.[1] Between 1964 and 1969, one million new black voters were registered; the proportion of eligible black voters rose from 35.5 percent to 64.8 percent for the southern states. Mississippi, Alabama, and Georgia had black voting registration percentages of 6.7, 19.3, and 27.4, respectively, in 1964. By 1969, they had black registration percentages of 66.5, 61.3, and 60.4 (see Table 4).

While fewer than 300 blacks held offices in the southern states before the passage of the Act, by 1980, the figure was over 2,000.[2] Mississippi, the state that was outdistanced by all others with respect to black voter registration prior to 1969, was now the state with the most black elected officials (see Table 5).

The raw figures are impressive when compared to the pre-Act figures. Nonetheless, blacks continued to hold a disproportionately low number of public offices. For example, Georgia's 249 black elected officials account for only 3.7 percent of the total number of elected officials while the state was 26.8 percent black (see Table 6). Within the specific categories of state and local offices, there was still a lack of proportional representation. Again, while Georgia blacks were 26.8 percent of the population, the House and Senate of the state legislature was only 11.7 percent and 3.6 percent black, respectively. Blacks held only 3.4 percent of the positions on county governing boards and 5.2 percent of those on municipal governing boards (see Table 7).

The black belt South provided the greatest hope for the proponents of black political empowerment. Blacks made up the majority of the population and, it was believed, would wield political power once enfranchised. However, even in the black belt, this political empowerment has not been realized. The 1980 U.S. Census reports that there are 87 predominantly black counties in the Southern states. Table 8 shows that in 21 percent (18) of these counties, there are no black elected officials; in 44 percent (38), there are no blacks on the county governing board; in 44 percent (38), there are no blacks on the school board; and in 59 percent (51), there are no black law enforcement officials.

What happened to the dream of black political empowerment in the black belt South? With all of the efforts that went into the passage of the Voting Rights Act of 1965 and subsequent extensions, it is apparent that the black political empowerment efforts have been largely unsuccessful, i.e., the majority of officials in predominantly black areas of the South are not black. A review of the literature on this process offers some answers.

The literature on black political empowerment in the South since 1965 can be divided into two primary categories: (1) the micro-behavioral literature which focuses on the individual aspects of political participation; and (2) the macro-structural literature which focuses on the structural aspects of government and the rules of the game.

The Socioeconomic Status Model

The area of strongest agreement in the literature on political behavior is perhaps that dealing with the importance of socioeconomic status (SES) in determining the extent of political participation. The SES model of political participation states simply that the social status of an individual—his or her job, education, and income—determines to a large extent how much he or she participates. It does this through the intervening effects of a variety of "civic attitudes" conducive to participation: attitudes such as a sense of efficacy, psychological involvement in politics, and a feeling of obligation to participate.[3]

Thus, despite the optimism of the civil rights community concerning their model of black political empowerment, there were those who questioned it from the beginning. Matthews and Protho wrote in 1966 that "most southern Negroes have low social status, relatively small incomes, and limited education received in inferior schools. These attributes are associated with lower-voter turnout among all populations. . . . Negro voting in the South is not, according to this reasoning, easily increased by political or legal means. The rise of a large, active, and effective Negro electorate in the South may have to await substantial social and economic changes."[4]

Pat Watters and Reese Cleghorn expressed the same sentiments when they wrote in 1967 that " . . . the commonly accepted laws of voting suggest relatively little future participation by Southern Negroes. If a low income, low education, lack of a middle class, and a lack of a sense of identity with the larger community are necessarily deterrents to voting, as they seem to have been with whites, and perhaps with Negroes in the past, Southern Negroes will come to the polls very slowly indeed."[5]

More recently, there have been studies which continue to emphasize the legitimacy of the status model as a predictor of voting patterns. Wolfinger and Rosenstone, in their study of voters in the 1972 national election, found that education was by far the most important determinant of one's decision to vote.[6] Abney found that the median education of blacks had the highest partial correlation with aggregate turnout among blacks in Mississippi elections.[7] Gerald Wright found a linear relationship between levels of education and the black turnout in the presidential election of 1968.[8] Thus, the socioeconomic status model argues that the lack of black political participation is a function of the disproportionate low ses levels in the black community.

Organization, Group Consciousness, and Specific Efficacy

The path from high socioeconomic status to political participation is not a direct one. High ses individuals tend to possess characteristics (e.g., confidence in their ability to effect change and feelings of personal efficacy) that lead them to the activity of political participation. Thus, people with low ses are not necessarily doomed to low levels of political participation; however, some other facilitating factor must replace high sᴇs. Organization, with an emphasis on group consciousness and a sense of specific efficacy, is a bypassing agent. Research has shown that "group consciousness" can cause blacks to participate at rates beyond what one would normally expect based on socioeconomic characteristics.[9]

"Political efficacy is the feeling that one is capable of influencing the public decision-making process."[10] While few individuals may feel that they have widespread influence in all areas of the public policy formation process at any given time, it is common for individuals to believe that under certain conditions and at certain times they can have an impact on the outcome of a decision. Thus, we have the concept of "specific efficacy." This notion motivated the coꜰo (Council of Federated Organizations) during the Freedom Summer of 1964—under the specific conditions of a black majority and the passage of a voting rights act, blacks could formulate public policy by electing blacks to office. When leaders can make clear what is possible under specific circumstances, otherwise apolitical individuals will often participate.[11]

Fear and Apathy

The socioeconomic status model of political behavior assumes that individuals are living in a basically free and open society, i.e., that one will not suffer reprisals for the exercise of the franchise. Under such circumstances, non-voting is usually attributed to apathy.[12] Since the Voting Rights Act did not remove the threat of violence or economic intimidation, it is questionable just how open the new black belt South really is.

Salamon and Van Evera doubt the usefulness of the standard "income-education-apathy thesis" as an explanatory model for political behavior in an area where participation is not truly open. Since participation in a closed society requires more than understanding and time, these authors posit that, in the South, fear may be a more powerful variable than apathy in explaining black participation rates. Salamon and Van Evera also assert that political inequality is a manifestation of discrimination. Operationalizing discrimination as educational and economic inequality, they found that the greater the disparity, the less blacks participated.[13] By 1978, fear appeared to be less of a factor. A study by David Garrow replicated the Salamon-Van Evera study using heavily black counties in South Carolina. He applied the model to five elections over a six-year period. For the first election in 1970, the Salamon-Van Evera analysis predicted the outcome well. However, the usefulness of the fear model almost disappeared when applied to the four elections held between 1972 and 1976. While Garrow did not offer an explanation for the sharp decline in the fear model's predictive power, he did suggest that "the possibility that changes in the characteristics of rural black southerners have been so rapid in the past eight years [1970–78] as to make the 1970 [census] misleading is highly substantial."[14]

Context versus Personal Characteristics

The most recent literature on black participation posits that the legacy of repression in the South is no longer the primary explanation for low black political participation. James Carlson, who looks at black political participation in the South using aggregate data on individuals, as well as a community context measure, states that " . . . contextual effects seem to have the greatest impact on those blacks with personal characteristics that would not impel them to participate in politics. Those whose personal characteristics predispose them towards participation seem to participate at relatively high levels regardless of context."[15]

This view recognizes that barriers still exist but that they simply make it more difficult for blacks to participate—not impossible. The present barriers in the South only reinforce the traditional relationship between SES and participation where more hostile forms of violence compromised this relationship.[16]

This view is based on the notion that obstacles to political participation have become increasingly benign since the Voting Rights Act. However, much of the "obstructionist literature" offers counter-evidence. Brian Sherman lists the various pressures, threats, and reprisals that still deter black political participation,[17] and a 1982 Voter Education Project (VEP) study listed "physical, economic, and other forms of intimidation" as barriers to black registration, voting, and candidacy. Moreover, the low rate of black political participation is also attributed to a lack of fair and effective representation.[18] Laughlin McDonald, in his 1982 ACLU study, also cites intimidation as a continuing barrier to equal political participation.[19]

Thus, there appear to be multiple factors that inhibit black political participation in the black belt South. The scholars minimize the influence of intimidation, whereas the writings of groups closer to the problem continue to document cases of intimidation. Although people with high political participatory profiles may suffer inconvenience in order to participate, it is questionable whether or not they will submit to the consequences of threats and other reprisals. After all, the decision to participate does involve a rational calculation based on cost and benefits. Thus, if intimidation continues to exist, political participation is still influenced by context. If intimidation no longer exists, the standard SES might be an accurate predictor of participation.

Nonetheless, as Stekler points out, many of the barriers listed by voting rights activists belong in the category of inconveniences.[20] Since many decisions about elections—location of polling places, who will work at the polls, time of registration, etc.—are made by the incumbents who have no interest in politicizing blacks, they are often made inconvenient, but not necessarily illegal. If blacks would go the extra mile, register, and vote, empowerment could occur. However, this view overlooks the power of racial bloc voting coupled with at-large elections in areas where whites predominate—blacks will invariably lose in such conditions.

At-Large Elections and Other Features of Reform Government

At-large elections have the power to mitigate black political power regardless of the rate of participation. Thus, proponents of black political empowerment have campaigned against at-large elections as being detrimental to black political empowerment efforts. Most scholars support this view and argue that other structural impediments contribute to the under-representation of blacks.[21]

Lee Sloan, in his study of America's twenty-eight largest cities, found that "the percentage of blacks serving on municipal governing councils approached that of blacks in the overall population in cities that employed district elections." In other cities, blacks were significantly under-represented. This 1969 study was followed by a series of supportive studies.[22]

Clinton Jones found that "at-large elections, especially in the South and the Northeast, small council sizes, and the use of larger districts, under ward plans, were all associated with black under-representation.[23] Karnig found that "at-large elections distill minority voting power," with negative impact being greater in the South.[24] However, methodological problems in each study made their conclusions questionable: they both used the reputedly unreliable municipal yearbook as the source for determining electoral method, and Jones used cities that had a very small number of blacks.[25] Nonetheless, studies without these flaws continued to support the thesis that political structure has an impact upon black representation.

Robinson and Dye found that at-large elections were the single greatest factor in black under-representation. Moreover, they found that mayor-council governmental usage and especially higher black median educational levels were also associated with gaining minority equity with respect to being elected to city councils.[26] Taebel found that blacks benefit from district election; blacks' representational equity is greater in the city; and overall under-representation of minorities was significantly greater in the South.[27]

In a more recent study, Karnig found that at-large elections were not as powerful as suggested by the Robinson and Dye study, although there was a strong association between at-large elections and black proportional representation. However, the greater associations were between indicators of black socioeconomic status and indicators of black organization. Thus, Karnig concludes that while the existence of at-large elections is an important factor in promoting under-representation, it is not the most important one. However, a more recent study by Stekler supports the earlier Robinson and Dye which shows the existence of at-large elections as having the greatest impact on under-representation. In his summary, Stekler concludes, " . . . while the socioeconomic characteristics of the black community do have an impact on black electoral success, much as has been found in earlier studies, the electoral structure used by cities, having at large versus district elections, has the more consistent and greater impact."[28]

The political behavior literature leads one to expect the following: (1) the rate of black political empowerment should correlate positively with increases in ses; (2) political empowerment should correlate negatively with the presence of fear; (3) positive electoral structures, i.e., district elections, partisan elections, and mayor-council forms of government have a positive effect on black political candidacies; and (4) organization is fundamental to successful black political empowerment. The purpose of the following section is to test how well these explanations apply to a specific area, Georgia's black belt.

Georgia: A Case Study

W. E. B. Du Bois wrote in 1903 that the problems of blacks seemed to be centered in the state of Georgia.[29] This statement is especially appropriate with respect to the state of black political empowerment in Georgia's black belt counties. A reading of the average number of black elected officials from 1972–82 offers a dismal picture of progress: Table 9 shows that 35 percent of the counties (8) had no officials; 35 percent (8) averaged only one official; 13 percent (3) averaged only two officials; 9 percent (2) averaged 4 officials; 4 percent (1) averaged 6 officials; 4 percent (1) averaged fourteen officials. Georgia had the largest proportion—65 percent—of counties with no blacks on the major county boards—more than any other southern state with a 20 percent or more black population. Moreover, Georgia had the largest number of counties with no black elected officials.[30] Since the problems are apparently greater in Georgia, an examination of the problems there should have relevancy for the black belt South in general.

Socioeconomic Variables
The socioeconomic model hypothesizes that the higher black ses counties are likely to have greater voter participation and there-

fore more black elected officials. Using median income, median school years, and the percentage of high school graduates as measures of socioeconomic status, one would think that Peach County would have elected the most officials. Blacks in Peach County have the highest median income (Table 10) and the highest percentage of high school graduates (Table 11). Nonetheless, Hancock outdistanced Peach in electing black officials, although the population of the former was poorer and less well educated. In fact, contrary to traditional SES predictions, there is no significant relationship between number of black elected officials and median income nor percentage of black high school graduates in the electorate. The relationship between the black population's median school years and the number of black officials it elects is significant, but only slightly so (R=0.4)—not nearly as strong as one would expect given the importance attributed to the socioeconomic explanation of political participation (see Table 15).

Fear Variables
Salamon and Van Evera have operationalized the fear variable as a function of economic vulnerability. Black agricultural workers and black families in poverty are vulnerable to economic intimidation. Thus, they tend to be inactive politically.[31] Blacks who are economically independent, on the other hand, tend to participate more. Tables 12, 13, and 14 show that Peach County is superior to Hancock on two of these measures: whereas only 37.6 percent of Peach's black families live in poverty, 54 percent of Hancock's blacks do; while 18.1 percent of Peach's blacks are economically independent, only 7.6 percent of Hancock's blacks are; and while 9.7 percent of Peach's blacks are employed in agriculture, 3.3 percent of Hancock blacks are. Nonetheless, it was Hancock that had the most successful political empowerment effort. Moreover, Table 16 shows that the correlations between these variables are not statistically significant.

Structural Variables
The structuralists argue that the features of reform government are detrimental to the aspirations of black elected officials. These features include at-large elections, partisan elections, and commission forms of government, rather than the mayor-council

form of government. All of Georgia's black belt counties had
at-large voting for county commissioners, partisan elections in
the county and city, the mayor-council form of government in
their county seat, and district elections for city councilpersons.[32]
Yet Hancock and Peach stand out for their respective county
and city successes. Hancock achieved majority control over the
county government, while Peach achieved potential control over
the city government.

Organizational Variables
Salamon and Van Evera's organizational index employed four
variables: (1) percentage of blacks economically independent;
(2) the absolute geographic size of the county; (3) the amount of
outside assistance; and (4) the percentage of the voting-age
population that was black.

Table 17 shows that the expected positive relationship between economically independent blacks and black elected officials does not exist and that the expected negative correlation
between absolute size of the county and the number of black
elected officials does not exist: the relationship is positive and not
significant. Moreover, Table 18 shows that Hancock, which has
the largest number of black elected officials, is the fourth largest
in area of the black belt counties, while Quitman County, the second smallest, has averaged only one black elected official.

The outside assistance variable and the black percentage of
the voting-age population have more *prima facie* explanatory potential. Table 19 shows that Hancock blacks account for 70.3 percent of the voting-age population. This means that in Hancock
there are clearly more blacks to spare for a mobilization effort;
Talbot, where blacks account for 65.3 percent of the voting-age
population, is the only other county which meets the Justice Department's "safe district" standard, i.e., a 65 percent or more
black population. Thus, it becomes clear that Hancock and Talbot
have a resource—large numbers—that other counties cannot
match. In a comparison of Hancock and Talbot, however, it became apparent that more was at work than numbers: Hancock
averaged 14 black elected officials for the 1972–82 decade, while
Talbot averaged only 2.

A partial explanation lies in the fact that Hancock was the

focus of more widespread outside assistance than the other counties. Table 20 shows that seventeen counties received financial and technical assistance only from the Voter Education Project; four counties received outside assistance from SNCC and VEP, while Hancock received support from SCLC, VEP, The Urban League, The Georgia Council on Human Relations, and the Ford Foundation. It is clear that more organizational activity was occurring in Hancock.

The socioeconomic model, the structuralist arguments, and the fear model individually explain little about black political empowerment in Georgia's predominantly black counties. The organizational variables tell us that black political empowerment would be more likely in Hancock based on their "safe district" status, i.e., a black voting-age population that makes up over 65 percent of the electorate. Moreover, a good deal of outside assistance is evident in Hancock. However, there is nothing in the political behavior literature which explains the process of organization building, although it is a crucial factor in facilitating black political participation.

Lipsky complained that although there were countless narratives detailing the particular events of particular civil rights efforts across the South, there were few theoretical works that tried to create a general model for success or failure of these efforts.[33] The opposite is true for the study of black political empowerment—the literature on black empowerment comprises models primarily, without any detailed studies of the efforts to gain this power. Even if a quantitative model explained all of the variance, one could only surmise about the dynamic process of empowerment. In order to understand the process of empowerment, one would have to study black political empowerment efforts as if they were "social movements." Although efforts to gain political power are not usually thought of as social movements, they share the necessary ingredients for success: (1) interests; (2) opportunity; (3) leadership; (4) organization; (5) resources; and (6) collective action.[34] The interrelationship among these elements can make or break a black political empowerment effort.

Interests are special concerns that have the potential to cause individuals to participate. A basic interest of all individuals is to have a better quality of life. The vote, historically, and to a lesser extent presently, is championed as an instrument of social change. To the extent that individuals accept the potency of the ballot as a tool of social change, voting and other forms of political participation follow. However, the efficacy of political participation as an agent of change is premised on the availability of the vote.

The post-WWII Civil Rights Movement created the opportunity to make voting and other forms of political participation potential tools to effect change.[35] Before the Voting Rights Act of 1965, disenfranchisement was reinforced by the government; however, it was also the government that later facilitated the move toward empowerment by enforcing the Fifteenth Amendment. Given the opportunity and the interest, someone must provide leadership.

Leaders are responsible for articulating goals and for developing strategies for reaching those goals. They articulate the interests and provide strong support for the rank-and-file who need the encouragement to participate. Their duties include: (1) developing and maintaining an organization; (2) mobilizing the resources; and (3) coordinating the collective action. In essence, they are responsible for "pulling it all together."

The goal of black political empowerment can be best achieved by a coordinated effort: the requisite political education, consciousness-raising, and turning out the vote does not happen alone. Organization provides a forum for the articulation of interests as well as a mechanism through which the resources can be mobilized.

Numbers are only one political resource. Time, money, experience, energy, expertise, access to elites, and popular approval are all potential resources which can be utilized in the process of attaining black political empowerment. These resources must be coordinated for maximum effectiveness. The maximum coordination of the resources, i.e., mobilization, sets the stage for collective action.

Tilly states that collective action consists of people acting together in pursuit of common interests. It is the result of successful coordination of all of the other elements that make for a successful social movement. With reference to black political empowerment, a major element of collective action is gaining high black voter turnout in a bloc for the black candidate. The dynamism of these variables has never been applied to the process of empowerment. However, Lester Salamon explicated a model of activating political participation in the black belt South which focused heavily on the organization component. Salamon cites leadership, organization, and popular support as key ingredients to lower-class protest. Violence, economic intimidation, patron-client relationships, and black class antagonism are barriers to black organizational development. Once the group is organized, they must meet effectiveness goals. Salamon argues that the following goals must be met in order for the organization to continue to exist: (1) management of fear; (2) education and communication; (3) political mobilization; (4) provision of services; (5) conflict resolution; (6) economic development.[37]

Salamon analyzes events in three Mississippi counties (Holmes, Sunflower, and Wilkinson) from the perspective of his organizational model, but does not provide a descriptive historical account of the political events. Herein lies the problem with his model; a greater appreciation for the process of organization building is gained when the historical context is adequately considered.

Salamon's organizational analysis has two other drawbacks: (1) his analysis does not allow the reader to appreciate the dynamism that exists among leadership, organization, overcoming barriers, meeting effectiveness goals, and resources—his analysis is largely static, whereas these components are dynamic; (2) since it focuses on factors relevant to the organizational components, the analysis could possibly overlook other salient factors which affect participation.

Case studies of counties which focus on social movement variables and avoid the drawbacks of Salamon's organizational analysis could shed light on the dynamism of the empowerment process. Hancock, Peach, and Clay stand out as especially good candidates for such studies, in that they provide examples of black belt counties with three different rates of black political empowerment: Hancock County averaged 14 black elected officials for the 1972 to 1982 decade; Peach County averaged 6 black elected officials for the same period; and Clay County failed to elect a black public official.[38] The review of the literature has revealed little to explain the variance in number of black elected officials in these counties. If social movement variables provide a useful perspective from which to view black political empowerment efforts, they should vary within these counties. The present study covers the 1960 to 1982 period. The research material that will be used to test the usefulness of this perspective was collected primarily from interviews conducted between September 1980 and August 1981. Four months were spent in each county. The informants were all activists in the black political empowerment efforts in their counties. Many non-activists were informally interviewed in order to obtain a more general perspective on black political activity in the county. In each county, the primary question to answer was "what factors facilitated or repressed black political empowerment?"

Hancock County, with an average of fourteen black elected officials for the 1972 to 1982 decade, did not have any black elected officials in 1964. Table 21 shows that, by 1974, blacks held sixteen of the eighteen elective public offices. Moreover, Table 29 shows that in 1966, Hancock's black registration rate was only 51.8 percent of those eligible. It rose to 77.8 percent in 1968, and, by 1974, Hancock's black registration had risen to 94.3 percent. The chapter dealing with Hancock County will seek to uncover the factors behind this mobilization and successful empowerment effort.

Peach County, with an average of six black elected officials for the 1972–82 decade, elected its first black official in 1970. By 1980, Fort Valley had a black mayor, and Table 36 shows that three blacks were on a city council of three persons, while two blacks were on the four-person utilities commission (Table 37). Thus, blacks had the potential to control public policy. However, this lasted for only two years. Rudolph Carson, the first black mayor, two long-term city councilmen, and a black on the utilities commission all lost their bids for re-election in 1982. The Peach County chapter will seek to uncover the factors behind this rise and fall of black political empowerment.

Clay County failed to elect any blacks to office during the period of the study. Although Table 38 shows that 80 percent of Clay's blacks were registered to vote by 1980, these numbers did not translate into black elected officials. Although the black registration rate in Clay County was higher than Peach's, Peach was relatively successful, whereas Clay achieved no measure of success. The Clay chapter will attempt to flesh out the factors which are responsible for this depressed level of black political empowerment.

The three chapters devoted to Hancock, Peach, and Clay counties will combine a descriptive historical account of the events in each county from 1960 to 1982 with an organizational analysis which utilizes the Salamon paradigm. The descriptive analysis serves two main functions: (1) it creates the possibility for the emergence of other salient factors which could have had an impact on black political empowerment; (2) it shows the dynamism among leadership, organization, overcoming barriers, meeting effectiveness goals, and resources. The organizational analysis presents a strong case for the importance of organizational development with respect to black political empowerment.

This book argues that black political empowerment is dependent upon the proper interrelationship between leadership, organization, and resources. These components mesh to create a state of organizational effectiveness. Organizational effectiveness can overcome the problems associated with low socioeconomic status, fear, structures, and other barriers to participation. The chief objective of this book is to show how three different levels of organizational effectiveness yielded three different levels of black political empowerment. This book does not seek to depreciate the importance of socioeconomic status, barriers, and structures. However, the focus here is on how organizational effectiveness can overcome other repressive influences on black political participation. The case studies of Hancock, Peach, and Clay reveal that leadership, organization, and resources were pivotal in the political empowerment process. Thus, the thesis of this work is as follows:

Hancock County blacks achieved political empowerment as a result of successful organizational development; a leadership group was organized and successfully overcame the barriers to its development: (1) economic intimidation, (2) fear of violence, (3) the angel system, and (4) black antagonism. After having established themselves as a meaningful and viable organization, they gained popular support largely because of their program of economic development and service provision. Because of the popular support, they were able to: (1) enhance their program of fear management, (2) resolve internal and external conflicts, (3) politically educate the masses, and (4) provide the catalyst for political mobilization. To the extent that these factors were not present in Peach and Clay, black political empowerment was not achieved there.

3. Black Political Empowerment in Hancock County, Georgia, 1960 to 1982

With the election of two blacks to a three-person board of commissioners, the 1968 election made Hancock the first biracial county in America to be controlled by blacks.[1] In 1964, there were no black elected officials in Hancock. By 1974, sixteen of eighteen public elected officials in Hancock were black (see Table 21). This political transformation did not occur at random; it was the result of an organized effort to gain black political empowerment. This chapter is an explication of how this empowerment was achieved.

Long before the opportunity structure[2] materialized for an attempt at black political empowerment in Hancock County, conditions which were conducive to an empowerment effort were present. These conditions were: (1) an overwhelmingly black population; (2) relatively little racial antagonism;[3] (3) the highest rate of black land ownership in the state; and (4) a group of black educators who stressed group accomplishments.

Hancock County has always been predominantly black. Slaves outnumbered planters,[4] and Table 22 shows that the county maintained a substantial black majority into the 1960s and to the present. A substantial black majority, defined by the Justice Department as a 65 percent black majority, is necessary for black political empowerment.[5] The assertion that such a sizable majority is needed is premised on the well-documented existence of high levels of white racial bloc-voting.[6] Thus, since it is not realistic for blacks to strategize for white votes, the black vote becomes the sole support base for empowerment. A substantial black majority is necessary also because there are at least three factors that reduce the number of potential black votes that will be cast for the black candidate: (1) since blacks on the average are younger than whites, the black voting age population is usually lower than the overall black population; (2) blacks tend to register and vote at lower rates than whites; and (3) blacks bloc-vote for blacks at lower rates than whites bloc-vote for whites: whites tend to bloc-vote at a 90 to 99 percent rate, while blacks bloc-vote at between 80 and 95 percent.[7] Because of such factors, large numbers are a valuable resource since they can absorb these losses. Hancock had the numbers, and was given the opportunity to use them.

Hancock blacks recount numerous stories about blacks from slavery to the present who refused to be subservient; they were known by the white and black communities as "crazy niggers." They were individuals who challenged the authority of whites, demanded a certain amount of respect, fought—and even killed— white people in defense of their principles. Robert Ingram, Sr., provided the following story:

> One time a black woman brushed up against a white man and she didn't apologize. A group of whites were coming into the black neighborhood to arrest the woman. Meanwhile, she had told her neighbors what had happened. They armed themselves with bottles and sticks and were waiting on the white men to come. A white man who had seen the armed blacks met the white mob and told them, "All of you can go down there if you want to but all of you won't come back." The group decided not to come.[8]

Such stories as these offer strong support for a neutral-to-positive political climate, i.e., an environment where intimidation is not rampant. Many counties across the South would have punished this assertiveness so severely that it would have disappeared. The local debate is not about whether or not the neutral-to-positive political climate ever existed—that is accepted. The debate is about *why* it existed.

One argument posits that Hancock was more neutral because it was "never in the redneck tradition." During and after slavery, Hancock was a "cultured, refined, and genteel community." The planters in Hancock were Whigs and voted for Alexander Stephens, the vice-president of the Confederacy, to stay in the Union; the only Klan in the county was organized for a brief period after WWI by a newcomer; and the county has no record of lynching. Thus, according to this argument, Hancock had a neutral-to-positive political climate for blacks because its white population eschewed the more extreme forms of racism.[9] The opponents of this view argue that the neutral-to-positive political climate is a function of black assertiveness not white benevolence. They cite documentation of lynchings and Klan activity in Hancock as evidence that Hancock whites were only different to the extent they were forced to be different.[10]

For a lengthy period after slavery, Hancock was known as a "white man's playground."[11] Interracial concubinage was an integral part of Hancock's early race relations. There are contemporary black families in Hancock whose roots originate with white planters. It was not rare for many of these men to leave their mixed children land in their wills. The most well-known example of black land inheritance is that of David Dickson. After the Civil War, he owned over thirty thousand acres of land, railroad stock, plantation stock, and farming equipment. When he died in 1885, he left his mulatto children his estate. Moreover, land was more accessible to blacks in Hancock by comparison to surrounding counties in Georgia. With these factors in operation, blacks in Hancock have always led in the state in the percentage of blacks who owned and operated their own farms.[12] As late as 1972, the *Atlanta Constitution* reported on the controversy caused by the rumor that blacks owned 60 percent of the land in Hancock.[13] Land ownership provided a measure of security from economic intimidation. Thus, those blacks who had land were often found among the leaders of black political empowerment efforts. The presence of more black landowners than any other county provided a valuable resource for Hancock.

Hancock County lays claim to being the home county of several outstanding blacks who were influential on the local, state, and national levels. The most prominent of these were educators: Henry Hunt, the founder of Fort Valley State College; Benjamin Hubert, a former president of Savannah State College and Charles S. Harper, who was the executive secretary of the Georgia Teachers Educational Association. These men were most influential following the turn of the century and through the 1950s. They were inspired by the examples of Burl S. Ingram, a former slave and pioneer school teacher; by Lucius H. Holsey, one of the founders of Paine College; and by Zach Hubert, the father of Ben Hubert, a very successful farmer during the late 1890s.[14]

Burl S. Ingram (ca. 1850–1926) was twenty before he could go to school, since it was illegal for blacks to read during slavery. He learned to read by playing school with white youths on the plantation before he was large enough to work in the fields. Despite Ingram's small stature, his master sent him to work in the fields when he was made aware of his academic pursuits. Nonetheless, Ingram continued to have an interest in learning—even though he was severely whipped once for reading a book while plowing. Since it was such a struggle for him to obtain basic reading, writing, and mathematical skills, he had a deep appreciation for learning that he proudly expressed to his friends and neighbors.[15]

Lucius H. Holsey (1842–1920) was born near Columbus, Georgia, in 1842. He was taught to read by his master's children and by an old black man, with the help of two Webster blueback spellers. Holsey became a minister after the Civil War and was instrumental in organizing the Christian Methodist Episcopal Church in America. He was elected bishop of this church in 1872 at the relatively young age of thirty. Undoubtedly influenced by his struggle to acquire an education, Holsey was one of the cofounders of Paine College, a small private black college in Augusta, Georgia.

Zach Hubert (?–1926) was born in slavery on the Hubert Plantation in neighboring Warren County. After the Civil War, he and his family were freed, and their former master aided them in securing a farm to rent. The Zach Hubert family was extremely successful with the farm—so successful that he struck out on his own in 1869.

Hubert rented a farm in the Powellton section of Hancock; he was the first black man to have land there. He joined the white Baptist church in Powellton and became a liaison between the black and white communities; he was generally credited with helping to maintain the harmony that earned Hancock the rare distinction of being a "lynchproof county."

The Sparta *Ishmaelite,* the local paper, wrote that Hubert was "the most remarkable Negro in the section of the state" when he died in 1926. The paper estimated his estate to be worth at least $100,000. This was remarkable, considering that he was born in slavery. Moreover, he sent all twelve of his children to college. All of his children, with the exception of one minister, were educators. Among them were two college presidents and a college professor.[17]

Hubert's son Benjamin (1887–1959) organized the Association for the Advancement of Negro Country Life as a memorial to his parents. George Foster Peabody, Dr. William H. Kilpatrick, and Eleanor Roosevelt were recruited to promote the work of the center. From 1934 to the beginning of WWII, Springfield, the site of the center, was a thriving community. The center contained a swimming pool, a community center, a farm shop building, a store, a health center, a home for teachers, a dairy farm, a boy's camp, and a cafeteria. The Log Cabin Center, the headquarters for the Association for the Advancement of Negro Country Life, was praised by a CBS commentator in 1938 as a cordial meeting place where blacks and whites gathered in a relaxed environment to discuss farming, politics, and local affairs. Although Benjamin Hubert tried to reactivate the excitement of the Log Cabin Center after the best young farmers left during WWII, he was largely unsuccessful. However, the center still serves as a community meetinghouse and voting place.[18]

Benjamin Hubert and Henry A. Hunt (1886–1938) both encouraged black Hancock Countians to attend school. Though the center did not reach its pre-WWII vitality, Hubert was successful in establishing a summer branch of Savannah State College at the center. Many Savannah State and Fort Valley State College graduates would return to Hancock to teach in the public schools there. Both of these men constantly asserted that land, education, and hard work would lead to progress for blacks in Hancock.[19]

Charles S. Harper (1877–1955), the executive secretary of the Georgia Teachers Educational Association, had a tremendous influence on public schoolteachers in Hancock County. The fear of losing one's job for politically motivated reasons was sharply lessened after Harper's organization became known for supporting its members in cases of unscrupulous firings. In the early 1950s, black female schoolteachers led a boycott that eventually caused the demise of a local dress shop. A boycott member explained that " . . . it was covert, not with pickets. There was a gubernatorial race between Herman Talmadge and M. E. Thompson. They were to speak at the courthouse. At the rally, a local lawyer said that the most educated black teacher was not capable of teaching a second grade white child. The black teachers patronized his wife's shop. The shop had to close when we boycotted."[20] Although the campaign was conducted covertly, the initiation of the boycott by the public schoolteachers went against the established norms of behavior for black schoolteachers in small rural areas.[21]

The presence of these black educators had inspirational as well as practical effects. They served as role models of success and articulated a plan for success. One community activist explained how " . . . they stressed that getting the ballot, some land, education, and hard work would lead to black progress in Hancock. Ben Hubert verbalized those values fervently. I think that they may have even motivated me."[22] On the practical level, Hunt and Hubert encouraged black Hancock youngsters to go on to college. Many of them returned to Hancock upon graduation. In sum, Hunt and Hubert provided a unique brand of leadership during their era.

With the demise of the white primary, a few blacks were allowed to vote in 1946. Against the will of the protesting Klan, blacks walked around burning crosses to register and vote.[23] However, the chances for substantial black influence did not materialize until the passage of the Voting Rights Act of 1965.

Hancock County and the Approaching Opportunity To Act

The Greensboro Movement began February 1, 1960, when Ezell Blair and Joseph McNeil challenged the system of segregation at Woolworth's in Greensboro, N. C. The movement spread across the South; between February 1, 1960, and September 1961, the sit-ins brought desegregation to more than one hundred cities and towns in the South. Moreover, The Student Non-Violent Co-ordinating Committee came into existence out of the need to peacefully manage the desegregation efforts.[24]

Hancock did not escape the winds of change sweeping the South. Three events facilitated the first local organizational effort toward empowerment: (1) persistent and inquisitive black students at Hancock's all-black Hancock Central High; (2) discourteous treatment of blacks at the county courthouse; and (3) the excitement created by the forthcoming Civil Rights Act of 1964.[25]

After hearing about events in Greensboro and other places, Hancock Central students began to ask why things were still the same in Hancock, according to E. R. Warren and James McMullen, two teachers at Hancock Central during this time. The students' curiosity found expression in their civics classes immediately following the beginning of the Greensboro Movement. They were full of questions: Why were all of Hancock's public officials white? Why did they get used books from the white school instead of new ones? And why were most of the prisoners in Hancock black, while the security guards were white?[26]

Hancock's black civics and social studies teachers were suddenly confronted with these questions. It is noteworthy that the public schoolteachers in Hancock would entertain such questions—most black schoolteachers in black belt southern areas would avoid sections of textbooks concerning citizenship rights and responsibilities. Many southern counties prohibited the teaching of civic responsibility in black public schools.[27] Black Hancock teachers were not typical—they faced the challenge of bright and inquisitive students asking difficult questions.[28] Warren and McMullen were especially disconcerted and often spent time in the teachers lounge discussing the problems raised by the students.[29]

The teachers usually responded by explaining slavery and its legacy of discrimination and segregation. They discussed the impact of discrimination and segregation on race relations in America in general and their impact on life in Hancock specifically. The teachers were not satisfied with their own answers, in that they simply offered a descriptive analysis without a prescriptive plan of action. They felt somewhat powerless, since the *Brown*

Decision was being evaded by massive resistance, taking cover behind the "all deliberate speed" phrase. Moreover, the Civil Rights Act of 1964 was doing little to deter discriminatory practices of local county registrars.[30] Meanwhile, black mistreatment at the hands of white county officials seemed to increase after the beginning of the sit-ins. Black frustration began to mount as the mistreatment became more commonplace. The Civil Rights Act came at a time when frustrations were peaking. While Warren and McMullen constantly discussed their frustrations concerning the gap between America's democratic theory and Hancock's political reality, Robert Ingram, Sr., a state hospital worker, and Merilous Roberts, a local businessman, were concerned about the continued abuse faced by blacks at the courthouse. When they became aware of their mutual frustration, they decided to meet to discuss what could be done about the problems.[31]

Meeting in late 1964 in the annex of the Macedonia Baptist Church, they decided that an organization was needed to develop the political potential of the black community. They also agreed that proposals for such an organization could be circulated best by the church. This proved to be a fruitful idea. With the support of the church and its affiliated groups, large crowds began to attend the meetings. It was apparent that the timing of such an organizational venture was excellent. The members soon decided that their chief focus would be on voter registration and on increasing political awareness in the black community. The organization was officially named "The Hancock County Democratic Club" (hereafter referred to as HCDC). Its members exuded a great deal of pride whenever they were given the opportunity to show off their membership cards. Within a three-month period, there were 300 members who paid dues of $5.00 each.[32]

The HCDC averaged approximately two hundred members per year from 1964 to 1974. With small voter-registration grants from the Voter Education Project (less than $500.00) and the membership dues, the annual budget averaged $1000.00 to $1,500.00 per year during the 1964–74 period. Approximately 50 people attended the meetings regularly, but members as well as non-members would turn out at approaching elections or during times of crisis.[33]

Hancock's black youth were also organized. Acting independently, they attempted to integrate public accommodations in the city of Sparta after the passage of the Civil Rights Act of 1964; they also held their own voter-registration drives. Robert Ingram, Jr., explained:

> We decided to integrate the Old Reese Drugstore. Blacks previously patronized the place but were not allowed to sit and drink at the soda fountain. So one day we bought sodas and attempted to sit down. The proprietor jumped up and moved the chairs—there are still no chairs in that drugstore. He hauled them to the back. We left there, going to the hotel. The drugstore man told them that we were coming and he had the doors closed . . .
>
> We would take people to get registered. We would go to town on Saturday and get people off to register. It would be open then. They soon stopped that practice. People would call my mother and ask who was getting her son to register people. They said that the FBI had asked them. I was even told by the police that I would be killed. I told them that they would have to do it. I eventually got labeled a "crazy nigger."[34]

Phase Two: External Organization and Mobilization

The purely internal phase of the Hancock effort toward black political empowerment came to an end during the summer of 1965. With a 75 percent black population and a black political organization going through its birth pains, the Southern Christian Leadership Conference (SCLC) felt that Hancock would be the perfect place to invest some of its resources. It initiated a voter-registration program called SCOPE (Summer Community Organization and Political Education Program) during the summer of 1965. Carl Farris, a young black sociologist from St. Louis, was sent to Hancock to help organize. Although he lacked rural organizational experience, he had organized extensively in the urban North with the Congress of Racial Equality.[35]

Although Farris met some fear in Hancock, he was steadfast in his mission. He intended to increase the inhabitants' knowledge of how politics worked in this largely apolitical black community. Thus, he was mainly a civic educator as he spread his message and encouraged more blacks to participate. One of his goals was the elimination of the literacy test, since it kept a disproportionate number of blacks from registering. His organizational efforts, in conjunction with those of HCDC, were fruitful— Hancock County was one of the few counties where blacks stood in line to register on the first day the Voting Rights Act became effective in Georgia. Despite the Klan's burning of two crosses in an attempt to provoke fear, the potential registrants would not be deterred. Carl Farris soon left to organize neighboring Warren County.[36]

The HCDC accelerated its mobilization activities after Carl Farris left during August of 1965. They wanted to run candidates in the 1966 Democratic primary, and they wanted to start early. Canvassing the communities, discussing the quest for empowerment, and promoting registration drives were their primary objectives. Ministers encouraged political participation from the pulpit, and workshops were held to instruct new voters in the details of using the regular and absentee ballots.[37]

As the election drew near, HCDC decided to run three candidates: one each for the board of education, the county commission, and the Democratic executive committee. Despite the time and energy devoted to registration drives, only 51.8 percent of the black voting-age population was registered to vote.[38] Although they held a slight majority—a majority of less than one percent—of the voters, an extremely high turnout of black voters bloc-voting for the black candidates was necessary to assure victory for the black candidates.

Moreover, blatant repressive measures were being utilized to discourage black voters. Reverend Edwards, a schoolteacher and minister, was very active in showing new black voters how to use the ballot. He was forcefully taken from his home by a group of white men in the midst of the campaign and warned to discontinue his activities. He was not physically harmed, but this act made the black community aware that some of the local whites were serious about protecting their exclusive control over governmental decision making in the county. Moreover, on the eve of the 1966 election, the KKK paraded down mainstreet in an attempt to dissuade the black voter turnout by arousing fear. Despite the burning of several crosses, they were decidedly unsuccessful.[39]

All three of the black candidates were victorious in their races: Robert Ingram became the first black member on the board of education; James Smith was the first black county commissioner; and E. R. Warren became the first black on the Hancock County Democratic executive committee. This was an important step for black Hancock Countians because, for the first time in the history of the county, a black political organization ran candidates. Moreover, they were victorious.[40]

An analysis of the registration figures reveals that the overwhelming numbers of Hancock's blacks were crucial to their victory. Table 28 shows that in 1966 blacks composed 66.4 percent of the total voting age population and 50.7 percent of the registered voters. Table 29 shows that only 51.8 percent of the black voting-age population was registered to vote, while 99.5 percent of the white voting-age population was registered. The black vote turned out in full force and apparently bloc-voted heavily. They elected the first black officials in the county with only one-half of their number registered—a feat that would have been impossible anywhere else. But because Hancock had so many votes to spare, the election of blacks became a reality there.

HCDC and the Arrival of McCown

The electoral victories of 1966 brought a tremendous amount of encouragement to black Hancock Countians. Encouragement also came in the form of a young twenty-eight-year-old man named John McCown. Although his impact was minimal on the 1966 elections, he would assume the major leadership role in black political empowerment efforts for the next ten years.

John McCown was a professional civil rights worker. When he decided to live in Hancock, he had an extensive résumé of civil rights affiliations. After the infamous Birmingham Bombing of 1963, he led the first civil rights demonstration in Colorado Springs, Colorado, while he was in the military. Moreover, he began to write letters to the editor of the local newspaper about racism in the military. After leaving the military, he tried to organize blacks on Hilton Head Island, South Carolina, before it was developed into a resort island. Because of his organizational efforts, he lost his job with the Equal Opportunity Administration in Savannah, Georgia. McCown was then employed by SCLC in Atlanta and worked on projects with Martin Luther King, Jr.

McCown grew disenchanted with King's tactic of going into a community briefly and then retreating. McCown felt that if organizers reasonably expected to change matters, they had to plant roots. Thus, while working as the field coordinator with SCLC, he began to look for a county with a significant number of politically undeveloped blacks. It was during this period that McCown became affiliated with the Georgia Council on Human Relations.[41] McCown was hired as an organizer with the Citizens Crusade, a council project designed to politically educate black communities around Georgia. While visiting Hancock County during Farris's tenure, he developed an interest in the people and became fascinated with the potential for black political and economic empowerment. Thus, when Farris left the county, McCown decided to move himself and his family to Hancock.

Of the three offices filled for the first time by black officials, the school board and the county commission positions proved to be subject to the closest public scrutiny; the Democratic executive committee met primarily during the pre-election season to assess the eligibility of the candidates and was, hence, less visible. As the HCDC watched the voting patterns of the black commissioner and the school-board member, two distinct patterns emerged: the black county commissioner voted consistently with his two colleagues, even on issues that the black community considered against its interest; whereas the black school-board member made constant reports to HCDC and consistently voted against any measures that he felt were not in the best interest of Hancock blacks.[42]

This situation brought the HCDC members to another level of awareness concerning politics. Through hard work and staying on top of the major issues and decisions of the school board and county commission, an important lesson was learned: black officials needed a philosophy guided by "black interests" if they were to make progress toward black empowerment. One black on a school board of five and one "undependable" black on a commission of three would not be enough to have a real impact.[43]

An organized segment of the white community wanted Ingram, the "radical" school-board member, removed from the board of education. Initially, the chairman of the board of education challenged Ingram's eligibility to serve, since he had been convicted by a Hancock superior court in 1945 for liquor law violations. In early February, the Georgia attorney general ruled that this conviction did not disqualify Ingram from holding office. His eligibility was then challenged on the basis on his employment at the Milledgeville State Hospital; he was told that Georgia law forbade state employees from holding public offices. Thus, he had a choice to make: he had to either give up his position on the school board or his job at the hospital. He could not keep both. After explaining his predicament to HCDC, he was urged to continue to serve on the board of education. Moreover, HCDC promised to pay his major bills until he could find other employment.[44] The decision was a pivotal one for HCDC: it was the first time they had taken active steps to help alleviate the fear of economic intimidation. Moreover, it was in keeping with other acts of assistance HCDC had performed soon after the election. "Some blacks lost housing, credit, and jobs. But John and others came to the rescue. We took them out of town to get credit and groceries. We also gave food and wood to the people who needed it."[45]

Robert Ingram, Sr., eventually found employment, but it took approximately three months; "the word" had been spread throughout all surrounding counties. Thus, his notoriety had to decrease before he could gain employment. Members of HCDC suggest that the intimidation materialized mainly because of Ingram's advocacy of black community interests. This view gains additional weight when one considers that James Smith, the black county commissioner who allegedly was coopted by white interests, was similarly employed, yet the white community did not give him the same ultimatum presented to Ingram. After continual displeasure with Smith's voting record, the black community successfully initiated the "work or serve" option against Smith. He also remained in office—he was hired by the local doctor who also served as a commissioner.[46]

The contrasting performances of Ingram, Sr., and James Smith made HCDC realize that they needed more officials in order to gain more effectiveness. The group decided that the black community needed a majority of elected officials: two seats on the county commission, the office of probate judge, the office of clerk of the superior court, and three of the five seats on the school board.

The county commission makes the major decisions for the county. The HCDC leadership reasoned that having two blacks on the county commission would be a major step toward sharing equally in the decision making. Since the present black commissioner seemed to be out of touch with the pulse of the community, they wanted to replace him. McCown and another HCDC member would run for these two commission seats.[47]

The offices of probate judge and clerk of court were viewed as being crucial. The probate judge is the superintendent of elections, and the clerk of court is responsible for keeping an accurate record of all proceedings in the superior court. These two positions could make the courthouse much more accessible to blacks. The HCDC nominated Edith Ingram, a young schoolteacher, as their candidate for probate judge, and Leroy S. Wiley was nominated as a candidate for clerk of the superior court.[48]

McCown, HCDC, and the Process of Empowerment

The decision to run a slate of black candidates was not a spontaneous one. The foundation for this effort evolved over the two years after the 1966 election. McCown, as a member of HCDC, began to lay the foundation for the transfer of power. Although other activists were crucial to the empowerment process, McCown was the most outstanding due to his charisma and resourcefulness.

Community organizing was one of McCown's major strengths. His first organizational effort in Hancock was directed toward the youth of the black community. Although HCDC already had a youth group, McCown started another one. This potential source of conflict never created a problem—the two groups eventually merged, and McCown had his first group of loyal constituents.[49]

The youth met after school and on Saturday, working on various projects. With financial assistance from the Georgia Council on Human Relations, McCown started a program that taught kids how to make silk-screened t-shirts. However, their major project—the building of a model house—was much more practical and ambitious, as Robert Ingram, Jr., explained. "We are trying to show that we could build a house for less than $5,500.00. We use a 'tunnel and groove' method. We made our own blocks and mortar. There was no mortar between the joints. Brick masons said that it would not stand but it is still there. He was trying to get federal aid to do this on a mass scale."[50]

It is important to remember that HCDC's youth group was involved in voter registration and public accommodations desegregation efforts after the passage of the Civil Rights Act of 1964. McCown was honing the political potential of an already organized group.[51]

McCown was primarily responsible for the continued activism between 1966 and 1968. He continued to prod the ministers towards activating their congregation, with such quips as "how can you lead someone to heaven and you can't lead them downtown with their heads up." With the strong influence that black ministers had over their congregations, gaining their support was crucial.[52]

Another of McCown's strengths was his expertise. Much of his knowledge was in the area of government antipoverty programs. As a member of his college debate team, he researched the area and studied grantsmanship. Moreover, he developed a network of contacts in Washington and in the regional offices of the various programs across the country. Thus, when McCown came to Hancock, he brought HCDC a valuable resource—expertise and access to financial resources.[53]

Relying on the resourcefulness of McCown, HCDC organized around the issues of Headstart, Federal Housing Administration (FHA) loans, and welfare benefits. Their advocacy in these areas laid the basis for the forthcoming mobilization effectiveness.[54]

McCown felt that there was a dire need for a Headstart program in Hancock County. The county superintendent of schools did not share his enthusiasm. Although it was widely believed that the program could not be established without the superintendent's blessing, the program eventually did come to Hancock. With the help of a McCown contact in Mississippi, a proposal was written and approved without the approval of or input from the superintendent.[55]

McCown discovered that out of the hundreds of loans approved through the FHA, only one black person in Hancock had received a loan for a new house—a small number of loans had been extended to blacks for minor refurbishment. McCown started an investigation of the FHA's lending practices in Hancock County to discover why blacks were not getting FHA loans. The investigation discovered that discriminatory practices were indeed in effect. Those practices were terminated, and it became commonplace for blacks to get FHA loans. Between 1966 and 1968, blacks received approximately twenty-five such loans.[56]

McCown was also surprised to discover that only a small percentage of blacks who qualified for public assistance benefits were actually receiving them. Thus, he began a personal crusade to find out who qualified for public assistance, even taking individuals to the office and assisting them in filling out applications. With his knowledge of welfare regulations, he often successfully challenged the decision of the welfare board.[57]

Having gained a reputation for providing some very basic services, McCown soon became known as the person to contact if a problem developed. He was approachable—even charismatic—and he enhanced these qualities by making himself available to everyone. He had a reputation for frequenting night clubs with his political message on Friday and Saturday nights, and he would take the same message to church on Sunday. McCown would do practically anything to make a person more at ease with him—"anything from playing billiards to picking cotton."[58] His wife offered a vivid description of the commonly held view concerning McCown and his organizing techniques: "He was always a little leader. He had a special way with people; he would make everyone feel like they were somebody; he always took time with people here."[59]

McCown constantly asserted that the objectives he achieved were the results of learning the art of politics. His efforts towards civic education were greatly enhanced by his uncanny ability to provide positive results.[60] The fact that McCown produced results as a private citizen had a powerful impact on the level of black political efficacy in Hancock. Interest in more black political empowerment increased since McCown argued that the powers of elected officials were considerable.

The period from 1966 to 1968 was crucial for the survival of HCDC as a viable organization. Because McCown did all of his service provision under the auspices of HCDC, the organization gained widespread support (see Table 23). Barriers to organizational development were handled effectively, and fear and violence were not major inhibiting factors. Though there was a Klan presence in the area, most people did not take them seriously. One observer states that "when they [the Klan] paraded on the streets before the election in 1966, we stood on the street laughing and made a game of guessing who was under the sheets."[61] Black class antagonism was not a factor, and economic intimidation was managed through the mutual aid policy ("political participation insurance") of HCDC. Moreover, as Tables 28 and 29 show, HCDC was able to increase black registration by 26 percent above the 1966 figure. Blacks constituted 60 percent of the registered voters, and 77.8 percent of Hancock's blacks were registered. The HCDC organized the county into precincts in order to turn out the vote. The organization was growing and appeared to be healthy. By 1968, HCDC was ready to attempt to capture more offices.

Retaliatory measures began to intensify as the election of 1968 approached. McCown alleges that he was offered ten thousand dollars not to run for the county commission. When he did not take the money, he alleges that it was placed in the bank for anyone who would kill him. And Edith Ingram, HCDC's candidate for probate judge, had her life threatened. Mrs. Kathryn Ingram, the candidate's mother, related the story. "When Edith was running for office, someone called and said that if she won, she would not live to get in office in January. They would always call and say that they would bomb the house. They even sent a black woman here one day to deliver the message. I told her to tell them to do it and prove it! I was tired!"[62]

Great care was taken to post important pieces of mail from out of town, since, somehow, a substantial amount of HCDC's mail never reached its intended destination. Moreover, HCDC members had valid reasons to assume that their phones were tapped. Mrs. Ingram stated, "We were supposed to have a private line but at times we could hear breathing and other conversations on the phone. . . . And once when people were in the street campaigning, some of the white people said that 'the people in the street are not doing us nearly as much harm out here as Kathryn Ingram is doing to us back home on the phone.' Now, how would they know that?"[63]

The campaign of 1968 proved to be a racially divisive one.

With threats and counter-threats being hurled throughout the campaign, the CB radios which HCDC had begun to use to replace the undependable phones were now used to reduce fear. They also provided a sense of community for participants in isolated areas of the county. Moreover, the CBs became important tools for contacting a large number of people in a short time. During the peak of the movement activities, HCDC members were able to fill a church with one to two hundred people in the span of an hour.[64]

The apparent goal of the repressive acts was to diminish the increased level of black political activity. Despite this opposition, however, HCDC efforts proved successful in the November Democratic primary, and all of HCDC's candidates won their offices: John McCown won a seat on the county commission; Edith Ingram became the first black probate judge in the nation; and Leroy Wiley won the office of clerk of the superior court. McCown and Ingram had especially difficult battles: although they won the August Democratic primary, their opponents ran again as write-in candidates. Nonetheless, as Table 24 shows, Ingram and McCown's supporters returned to the polls to ensure their victory in the general election. The *Atlanta Constitution* ran a non-ambigious headline: "Negroes Take Over in Hancock Voting."[65] This "takeover" was more apparent than real. Black Hancock Countians, via the organizational effort of HCDC, had made another stride, but there was not a "takeover"; blacks held only five of the eighteen elective offices (probate judge, one school-board member, clerk of the superior court, and two county commissioners). Although they had a majority on the three-member commission, the chances of McCown and Smith cooperating were slim. Nonetheless, a new phase of political development was beginning in Hancock County.

Post Election Reactions
Since it appeared that blacks were "taking over" county government, a campaign was initiated to try to save the white political power in Sparta, Hancock's county seat. Whites were encouraged to move into the city to insure a white majority and, thus, continued white dominance of city politics.[66] Gerrymandering was also an issue: "We have never been able to elect any black to

city government because every time there is an election, the mayor moves the town line to exclude any large settlement of blacks. The mayor does this at will. . . . "[67]

The feeling in the white community ranged from fear to indignation. (Edith Ingram's defeated opponent ran her out when Judge-Elect Ingram asked to be shown around the office before her official duties began.) Whites simply did not know what to expect. Some were afraid that blacks would resort to violence, and others were uncomfortable with the idea that they would have to transact business with blacks in authoritative roles. As one courthouse employee said to a *Constitution* reporter, "being a minority was not a problem as long as the white minority had the political power."[68]

The newly elected black officials took office in January of 1969. The eyes of Hancock were focused primarily on the probate judge and the clerk of court, since their courthouse offices were highly visible. The whites soon realized that they would be treated fairly when they had to use the offices. Many of their worst fears began to dissipate. Although Judge Ingram was often accused of insisting on too much protocol (demanding to be addressed as "Miss Ingram" or "Judge Ingram" by those who were unfamiliar to her), she felt that no one could claim to have been treated unfairly in the offices of the black elected officials.[69]

The election of blacks to public office was a source of pride and jubilation in Hancock's black community. There was a new sense of familiarity about their county courthouse. Instead of being afraid to go there, many black residents enjoyed going to see the black elected officials in their offices. Many of them had never been in the courthouse because of fear or had avoided it because of discourteous treatment. Many of them did not know what the purposes of the offices were, and explaining their functions consumed a good deal of the new black officials' time. The offices soon became places where many questions were asked and answers provided. In essence, the black elected officials' offices became small-scale service provision centers (see Table 25). Judge Ingram elaborates:

I have people who come to this office like clockwork. "Mother's Day" is the day the welfare checks come. "Father's Day" is social security day. It's "Mother's and Father's Day" every month. I have to write checks for them, pay bills, buy groceries, take them to the doctors, balance checkbooks, certify them for welfare, make doctors' appointments, read letters, answer letters, and fix loan papers for houses. A good 85 percent to 90 percent of the work that we do is non-office related work but these people have no one else to depend on—they trust us, so we do it.[70]

The 1968 election was a watershed year for black political empowerment in Hancock County. The organizational effort had given blacks numerical control of the board of commissioners, the first black probate judge in the nation, and a black clerk of court; and Robert Ingram remained on the school board as well. These black elected officials provided the leadership for the subsequent school desegregation battle in Hancock.

Hancock County and School Desegregation

The school desegregation issue presented a dilemma for Hancock's black leadership: if they followed the desires of their constituents and fought for full desegregation, they would run the risk of alienating the few whites who were willing to work with them to attract industry; if they had pragmatically tried to satisfy the desires of their white county boosters and refused to tackle the desegregation issue, the blacks were certain to feel betrayed. Realizing that there was a heavy political price to be paid with either option, Hancock's black leadership decided to follow the desires of their constituents.

The newly elected black officials were swamped with complaints about the overcrowded conditions at Hancock Central, the county's all-black high school. Black citizens had begun to feel that somehow their rights were being violated by the workings of Hancock's public school system.

"Freedom of choice" was the method by which students selected their schools. In other words, all students were free to choose where they would matriculate. In practical terms, this meant that a small number of black students attended the predominantly white schools; no whites attended the black school.[71]

The black school was drastically overcrowded; several classes had to meet in the bleachers of the gymnasium while regular noisy gym exercises were in progress—there were empty classrooms in the white schools. Black bus drivers had to work from two to four hours longer than the white bus drivers because most of them had to make two round trips with their overcrowded busses—the white busses had empty seats on their single run. Moreover, the student-teacher ratio at the black school was alleged to be horrendous when compared to the sparsely populated classrooms at Sparta High.[72]

These conditions prompted the black citizens of Hancock to petition the superintendent to have at least a hundred black students transferred to the predominantly white school. The superintendent denied their request, stating that choices had been made for the 1969–70 school term. However, he did not explain why many of the black students had been denied their "freedom of choice" when they requested to attend Sparta High for the 1969–70 school year. The refusal led to a mass demonstration in Hancock. The Macon and Atlanta press covered the events extensively, but, like all other events concerning the black political empowerment movement, the demonstration was completely ignored by Sparta's local weekly newspaper. The editor felt that "they were noticed too much." Thus, The *Ishmaelite* carried none of the newsworthy events.[73] Nonetheless, Hancock was followed closely throughout the South as a result of the coverage by the *Atlanta Constitution*.

The school crisis erupted September 5, 1969, when McCown and the parents of two hundred black students marched into the auditorium of Sparta High School demanding enrollment under the freedom of choice plan. They charged that all-black Hancock Central was overcrowded. School officials denied the charges and closed the schools; they were reopened three days later after an injunction had been obtained barring further demonstrations. The injunction stipulated that McCown and Edith Ingram, the chief organizers of the daily marches, could not come within a specified number of feet from the school. Being careful not to violate the order, the organizers continued their daily trips.[74]

Upset by the injunction, Hancock blacks began boycotting the schools. The boycott cost the county approximately $5,000 per day, since the average daily attendance dipped severely. A compromise was reached after blacks threatened more demonstrations and a boycott of local merchants.[75]

The black community had good reason to feel victorious at the outcome: the board either met or made major concessions toward every demand made by the black elected officials and organization leaders. The board of education agreed to immediately transfer ninety-two black students and two black teachers to the predominantly white Sparta High School; moreover, they agreed to add ninety-two more blacks to Sparta High by December, which would make Sparta High 53 percent black. When the boycott began, there were seventy black students and no black teachers in the predominantly white schools. The board also agreed to develop a plan to integrate the county busses within ten days, and they promised that black students who had boycotted would not be punished. Black and white teachers would begin to receive equal salary supplements, and there would be a black visiting teacher at the white school.[76]

However, HCDC was still dissatisfied with the racial make-up of the school. Although Sparta High was 53 percent black, it was the feeling of the group that Hancock Central should also be integrated. Thus, a suit was initiated in mid-September to end the dual school system in Hancock.[77]

Although whites still controlled the economy of the county, the high level of activism in Hancock's black community had its effects on the white community in Hancock. A local white expressed his view concerning the impact of black elected officials: "White people didn't sense change too much when a few Negroes were elected to office last November, but they're now beginning to realize that the real changes are only starting and they're going to be painful to accept. We're seeing what black power is all about."

Everyone was not as rational and philosophical. Another local white man stormed into a local board of education meeting trembling on the verge of tears. He said that he had had enough, that he was ready to die, and that there were two hundred others who had the same feeling. The tension began to grow, even more as it became a common practice for everyone to carry weapons.

The federal government mandated that Hancock County, along with hundreds of other counties in the South, would have to desegregate its public schools in September of 1970. The federal ruling, however, left Hancock with a school system essentially no different from what was already in existence: the county would have two high schools, one all-black and the other predominantly black; all of the county's white students would still be at one school. The black community basically felt that the whites should be dispersed throughout the county's schools. The county superintendent objected that such a plan would create a 14:1 black-white ratio; moreover, he argued that white flight from the community would further diminish the miniscule 8 percent white population of the public schools.[79]

The federally mandated desegregation plan did not receive widespread acceptance in the black community; HCDC started an economic boycott to express their displeasure with the plan. To express their disfavor, black Hancock teachers began a second boycott of the schools on the first day of pre-planning, August 23, 1970. Students and black staff members soon joined in. Marvin Lewis, the black principal, spoke the conviction of the boycotters when he was asked about going back to school in the midst of the strike: "That will be a dark day in Hancock County because we are not going back. It is time for educators to stop worrying about their paychecks and get concerned about the education of children. Teachers, bus drivers, and students are together in this thing and we are not giving in."[80]

Again, the boycott was extremely effective: of the 2,350 black students, only 3 showed up for class; none of the 84 black teachers or 27 black bus drivers showed up for work on September 10, the first day of school. Moreover, the economic boycott was comparable in effectiveness. The owner of a convenience store north of Sparta remarked that all of his customers were "run off" by the protestors.

Members of HCDC and other blacks were upset mainly because they had not been consulted about their views with regard to the desegregation plan. They objected that the plan was submitted to federal officials as though the black community had approved of it.[81] Representatives of the school's officials and the black leadership were eventually summoned to a federal court hearing in Atlanta. A compromise was reached: some of Sparta's white teachers would have to teach at Hancock Central, although the superintendent had previously argued that none of the teachers would make the transfer. Since most of the whites had left to attend the newly built Hancock County Academy, there were few students to transfer.

The brief stab at achieving some type of interracial cooperation suffered tremendously as a result of the black elected officials' involvement in the desegregation effort. The strategy had been to gain political control, but still keep some input and participation from the white community. This would be good for attracting industries, which would not want to locate in a racially tense county. Instead, the school desegregation conflict disrupted the tenuous, calculated "harmony" which existed in Hancock before 1969. After the disharmony, the black strategy was to gain more offices and pursue economic development alone. Heretofore, even during the midst of the crisis, McCown was trying to orchestrate a biracial attempt to economically develop Hancock County. Although Hancock blacks benefitted economically from welfare and FHA loans, McCown was interested in a more fundamental type of empowerment. He wanted black Hancock Countians to work on private sector jobs, to own their own businesses, and to become economically independent.[82]

John McCown and Economic Empowerment

McCown was a proud advocate of instrumentalist politics. From his perspective, political offices were platforms from which elected officials could help their constituents. Having won a seat on the county commission in the 1968 election, McCown used his position as a county commissioner to initiate a program of economic development for the county. He felt that economic development and political development were interrelated and that it would be self-defeating to pursue one without the other. He wanted to attract private and public sector jobs to Hancock. His first project was to try to persuade the Georgia Council on Human Relations (GCHR) to become interested in Hancock County.[83]

McCown became the first black president of GCHR in late 1967. The council was an organization of mainly middle-class whites who were interested in improving race relations throughout Georgia. Standard practice for GCHR was to fund several projects across the state. McCown felt that the council could be more effective if it concentrated its resources in one particular spot, and he convinced the council that Hancock was that spot.[84] Simultaneously, McCown was trying to convince national government officials, as well as the National Urban League, that many of the problems in urban areas could be attentuated by making the rural South a more attractive place to live.[85]

McCown invited Whitney Young, the executive director of the National Urban League, to Hancock during February of 1969 to gain his support for the economic development of the county. As a result, the National Urban League opened an office in Sparta to work with local, state, and federal agencies in developing social and economic advancement programs.[86]

The Urban League, with its advisory committee of three whites and four blacks, was putting forth efforts to help the county attract industry and secure funds for a recreation program. While in Sparta at an economic development conference organized by Sparta's Urban League, Whitney Young called on Nixon to make Hancock a model demonstration area for a crash program of economic, social, and political development. He said that he would request the president to send a task force from federal departments to undertake demonstration area programs in Hancock. He said that it would be similar to demonstration programs undertaken after floods, tornados, and other disasters.[87]

With the backing of the National Urban League, McCown took the problems of Hancock to Washington. As a result, the U.S. Department of Commerce provided more than $68,550 to finance the Hancock County Committee for Social and Economic Development. This group was a biracial organization established to attract industries to Hancock and to make studies identifying the county's resources. For example, the county commissioned Georgia Tech to conduct a feasibility study on reactivating a defunct mattress factory.[88]

Despite the initial hostility that accompanied blacks to their elected offices, the more extreme white fears began to wane with the attempt at racial cooperation. The biracial committee was an encouraging symbol of interracial harmony. However, the subsequent school desegregation crisis erased all dreams of racial cooperation.

The Eastern Central Committee for Opportunity (ECCO), a

community-development corporation, was founded by McCown to serve as the economic arm of HCDC. McCown founded ECCO in early 1970 to pursue the noble goal of eliminating poverty from the county. By acquiring money for a variety of economic ventures, McCown hoped that Hancock would soon be an economic oasis. Having run and won as a Republican in 1970, McCown and ECCO were to get a tremendous amount of money from the Office of Economic Opportunity which was being phased out during the Nixon administration. It did not take very long before ECCO was the center of attention in Hancock.[89]

The most ambitious project ECCO undertook was a 357-acre catfish farm. McCown projected that the farm would put $325,000 yearly into the county's economy. The local residents could buy shares in the farm for as little as five dollars, in monthly installments of twenty-five cents. The committee had a credit union which would allow at least three hundred local farmers to borrow money to begin catfish farming. Like all of ECCO's programs, the goal of the catfish project was to increase the economic power of Hancock's black community. McCown reasoned that the catfish farm alone would create enough jobs to significantly lower black dependence on welfare in Hancock. He had visions of eventually distributing fish to major wholesalers and owning fish-and-chips fast-food chains.[90]

McCown's ECCO was the centerpiece of the fruits of political empowerment. It held the potential for large-scale black economic independence, which would reinforce black empowerment. The founding of ECCO climaxed four long years of organizing and added an economic component to the changes that had swept the county beginning in 1966.

Four Years of Changes:
Political, Social, and Economic

Starting in 1966, there were tremendous political, social, and economic changes in Hancock. The trend continued as the seventies arrived, and Hancock was touted as a place where black political and economic power had been achieved.

Political Changes

The four years had seen significant political change in Hancock. Before 1966, there had been no black elected officials in the county. By 1970, the county government was predominantly black: the probate judge and the clerk of the superior court were black; blacks held two of the three seats on the county commission and three seats on the five-seat school board. The county superintendent of schools and the tax commissioner were white, but there were plans to unseat them in 1972. Surprisingly, the white sheriff worked well with the black community and was not opposed. This suggests that an official's attitude toward certain policies and issues was more important than actual race.[91]

By 1970, HCDC was a formidable political machine. A group of leaders who had organized themselves and strategized to achieve black political empowerment as early as 1964 had managed to eradicate fear and economic intimidation as causes of nonparticipation. They had gained the popular support of black Hancock Countians by providing basic but important services, and this popular support created an environment conducive to political education. The black population's sense of specific efficacy was nurtured as they learned how local government worked and that blacks had the numbers to gain control in Hancock. Political mobilization included encouraging black racial bloc-voting, organizing registration drives, establishing precincts with captains, and making other efforts that would facilitate a heavy black turnout. With heavy turnouts in '66, '68, and '70, blacks became politically empowered in Hancock. In fact, a general paradigm for successful black political empowerment may be derived from the example of Hancock County (see Table 41).

Social Changes

The white population's reaction ranged from resignation to rage. Although to obtain white cooperation would have been a challenge under any set of circumstances, the role played by the black elected officials in the school desegregation effort complicated matters further. Before their drive for school desegregation, interracial cooperation was being attempted with a fair amount of success. After the desegregation effort, no local whites could be found publicly in the McCown camp. The desegregation process created so much turmoil and fear that most of the whites fled to the newly established John Hancock Academy, leaving the public schools almost all black.[92]

Economic Changes

Even before McCown's ECCO idea, blacks had begun to feel more economically secure. Welfare benefits and social security benefits could no longer be held as hostages in return for political apathy; McCown knew the regulations and he did not mind insisting on benefits for the applicants whom he often personally escorted to the offices. After the county commission became predominantly black, Hancock blacks became even less afraid of unfair social security and welfare decisions, since the county commissioners had review power over these boards.[93] And after the formation of ECCO, every event in Hancock had two versions—a black one and a white one. The mere mention of the county's name throughout the state was a sure bet to spark controversy. The eyes of the state and much of the nation were centered on Hancock County.

McCown constantly argued that whites were welcome to take part in all aspects of ECCO's operation. Nonetheless, the McCown style proved to be too "abrasive" for the majority of Hancock's whites, who had been heretofore unchallenged. Although this same "abrasive" style proved to be charismatic for many of the county's blacks, it offended a small minority of them, as well, and hampered efforts toward black-white cooperation.

There were white members of ECCO's board from its inception, but they were criticized severely by the white community. Some were even physically threatened and decided to resign after having asked "to be excused from participating." White businessmen refused to accept assistance from the agency's program that aided small businesses, although they could have used the help. McCown also tried to get three hundred low-rent housing units into the city of Sparta—with no success. White city officials and the other black commissioner refused to cooperate, although the housing would have been free for the county. Some speculate that the addition of three hundred black families did not appeal to the protectors of white political dominance in Sparta.[94] This tense environment led to the arms race of 1971.

The Hancock County Arms Race. During the spring of 1971, automatic weapons fire was heard in the county. The whites accused the blacks of being the source of the firing sounds heard throughout the night; the blacks accused the whites of having the weapons. After four years of constant change whites seemed to feel physically intimidated. An allegation that "thirty or forty blacks had threatened to kill a policeman" contributed to the charged atmosphere. And the situation was made worse when a white policeman was injured in a scuffle with a black.[95]

Sparta's mayor ordered his three-man police department ten machine guns to protect the citizens of the city. Most blacks felt that this was a reaction to black political and economic empowerment. With blacks behaving considerably less subserviently, whites may have felt that violence could not be far away.[96]

The Hancock County commissioners announced that they were ordering twenty machine guns from a dealer in Miami. And the arms race was on. McCown and Judge Ingram organized a hunting club—The Sporting Rangers—and urged their prospective members to buy guns. Although they argued that the formation of the club had nothing to do with the purchase of the machine guns, most observers viewed the club's formation as a method of escalating possession of firearms in the black community.[97]

The state news media, primarily the *Atlanta Constitution* and the *Macon Telegraph*, focused on Hancock again. The whole state was watching to see what would eventually unfold in the state's only black-controlled county. The arms race was eventually arbitrated and stopped by Governor Jimmy Carter and his negotiating staff. The city officials agreed to send their guns back; the Hancock commissioners agreed to cancel their order and discontinue the formation of The Sporting Rangers;[98] and the conflict was resolved. However, the conflict only exacerbated the negative relations between the white public officials of Sparta and ECCO.

The city of Sparta's public officials were basically negative toward McCown and his political views. Although he made efforts to get industry into Sparta, he could never get the white officials to support him. Some fault McCown for being "too abrasive," and others fault the county's whites for refusing to be led to prosperity by a black man—it was felt that Sparta officials welcomed new industries but resented McCown's role as prime mover. Since relations were bad with the city officials, McCown decided it would be best to center the operational base of ECCO outside the city limits of Sparta, where the black county officials would have more jurisdiction.

The placement of ECCO's headquarters in Mayfield created a major controversy. After publicly announcing that efforts to win cooperation had failed, McCown announced that ECCO would begin to build a town with a $7 million grant from the Ford Foundation. McCown summarized the struggle to secure white cooperation by saying " . . . some people would rather die and go to hell than be pulled to prosperity by black people." With the formation of the new town, the Ford Foundation said that this "would make Hancock County a national showcase for blacks." In response to this assertion, the *Constitution* reported that ". . . while it may be a showcase for blacks, it could mean economic trouble for white business in Sparta, the county's largest town with a population of 2,000. Seventy-five per cent of the county's 10,000 residents are black and white merchants freely admit that they would be forced to close without black customers."[99]

McCown attacked the *Constitution* on the grounds that the statement jeopardized the project. Arguing that the story made it appear that the Ford Foundation "was being duped into building a town for blacks by killing a white town [Sparta]," he claimed that the Ford Foundation and several other private and governmental agencies had second thoughts about financing the project.[100] Nonetheless, the move to Mayfield was made and funds began to flow in.

The headquarters of ECCO was located in Mayfield, a small unincorporated area of the county, which had once been prosperous. Turning an old railroad station into a temporary headquarters, ECCO began to acquire property and to start several ventures: a concrete block plant, a lumber company, a low-income housing project, a movie house, a grocery store, and the county's only airport. The black community began to associate political participation with economic development. Moreover, blacks became less subservient to whites. As ECCO began to expand, so would the problems of racial tensions.

ECCO: The Center of Attention. In the face of increasing opposition, ECCO and HCDC had grown weary of trying to cooperate with the white community in efforts to revitalize the county. The city refused to run water to the concrete block plant; ECCO employees had often been hassled by Sparta's policemen; phones were believed to be tapped; the whites boycotted the fish farm owned by ECCO; and the major fish pond was sabotaged. Black frustration showed at the polls, and the black percentage of elected officials began to increase as it became apparent that little could be gained from working with whites. The election of 1972 increased the majority of black elected officials: there were four blacks on the five-member school board; a black county police officer; a black school superintendent; four blacks on a seven-member welfare board; four blacks on a seven-member hospital board; and the probate judge, the clerk of superior court, the county coroner, and the prison warden were all black.[101]

The white leaders in Hancock continued to be concerned about McCown and ECCO. How could he get grants so easily from OEO and other agencies in Washington? What was his relationship with "militant" Stokely Carmichael, who visited the county to meet with McCown? How could he afford his Cadillac, his plane, and fast-paced lifestyle? Why wasn't he afraid for his life, since everyone knew that several people wanted him dead? The speculation continued and so did the harassment of black citizens involved with the movement: Judge Edith Ingram was arrested in a nearby county on a false charge of shoplifting that was later apologized for and dropped; and Bertha Thomas, an ECCO employee, was placed in jail for a parking violation. This incident created a major disturbance.[102]

Beatrice Thomas confronted the meter maid who gave her a ticket for parking at a damaged meter. The confrontation ended with Ms. Thomas being placed in jail for "sassing the meter maid." Upon being notified, practically all of the ECCO employees came to get their co-workers out of jail. The big crowd created a huge traffic jam, and McCown was charged with unlawful assembly, failure to disperse, and obstructing a police officer. McCown was jailed when Ms. Thomas was released on May 10, 1974, and ECCO workers held a twenty-four hour vigil while McCown was in jail. They feared for his life because a group of whites had threatened to lynch McCown when he was jailed in 1968.[103]

While McCown was in jail, three fires broke out on the morning of May 11; one of the sites was the historic Clinch House. Moreover, sporadic shooting could be heard during the night. Both sides blamed each other for the fires and the shootings. McCown was released the same night supposedly to see if he could use his influence to dissuade the arsonist from burning the city down. Although he accepted his release, he proclaimed that the mayor and police chief set the fires and shot into the homes just to get help from the national guard. Governor Carter eventually came to Sparta to try to bring about a truce.[104]

Hancock County and the Press

The press was interested in Hancock for three main reasons: (1) the county was controlled by blacks; (2) there were continuous controversies; and (3) ECCO was attracting tremendous amounts of money. By 1974, HCDC had managed to secure over 10 million dollars from the federal government and from various foundations, while ECCO had hired approximately fifty Hancock citizens, sponsored economic ventures, and provided important services to Hancock's black community (see Tables 26 and 27).

Because of the tremendous amount of funding and the high level of distrust engendered by McCown and HCDC, Sparta's white community pressured Governor Carter for an audit of ECCO. While Carter was in town to mediate the meter maid dispute, he announced that his audit of ECCO revealed no discrepancies. However, Carter stated that if he were running ECCO, he would not use many of the same procedures currently employed by the staff. Carter was holding an OEO grant pending the outcome of the audit. Since the audit revealed no discrepancies, Carter released the grant to ECCO. This did not end the case, however; the extensive, but not very accurate reporting of the *Constitution* concerning the grant would create severe problems for ECCO[105]

The *Constitution's* method of reporting the story of Carter's temporary hold up of the OEO funds for Hancock created a great deal of suspicion and controversy. Three major news stories provide good examples of the paper's incomplete method of reporting.

On April 10, 1974, the *Constitution* reported that "county commissioners in rural Georgia have been approved for federal poverty funds to pay themselves salaries."[106] Although this was true, it was not the whole truth—they did not report two important points: the article failed to mention that OEO's rationale was that commissioners needed to work full time as commissioners and give up their other jobs; and they also neglected to report that Carter's own staff approved the proposal. Their reporting portrayed the commissioners as being recipients of two salaries, with no rationale provided.[107]

The *Constitution* also ran an article titled "Nightclub Getting Hancock Poverty Funds." The article did not reveal that this was an enterprise funded by the Minority Enterprises Small Business Improvement Corporation (MESBIC), a government program established to help finance the development of minority business enterprises.[108]

And, in a report titled "ECCO Audit Pressed for in Hancock" printed on April 22, 1974, the *Constitution* reported that "OEO officials have refused to provide Governor Carter with an audit of how federal money is being spent in the county."[109] They failed to mention that OEO in Atlanta did not have the records to conduct an audit, since the grant came through the national office. They left the impression that OEO in Atlanta had an audit of ECCO that it was not providing. The Atlanta office had petitioned the national office for an ECCO audit.[110]

Although Carter found no discrepancies in the internal audit that McCown provided him with around May 15, the clouds of doubt had been cast over McCown and ECCO. The *Macon Telegraph* published a series of articles June 9–12, 1974, that questioned the legitimacy of ECCO given that all of its projects were apparent failures.[111] Within three weeks, June 30–July 5, the *Atlanta Constitution* did an even more damaging piece focusing mainly on John McCown. McCown was portrayed as a shrewd profiteer whose antipoverty business ventures had failed. Mc-Cown was accused of using money from the Georgia Council for his personal use and misappropriating money and enriching himself instead of the poor people of Hancock. The series was introduced as follows: "In 1966 an ambitious and energetic man named John McCown went to rural Hancock County, GA to begin a massive poverty fighting program. After eight years of recurring turmoil and 5.5 million in federal and private donation funds, Hancock still has more than its share of poor people. But John McCown is not one of them."[112]

With the concluding article on July 5, even those who had the utmost faith in McCown began to question his credibility. The detailed examination of McCown's financial affairs led Senator Sam Nunn to press the General Accounting Office to speed up its audit of ECCO and to request a preliminary report.[113]

As publicity began to spread about the audit, practically all sources of funding for ECCO began to dry up. Simultaneously, ECCO staffers and black county officials were being audited individually by the IRS. The death knell for ECCO came on July 24, 1974, when the *Constitution* ran an article entitled "Discrepancies Turned Up in ECCO Audit Nunn Says." This information was part of the preliminary audit reports. By late July, the completed audit report found $280,000 in ECCO expenditures that OEO considered not acceptable, e.g., possible misuse of credit cards, salary overpayments, and undocumented travel expenses.[114]

A federal grand jury for the Northern District of Georgia in Atlanta began to hold hearings on the allegations that McCown and his employees had attempted to defraud the government.[115] All ECCO's records were summoned for scrutiny. The seizure of the records, coupled with the immediate lessening of funds, practically ended ECCO as a functioning organization.[116]

After reviewing the records of ECCO during May of 1975, McCown and eleven of his employees were accused of conspiring to misuse federal funds. The grand jury investigation took several twists and turns during its eighteen months. Finally on November 12, 1976, eight of the accused were indicted. Five defendants, with the advice of legal counsel, pleaded guilty to lesser offenses, since they felt that there was no way that they could get a fair trial.[117] Frustrated because the man they actually wanted, McCown, had been killed in a plane crash during January of 1976, the government ended by plea-bargaining.[118] There were many in the white community who felt that only partial justice had been served; they were happy that the accused parties pleaded guilty—this was *prima facie* proof that McCown and his associates were self-admitted violators of the law. They only wished that the punishment had been more harsh. The majority of the black community in Hancock felt that the news stories, the investigation, and the trial were all part of an attempt to discredit McCown and ECCO. They argued that since McCown could not be run out with noncooperation, hostility, and death threats, a concerted effort had been mounted to discredit him. The IRS audited key defendants before the grand jury proceedings without informing them of their rights and gave the information to the prosecuting attorney's office to use in the case. This illegality and other procedural irregularities were never fully exposed since the case never got to court.[119] The attorneys for the Hancock officials and ECCO employees felt that, despite any amount of evidence presented in their defense, the public sentiment for their conviction could not be overcome.[120]

Today Hancock County has settled down to a very non-eventful existence as a rural black belt county. As of this writing, blacks still control seventeen of the eighteen elective offices in county government. Sparta, the county seat, still has all white elected officials. The association between economic development and black elected officials no longer holds—all of ECCO's programs lost their funding long before the legal deliberation ended; the housing project in Mayfield still stands as the only tangible proof that ECCO did exist.[121]

The black elected officials are taken for granted now, and the HCDC is a shell of what it once was. The fervor for politics seems to have gone, although black registration is optimal and blacks make up 72.7 percent of the registered voters (Tables 28 and 29). Black officials have not had any opposition in the last five elections. Hancock blacks are trying to hold on to the political power that they hope can be translated into economic power at some point in the future.

"The McCown Era" will always be a controversial period: the

mere mention of McCown or ECCO is still enough to spark debate. Nonetheless, the general consensus is that racial resentment is waning in Hancock. The bad economy has forced blacks and whites to try to forget the past and cooperate in attempts to bring industry to the county.[122]

Hancock County: An Analysis of the Components for Collective Action

Hancock County blacks were politically empowered as a result of successful organizational development. That development was the result of the dynamics of five critical conditions for collective action: (1) interests, (2) the opportunity to act, (3) leadership, (4) organization, and (5) resources. Although "interests" and "opportunity" are important, this analysis will concern itself primarily with leadership, organization, and resources, in order to illustrate how the existence and degree of these factors led to black political empowerment in Hancock.

A discussion of interest and opportunity are not important here since they do not differ with respect to the three sample counties. Group interests always existed to the extent that racial discrimination and segregation were present. Moreover, the opportunity to act came to the counties with the passage of positive civil rights legislation culminating in the Voting Rights Act of 1965.

Leadership

Hancock was replete with black leaders before the opportunity to act materialized. Burls S. Ingram, Lucius H. Holsey, Zach Hubert, Henry Hunt, and Charles S. Harper provided outstanding leadership during their lifetimes. Hubert and Hunt especially emphasized the virtues of hard work, education, and land ownership. They recruited black Hancock students to Savannah State College, many of whom returned to Hancock to teach in the public schools. Two of this group of teachers—Warren and McMullen—provided the thrust for political organization.

The apolitical profile of black schoolteachers throughout the South is well documented.[123] Although local black citizens expect teachers to lead, since the common perception is that education makes you qualified and capable, black schoolteachers often feel that political leadership will jeopardize their livelihood. This feeling is usually based on personal or second-hand knowledge of incidents in which white school boards terminated the contracts of black teachers who had become politically active. Thus, the leadership offered by the two black schoolteachers was indeed rare. Warren stated that the practical consequences were not a factor in his decision: "it was time to stand up and be a man"[124]

After HCDC's founder laid the internal organizational foundation of their political action group in 1964, Hancock was noticed by SCLC in Atlanta in 1965. Carl Farris came to Hancock and headed the SCOPE project. The internal leadership was now enhanced by outside assistance, and registration drives were held prior to the passage of the Voting Rights Act. The passage of the VRA gave impetus to a movement already in progress, and the drive for black political empowerment was further enhanced by the arrival of John McCown.

McCown provided an entirely different style of leadership. While Carl Farris and the local leaders were getting results, they lacked the flare and excitement that were provided by McCown. Because McCown was charismatic, unorthodox, and knowledgeable, he was able to reach the die-hard nonparticipants.

The successful organizational development of the black community led to many of the HCDC members assuming the role of political leaders by serving as public officials beginning in 1966. By 1974, blacks held all of the county offices except sheriff. The leadership had been transformed from private citizens to elected officials.

Two Hancock teachers, a state worker, and a businessman, then, provided the basic elements of leadership. Their ideas were sufficiently popular to attract a following and to start an organization. This organization, with the help of its economic arm, ECCO, provided the necessary ingredients for the successful political mobilization which led to black political empowerment. Political mobilization and black political empowerment depended upon the survival of the organization. Our focus will now shift to how the organizations—the HCDC and ECCO—survived to bring about mobilization.

Organization

The Hancock County Democratic Club was organized in 1964 as a group dedicated to increasing the participation of blacks in politics through voting and office holding. The founders of this group provided effective leadership and maintained a high percentage of popular support. The HCDC was the vehicle through which the barriers of economic intimidation, violence, the angel system, and black class antagonism were overcome.

Although dependence on whites for employment was a reality, economic intimidation played a minimal role in thwarting efforts to organize the HCDC. Two schoolteachers, members of a profession traditionally considered highly vulnerable to economic pressure, were among the founders of the HCDC. When the HCDC went on record as being responsible for the major bills of Robert Ingram, Sr., during the time when his seat was being challenged, the small potential for economic intimidation was practically crushed. The black community felt that the HCDC would support them financially too if the circumstances dictated such a gesture.

Violence had never been a problem between the races in Hancock County. Some argue that violence did not occur because Hancock whites were aristocratic Whigs who treated blacks humanely during and after slavery; others maintain that the relative peacefulness may be attributed to the predominantly black population with its "crazy niggers" who would fight back. Whatever the explanation, all agree that the fear of white violence has never been an overwhelming concern in the black community— neither during the post slavery era nor during the organizational era of 1964. Their basic sense of security was reinforced by the sophisticated communications system of CB radios. Any isolated person was never far from help.

An "angel system" exists where there is a power group and a group or groups without power; a member of the group without power acts as an informant to a "guardian angel" within the power group. The informant is rewarded with favors by the power group since he provides the information necessary to combat any attempt of the powerless group to gain power. Without the threat of economic intimidation or the threat of violence, the angel system in Hancock was robbed of its foundation. Moreover, for an angel system to work, the "angels" must have the power to protect their clients from something. There were simply not enough Hancock blacks who were fearful enough to feel that they needed an "angel."

Like violence, the problem of black class antagonism has never been major in Hancock. The black teachers, preachers, landowners, and entrepreneurs chose to identify with the larger black community rather than with their own privileged status. Moreover, the churches and fraternal lodges broke down most of the remaining particles of differences based on class. Once more, McCown capitalized on this positive trait of Hancock's black community.

McCown was staunchly against class divisions in the black community. Much of his organizational skill lay in the fact that he had a tremendous appeal to Hancock's black lower class; he also had the knowledge and exposure that is usually associated with the middle and upper classes. Combined with his charisma, the aforementioned qualities allowed McCown to create an alliance between Hancock blacks that left little room for religious, class, or group-affiliated friction.

Although it survived the four obstacles to organizational development (economic intimidation, violence, the angel system, and black class antagonism), the organization would still have become dysfunctional had it not been successful at developing the following functions cited by Salamon as critical to the longevity of a protest organization: (1) management of fear, (2) provision of services, (3) education and communication, (4) political mobilization, (5) resolution of conflict, and (6) economic development.

Management of Fear. With the county's history and legacy of black assertiveness, fear has never been a major characteristic of black Hancock Countians. The strong sense of belonging and unity spawned by the formation of HCDC and ECCO helped to alleviate any remnants of fear as a dominant influence on individual political actions. Fear was managed in two ways: the fear of physical harm was mitigated via the constant communication by CB radios; and the fear of economic vulnerability was reduced by the organization's gaining control of the distribution of federal financial benefits.

By aiding eligible blacks to acquire social security, welfare, and FHA loans, HCDC allowed many heretofore intimidated blacks to feel that they could flex their political muscle, since their benefits were no longer dispensed at the discretion of a local white administrator.

Provision of Services. McCown strongly believed that the poor would not become political activists unless they could see some tangible benefits in their lives; lengthy impassioned explanations about voting rights and civic responsibility were not enough. Thus, McCown set out to convince the black community that his expertise in social security, welfare, and FHA regulations was a result of his own political involvement. Having produced tangible results, abstractions about democratic theory made more practical sense. It is important to note here that many of McCown's accomplishments came before his election to office. Unlike most activists, he had the savvy to produce results before actually securing an office.

In addition to McCown's services to the community, other Hancock black elected officials also went out of their way to be helpful. Judge Ingram stated that "constituency services" consumed a considerable amount of time. "Constituency services" include everything from arbitrating domestic quarrels to paying bills. The problem of widespread illiteracy also made the constituency service invaluable, and these services were very important to a constituency that was poor and depended upon social security and welfare. Historically, this group, all across the South, has been extremely vulnerable to economic intimidation. Through one-to-one civil education, poor citizens of Hancock were made to realize that they ultimately controlled the bureaucrats who administered their benefits. Since the county commissioners controlled the welfare workers, the citizens learned they could affect local welfare policy by electing black officials sensitive to their needs. McCown and HCDC had taught the poor to question authority.

Education and Communication. McCown was an extraordinary civic educator. He believed that knowledge of political affairs and the effective use of the ballot were resources to be used to make one's life better. Thus, he took his message of a "better life through political participation" to homes, bars, and churches. The acceptance of this McCown doctrine intensified the political mobilization that had begun before he came to the county. Communicating about the latest developments in the "movement" was never a problem. The HCDC, ECCO employees, the black elected officials, and the nonaffiliated members of the black community were constantly meeting. With everyone having a chance to express their concerns, the overwhelming majority of the black community was assured that they knew the current state of affairs.

Political Mobilization. Beginning with the formation of the HCDC in 1964, the Hancock County black community began to develop its political potential. By the time the Voting Rights Act of 1965 was passed, Hancock blacks were ready to take advantage of it: they stood in line waiting for the courthouse to open on the first day it took effect. After having elected a black school-board member and a black county commissioner in 1966, the black voters were to face an even greater challenge in 1968.

The winning of the Democratic primary had always been tantamount to election in the South, due to the nature of the one-party system. John McCown and Edith Ingram won the Democratic primary for the offices of county commissioner and probate judge, respectively. Ordinarily, since there would have been no Republican opposition, their campaigns would have been over. This was not the case: they would have to face their incumbent opponents as write-in candidates. The black community rose to the challenge; and, although McCown lost votes from the primary to the general election, Ingram increased her margin of victory by 135 votes.[125]

Conflict Resolution. McCown, working through the HCDC and ECCO, handled internal and external conflicts poorly. Many argue that, internally, McCown's managerial style was too abrasive. For a variety of reasons, a number of HCDC members left, and an anti-McCown black Concerned Citizens group formed a close alliance with a white Concerned Citizens group. Concerning procedural matters, McCown would insist on having things his way even when expert consultants advised him otherwise. Moreover, the external conflicts, i.e., the negative white reactions, were not handled in the most pragmatic fashion, though many of the aspects of events were out of his control. The McCown personality was full of irony: whereas it contained the charisma and vigor necessary to activate the deeply entrenched nonparticipant, it also contained a blatant disregard for "rules and procedures," a trait that would translate into trouble for him and ECCO.

The tragic flaw in McCown's leadership is that he refused to miss any opportunity to pour salt in the wounds of the whites who were freshly out of power. Although he appealed for a biracial coalition to economic prosperity, his inflammatory rhetoric aroused more fear than brotherhood. After the prize of black political empowerment had been won, the most pragmatic strategy would have been to try to heal the wounds and to attract industry into a peaceful community as opposed to a racially tense one. Although the Hancock whites were not angels, McCown unnecessarily provoked them at times. The failure to handle these conflicts better, along with McCown's inept system of bookkeeping, led to the demise of ECCO.

Economic Development. Economic development was at the heart of McCown's overall strategy of political empowerment. Throughout the rural South, it is common to find blacks who feel that their local officials are not interested in attracting industry to their area.[126] This alleged practice keeps wages low, work scarce, and the environment intimate. These conditions also lay the groundwork for economic intimidation. Based on this reasoning, McCown viewed the election of black officials as the first step toward the liberation of blacks from economic intimidation.

The classic problem is that "protestors usually need what they are trying to get in order to get what they want."[127] In the case of Hancock, blacks needed to be economically independent, or at least assured that life's basics would not be endangered, before they could elect black officials who would work to bring industries and to establish public policies that removed the ability of those who delivered federally sponsored assistance to threaten economic reprisals for political activism. McCown and the HCDC were able to overcome this problem: HCDC's policy of providing financial assistance to political victims and McCown's personal quest to challenge the decisions of local administrators freed many blacks from fear of economic intimidation. However, Mc-Cown wanted an organization specifically dedicated to overcoming economic deprivation and intimidation. Thus, ECCO was born. The dream of eliminating poverty with ECCO never became a reality. As with many aspects of life in Hancock during the Mc-Cown era, it is hard to obtain an objective account regarding the feasibility of ECCO's operations. Nonetheless, any hope of ECCO ending poverty in Hancock began to fade when their records were secured for the grand jury investigation. McCown's dream for ECCO died with him.

Resources
Resources, within the context of this book, may be defined as the characteristics and means which facilitate movement toward political mobilization of the black community. The black community in Hancock had considerable resources, material and nonmaterial. They included the following: (1) a positive to neutral political climate; (2) high rates of black land ownership; (3) a group of influential black educators who stressed group accomplishments; (4) an overwhelming black majority; (5) positive media coverage; and (6) a resourceful, charismatic black leader who was able to bring over 10 million dollars in aid to Hancock between 1970–1974. These resources enabled blacks in Hancock to achieve black political empowerment.

Black political empowerment, however, was only one goal on the way toward the elusive larger goal of black economic empowerment. Whites in Hancock stopped this movement by creating a cloud of suspicion over McCown and ECCO.

Ironically, McCown played a major role in the demise of ECCO. McCown's uncompromising stance with regard to black rights encouraged many blacks to participate politically. However, after the procurement of political power, McCown continued to antagonize many whites. His unbending attitude toward whites proved to be nonpragmatic. Finally, it was self-destructive.

On May 12, 1974, McCown led 150 other blacks in a "takeover" of the Sparta Baptist Church, the local white Baptist church, which had over 400 members. This needless church "takeover" led to an unfavorable series of newspaper articles. These articles led to an audit and the audit revealed "discrepancies" that led to a federal grand jury investigation. Even before a trial which would have proven ECCO innocent or guilty, funds evaporated and ECCO was a historic relic.

4. Black Political Empowerment in Peach County, Georgia, 1960 to 1982

Rudolph Carson became the first black mayor of Fort Valley, Georgia, in 1980. With a racially balanced city council and utilities commission, he had the power to break tie votes. Thus, blacks had the power to make public policy. This chapter is an explication of how this empowerment was achieved and lost.

Peach County and Fort Valley, its county seat, have always been predominantly black (see Table 30). The pre-sixties era in Peach County may be characterized by three major features which repressed black political participation: (1) a negative political climate, (2) the absence of an assertive black leadership, and (3) black economic dependence.

A 1956 study by B. R. Brazeal is perhaps the most widely circulated analysis of black political activity in Peach County prior to the post-WWII civil rights movement. In his report, Brazeal indicated that the presence of Peach's black majority population affected white attitudes in the typical southern rural black belt fashion. He asserted that ". . . the population pattern has resulted in whites resorting to subtle and overt methods which have not always been political in nature. On the other hand, Negro residents in this county, because of their dominant numbers, have felt compelled to reassure the white people that they do not expect to 'take over' in a political sense."[1]

When the white primary was ruled unconstitutional in 1944, only 33 percent of the voters in Peach, 1,200 of 3,300, were black.[2] Blacks were discouraged from voting and registering in two ways: registered blacks by the hundreds were subpoenaed to report to the registrar's office to explain why their names should remain on the qualified voters list; and many were purged when they were not able to read various constitutional passages to the satisfaction of the registrars. Thus, the local whites were largely successful in keeping down the black voting potential, even after the ruling against the Georgia white primary. In 1954, eight years after the ruling against the Georgia white primary and nine years after the repeal of the poll tax, blacks made up only 18.1 percent of the registered voters in Peach County.[3]

The president of the Civic League, a black political organization, gave three main reasons for the lack of registration and voting among all sectors of the black community: (1) blacks perceived their vote was not valuable, i.e., "my vote doesn't count"; (2) they felt a reluctance to compete with whites because of the perception that the former would always get their way; and (3) they felt a need to avoid the stigma of being segregated at the polls: black voters had to enter the rear of the city hall to place their ballots in a black box; white voters entered the front of city hall and placed their ballots in an unpainted box.[4]

The Brazeal study found that Peach County was in dire need of leadership. He concluded that the paucity of leadership was due partially to the absence of black economic independence:

> There are a few small, relatively new businesses conducted by Negroes. Except for the teachers in the college and public school system, a few ministers, and business people, most of the Negroes in Peach depend on menial, domestic, factory and farming jobs. Some are employed at Warner Robins Air Force Base. . . . The few Negroes who are most active in a political sense are those four or five who are ministers or run a filling station, grocery store or undertaking establishment. Very limited political leadership among Negroes is the prospect until the development of a larger number of relatively independent business, religious, and professional Negro people.[5]

The black leadership pool was already a shallow one; it would become even more so when Otis Wesley Smith, the county's only black physician, chose to leave town rather than serve an eight-month jail sentence for using obscene language in the presence of a white woman. The case evolved from a phone conversation that Smith made to Atlanta in June, 1957. His line was crossed with the plaintiff's, and the alleged obscene language was used in an argument which developed between them. Thus, a relatively independent black professional was removed from the Peach County scene.[6]

Teachers, as we have noted, represent a potential leadership pool for black communities. However, this potential was dormant throughout the pre-sixties era in Peach. With the exception of H. E. Bryant, the black high-school principal, and faculty member William M. Boyd, the black staff and faculty at the predominantly black Fort Valley State College and the black county schoolteachers offered "no active leadership in political affairs" in Peach County during the pre-sixties era. Although most of them were registered voters and NAACP members, they kept low profiles, since political activity involved risks.[7]

The idea of black political empowerment was not a widespread notion when the decade of the sixties dawned on Peach County. With almost 40 percent of the population living in poverty and educated at a median grade level of 8.9,[8] socioeconomic factors alone would forecast low rates of black political participation— one would not expect fundamental changes to be on the verge of taking place. This view is reinforced when one considers that the majority of the blacks who would rank high on the socioeconomic scale, such as educators and ministers, were unwilling to take the responsibility that accompanied advocacy for black political rights. Nonetheless, a movement would begin in the decade that would give the city of Fort Valley a black mayor and a racially balanced city council by 1980.

When the sit-ins to integrate the Woolworth's lunch counter started in Greensboro, N.C., black political consciousness in Fort Valley, as in many other areas in the South in 1963, was in a state of incubation. The students at Fort Valley State College were keeping track of the rapid spread of the movement, but they had not confronted the problems in Fort Valley. It is ironic that whites in Fort Valley made the first ostensible acknowledgment that a movement was taking place that could have an effect on life in Fort Valley and Peach County. In August 1963, twenty-five prominent whites of Fort Valley petitioned the Fort Valley mayor and the city council to create a racial coordinating committee. With all of the political activity occurring in other black college towns across the South, it is reasonable to assume that this petition was probably calculated to reduce the likelihood of a violent confrontation in Peach County.[9]

In September, the mayor and the city council passed a resolution establishing a committee to be composed of four blacks and four whites. According to the resolution, the committee's purpose was to "promote and maintain good will and relations between the races." Although a group of this sort was already in existence, it was apparently important to have a group that was a bit more ostensive than the informal, low profile group of black and white ministers who often met to "discuss local issues and the spirit with which they should be met."

Although the sit-in movement was undoubtedly the chief motivating factor for the formation of the committee, there was a local crisis that required immediate attention: the recent shooting of a black man in the county jail had caused some white concern and a substantial amount of black anger. The black community was convinced that a murder had taken place in the county jail—the black victim was handcuffed when he was shot.[10] Moreover, their anger was fueled by the memory of the plight of the black physician who, in their view, was given little choice but to leave town.

Blacks became active on a large scale in 1963, and the degree of participation never again dipped to the low levels of the pre-1963 period. After the killing of the black man in the county jail by a state trooper, the groundwork was laid for the first black civic club since the NAACP was dissolved due to internal problems in the early fifties. Blacks started to hold meetings and decided to wage a battle against all of the injustices that were being perpetrated against them. The group began to study the community to identify the white merchants who had a large black patronage and no employment record of blacks holding important positions in their business. A "Don't Shop Where You Can't Work" boycott resulted from the study. This group eventually became the Citizens Education Committee (CEC).

The CEC was formed under the leadership of Houston Stallworth, a Fort Valley State professor, who brought together black businessmen, public schoolteachers, and Fort Valley State's students. The boycott and the success of the biracial committee helped to bring about change: "Colored and White" signs on restrooms and above water fountains were removed; "the clean, polite, and orderly blacks"[11] were permitted to eat at white-owned and -operated restaurants; blacks were employed as sales clerks in clothing and grocery stores; and many blacks who were already employed were given promotion to higher status duties. The boycott ended in early 1964 when the biracial committee promised to deal with the situation and the merchants agreed to meet with the black representatives. After a black policeman was added to the police force in February of 1964, CEC changed its focus to electoral politics.

The Beginning of Efforts
Toward Black Political Empowerment

Politically, 1964 was a watershed year in Peach County. In February of that year W. S. M. Banks, a black sociology professor at Fort Valley State College (FVSC), qualified for the March 18 municipal Democratic primary. He became the first black in the history of Fort Valley to seek office; he chose to run for one of the three four-year seats on the city council.[12] In late February, a second black, A. J. Edwards, a self-employed mortician, qualified to seek one of the two four-year seats on the utilities commission. Banks and Edwards gave rise to biracial political campaigns in Peach County.[13]

Both Banks and Edwards lost their bids for positions in Fort Valley's government. Although some 950 blacks were qualified to vote in the primary, provided that their taxes were paid,[14] Banks received 680 votes and Edwards received 645—72 percent and 68 percent of the possible black vote. The election returns suggest that some blacks probably voted for the white candidates or did not vote at all, while the white contenders undoubtedly received a white bloc vote (Table 31).

The defeat of Banks and Edwards did not destroy the black community's desire for representation in their county and city government, and CEC continued its efforts to register black voters. With the passage of the Voting Rights Act of 1965, there was even more of an incentive to get blacks registered. The campaigns were financed by the Voter Education Project based in Atlanta. The FVSC students, including white exchange students from the University of Minnesota, canvassed the black community trying to register as many blacks as possible. The city clerk, Wilbur K. Avera, announced that the city's voters list was being purged of all ineligible names. Nonpayment of taxes was the official reason for purging the list. The clerk announced that anyone's name would be replaced on the list of voters after the payment of the taxes. There was a black man on the three-member committee, but that was not important with respect to the impact of the purge—which affected blacks more adversely than whites.[15]

The 1964 municipal Democratic primary was the last one held in Fort Valley.[16] Beginning in 1966, only the general and the run-off elections were held. Moreover, the 1965 Georgia General Assembly passed a measure allowing the city and the county officials to change their method of election from plurality to majority and from non-post to post where it was applicable. This new method would make it much more difficult to elect a black to office. State Representative Daniel K. Grahl, owner and publisher of the local paper and author of the 1965 law, felt that the new legislation was fair. Although the Voting Rights Act of 1965 did not pass until August, this new legislation still required pre-clearance—the change was never sent to the Justice Department for approval.[17]

Between 1966 and 1970, blacks would continue to lose at the polls. In his bid for a utilities commissioner's seat in April 1966, Roosevelt Arnold, a black plumber, won enough votes (547) to force a run-off. In the run-off contest he lost 604 to 990 votes.[18] Similarly in 1968, Benjamin S. Anderson, a FVSC professor, won a plurality of the votes in a three-way race for a city council seat. He lost the run-off 772 to 933.[19] His defeat was the first casualty of the 1965 majority rule law.

The 1970s: A Decade of Political Victory and Successful Litigation

The first real election victory for a black Fort Valley resident came in 1970. In the April 1, 1970, election, there were three black candidates: Claybon Edwards, son of A. J. Edwards, was in a two-person race for city council; Willie D. Sneed, a FVSC alumnus and public schoolteacher, was in a three-way race for a city council seat; and Ms. Hattie Banks, the wife of W. S. M. Banks, was a utilities commission candidate. Edwards won his race; Banks received the highest number of votes in her race; and Sneed won enough votes to be in the run-off (Table 32). Two weeks later, Banks and Sneed lost their races to their white opponents.[20] Moreover, the courts had to decide the Edwards race.[21]

Edwards's victory in the election was challenged because he had received votes cast by people who had not paid their city taxes as required by the charter of the city. Given the low economic status of the majority of black citizens in Peach, it was no surprise that 150 of 192 potentially questionable ballots were those of blacks.[22] When the charter provision was legally challenged by three blacks on the eve of the election, Peach County Superior Court Judge George B. Culpepper II ordered that all persons purged from the voter's list be restored. However, he indicated that the "nonpayment voters" must use a separate voting box. Moreover, he wanted the results of the election with and without the "nonpayment voters" ballots.[23]

When the results of the April 1, 1970, election were reported to Culpepper, he certified election results in all of the races except the one in which Edwards was a candidate. After hearing evidence and arguments from both sides on the legality of the charter provision, Judge Culpepper ruled on April 15, 1970, that ". . . voters who had not paid all taxes owing to the city as required by the charter thereof . . . are not entitled to be counted in determining the results of said election and the superintendent shall certify the result thereof without including in his count the votes cast by such voters on separate machines."[24]

Thus, the county courthouse declared Edwards the loser and his white opponent, J. W. Poole, the winner. Thirty-four votes were cast on the special machine; Edwards received thirty-one of them.

Two days later, Edwards and six blacks who had been disqualified from voting in Fort Valley because of the tax restriction filed a suit in the U.S. Middle District Court of Georgia. The suit challenged the legality of the charter provision and alleged irregularities in the April 1, 1970, election. Their major charge was that the tax restriction was unconstitutional.[25] The legal proceeding which followed ended almost two years later when Edwards appealed to the U.S. Fifth Circuit Court. On February 2, 1972, they reversed the lower court's decision and Edwards finally took his seat some eighteen months after having "won" the election.[26]

While Edwards and others were doing legal battle, the first black to win a primary nomination was defeated by a white bloc-vote. Houston Stallworth, the FVSC professor and CEC founder, made an unsuccessful bid for a commissioner's seat in November, 1970.[27]

The story of Stallworth's defeat is a good indicator of how race influenced voting in Peach County. In the August 1970 Democratic primary election, Stallworth defeated N. F. Smission by a vote of 1,254 or 51 percent to 1,203 or 49 percent. In the November 3, 1970, general election, Stallworth was defeated by William Alford, who had lost a 1968 race to a white Republican for a county commission seat by a 63 percent to 37 percent margin. Alford received 52 percent of the votes in November to Stallworth's 48 percent. Alford's victory was the first time an acknowledged Republican won a local election in Peach County.

The Election of 1972
The Georgia legislature voted to give college students the right to vote in the town in which they attended college; this measure was passed during the 1972 session. This created a potential pool of approximately two thousand new black voters, the students at the historically black Fort Valley State College. Mobilization began to take place in both the black and white communities.[29]

The Peach County *Enterprise* editorialized that the presence of Fort Valley State students at polling places during the August primary was a "gnawing problem"; open letters were also written to FVSC students informing them that their school had "been turned into an arena for partisan politics to the extent that any serious academic work was a near impossibility."[30] Figuring that the students would vote at a higher rate than the general population, white community leaders began to quietly increase their own numbers on the registration rolls.[31]

The CEC decided to run only two candidates for office in 1972; they argued that this was a means of insuring the election of the two blacks who would run for office. This caused a problem for the more aggressive students and faculty members who were members of the group. Although they did not view themselves as competitors with CEC, they wanted to run more than two black candidates, arguing that they could elect "ten just as easily as they could elect two."[32] However, they would not run a candidate against a CEC candidate.

They formed an organization called Citizens and Students for a Better Community (CASBC). This group conducted an aggressive voter registration campaign in all sections of the black community. If CEC refused to run a candidate, CASBC would. With the primaries approaching in August, the CASBC leadership knew that the vast majority of the college students would not be in the city for the election. This placed all of the black candidates at a distinct disadvantage since they relied heavily on the black student vote. To remedy this situation, the CASBC leadership called for a special secret meeting to plan a strategy; the presence of the angel system made the secrecy of the meeting crucial. Instead of running as Democrats, they decided to run as Republicans at the last minute. Since they had no Republican opposition, they could run again in November with the benefit of the black student vote.[33]

The only victorious candidates, however, were those candidates endorsed by CEC (Table 33)—most of Fort Valley's blacks were unwilling to support the CASBC slate due to the antagonism between the college and the town.[34]

Three of the four losing candidates were the plurality winners in their respective races, but they failed to get the required majority of the votes cast for their office and were defeated by their white opponents in the run-off elections. Even in the run-offs, the black challengers received a majority of the machine votes, but the results of the absentee ballots threw the election to their white opponents (Table 34).

The voter-registration drive in the black community rallied the white community to do the same. This unforeseen development led to the defeat of most of the black candidates. The white voters turned out and bloc-voted at a higher rate than the black voters.[35]

Sensing that the student voters would give the black community a majority of voters, white citizens set up block-by-block, house-by-house lists and added more than six hundred whites to the list of registered voters. Block captains were appointed to see that every white person got to the polls on November 7. The captains were also active on election day; they checked off every name on their list and furnished a ride to the polls if there was a need. The voter-registration drive made the voter's list a 50–50 split with respect to race.[36]

Approximately 90 percent of the white community went to the polls; the black community turned out approximately 60 percent of their voters. With these percentages, even given perfect racial bloc-voting, the white candidates would have easily won. Moreover, some sources argue that anywhere from 250–350 blacks voted for the white candidates. Although the sources fail to tell exactly how there was a substantial black crossover vote, other studies have indicated that blacks tend to vote for a white candidate more often than vice versa when black and white candidates oppose each other.[37]

Three lawsuits came about as a result of these hotly contested elections. The three defeated black candidates in the run-off election filed a suit alleging that absentee ballots had been misused; two black schoolteachers filed a suit against the white school superintendent alleging that they were terminated for supporting his black opponent; and a group of white citizens brought a suit against the Georgia Board of Regents to desegregate FVSC. They argued in court that the school was an inferior institution of higher learning and that its large concentration of black voters diluted the voting power of Peach County's white citizens. The three suits highlight the vigor with which both groups were willing to fight in the courts.[38]

Dixon et al. vs the Peach County
Election Commission
Black candidates Clinton Dixon, William Arnold, and Claude Lawson were the leading vote getters in their respective races in the April 5, 1972, general election. However they did not get a majority of the vote. Thus, they had to compete in a run-off (they would have been winners prior to 1965). In the April 19 run-off,

each of the three black candidates won on the machines, but with 86 percent of the 233 absentee votes going to the white candidates, the latter overcame their narrow losses at the machines. Thus, another close election ended with blacks going down in defeat (see Table 34).[39]

In early May 1972, the three black candidates filed suit in district court charging that there were irregularities in the absentee voting procedures.[40] This case was still pending when the Justice Department filed a similar suit in July of 1973. Among other things, the Justice Department complaint argued the following:

Election officials assisted with the application of absentee ballots for whites whom they knew or should have known were not eligible to vote absentee. . . . The acceptance . . . of absentee ballots cast by persons ineligible to vote absentee affected the election . . . and resulted in the defeat of the candidates for those positions who were the choice of black voters. The different standards, practices, and procedures applied to black applicants for absentee ballots had the effect of "discriminatorily abridging the right of black voters to vote for candidates of their choice."[41]

Paul Reehling, the mayor of Fort Valley, immediately argued that there was "absolutely no basis in fact" for such charges. He also questioned why the Justice Department would wait fifteen months to file a suit. He felt that they were pressured by the three losing candidates into filing a complaint with "shabby evidence."[42] The court eventually ordered city officials to stop issuing absentee ballots to nonresidents, but declined to set aside the election. The three defeated candidates wanted to push the issue further but their inability to meet the legal fees prevented this course of action.[43]

McCrary et al. vs Anderson

Black schoolteachers were politically active in Peach County during the period following 1963. The participation of teachers in the campaign to elect black officials, particularly Robert Threatt, to the office of county superintendent, led to the firing of four black schoolteachers.[44]

Ernest Anderson had been superintendent of schools in Peach County for twenty-four years without any opposition. Some say that he began to think of the office as being his. Thus, when

Robert Threatt decided to run for office, it was Anderson's personal turf (at least in Anderson's mind) and not a public office that Threatt was seeking.[45]

Anderson wrote letters to employees of the public school system asking for their support. He reminded the teachers of his "extraordinary powers" in the matter of hiring and firing. He also said that he expected their votes in the election.

Threatt did not win the election, but it was not because of a lack of support from many of the black teachers.[46] When contract time rolled around, several black teachers were terminated by the board of education despite recommendations for contract renewal by their principals. Since these teachers were veteran teachers in Peach County, they alleged that their firing was due in full measure to their support of Robert Threatt. Thus, four of them decided to bring a suit alleging that the board of education and Superintendent Anderson had violated their constitutional rights by denying them re-employment because of the exercise of their vote in a manner of their choice.[47]

The judge agreed with the plaintiffs. He ruled that the Peach County Board of Education would have to rehire the teachers. He found that "the letter to the teachers by Anderson could not have been interpreted by the recipients to mean anything other than that the superintendent expected them to go to the polls for him and not Threatt." However, the judge did not feel that race was a factor in the case, although black teachers were the only veteran teachers terminated that year. Nonetheless, after losing friends and burning huge amounts of gas commuting to other counties to teach, the black schoolteachers were reinstated in their jobs.[48]

Avera vs Georgia Board of Regents

The suit by white citizens to integrate the traditionally black Fort Valley State College was unprecedented in the history of higher education. The genesis of the suit, however, was not in the interest of furthering the cause of integration; the genuine purpose of the suit was to take away the voting strength of blacks in Peach County. The suit came after the students at Fort Valley State were enfranchised in the city of their matriculation.[49]

In the middle of the heated election of 1972, Wilbur K. Avera, Chief Registrar of the City of Fort Valley, filed a suit in the District

Court in Macon. Avera's civil action against the Board of Regents of the University System of Georgia alleged that ". . . the voting strength of plaintiff and other white minority electors of the City of Fort Valley has been diluted to such an extent that they have been substantially disenfranchised thereby."[50] Avera and other plaintiffs wanted a "meaningful white presence" on the Fort Valley State campus. Most black people felt that, since FVSC students, faculty members, and alumni were participating in the electoral process in Fort Valley, the registrar wanted to change the college student body from 99 percent black to 85 percent white. Although the black voters would have been in the majority without the black students, it is apparent that Avera reasoned that if there had been a "meaningful white presence" at the college, the white voting strength would continue to ensure a practically all-white city government.[51]

Judge Owens ordered a hearing on the motion for preliminary injunctive relief, but he denied Avera's claim that the unconstitutional action of the defendants had the effect of diluting the voting rights of Fort Valley whites.[52]

The whites in Fort Valley were not to be deterred from their goal of trying to neutralize the black student bloc at FVSC. On July 5, 1972, Jack R. Hunnicut, a white who was barely returned to his position on the city utility commission in 1972, and twelve other whites, including two faculty members, filed a second suit in the Owens court. They continued to argue that the school was segregated. Moreover, they argued that the college was an inferior academic institution because it was all black. Part of the sixteen-page complaint reads as follows:

Fort Valley State College has in the past, as a result of its operation as an indentifiable Negro college by the defendants, occupied a position academically inferior to the other non-black division of the University System which continues to exist. . . . The Board of Regents continue to use the institution virtually as an educational dumping ground for the admission of students primarily unqualified for college work and who are unlikely to improve or obtain even the minimum academic level for the receipt of a college degree due to the makeup of the school's faculty and student body.[53]

In other words, FVSC was inferior because it was composed primarily of blacks. The quickest way to remedy this situation was to make the school predominantly white.

Despite the fact that FVSC had admitted practically every white student that had ever applied, the judge ruled that the FVSC and the Georgia Board of Regents would have to submit a desegregation plan for FVSC's student body and faculty. Although the faculty was much whiter than the white schools' faculty were black, the judge did not find it strange to single out FVSC in its ruling concerning "minorities" on the faculties.[54]

The suit had the effect of curtailing much of the political activism on campus for a period; all attention was focused on the defense of FVSC as a viable institution of higher learning. To add even more instability to an already shaky situation, the activist college president was retiring. He was replaced by a much more conservative president. Some argue that the new president began to make life difficult for many of the activist professors in order to appease the Board of Regents.[55]

At the present, FVSC is in the process of desegregating. Although the school is still overwhelmingly black, most of the top administrative jobs, with the exception of the presidency, are held by whites. New "magnet" programs are being developed in order to attract white students to the school. Although Fort Valley will probably remain a predominantly black college, most agree that its role as a center of black activism and progressive thought might be seriously threatened in the years to come.[56]

The Justice Department Charges Non-Compliance

Two weeks before the April 3, 1974, city elections, the Justice Department informed city officials that they might be in violation of election laws if candidates were elected by a majority and by posts. After arguing their cases before Justice Department lawyers, Fort Valley city officials, including the two black city councilmen, returned home to await the decision of the department. Having promised a decision within a week, the Justice Department later informed Fort Valley officials that it would not decide. Mayor Reehling announced to the citizenry that ". . . in essence, the Justice Department informed the city to make its own decision and if they don't like it they would take us to court."[57]

Thus, in an effort to avoid a court battle, Reehling urged the councilmen to abide by the 1964 charter calling for plurality and non-post elections. The Justice Department viewed the combination of a majority vote requirement and post elections as factors working to the detriment of electing blacks, although two blacks were on the city council.[58] Two more blacks were added to the roll of black elected officials in Peach County as a result of the April 3, 1974, election. Robert Church, a retired county agent, came in second in the balloting, behind Edwards, to become the third black on the six-member Fort Valley City Council. Claude Lawson, a black plumber, won a post on the utilities commission. Twenty-five angry whites gathered in front of the courthouse the following day to protest to the Justice Department officials. They charged that the election of two blacks and the re-election of another was the result of a black bloc-vote. The Justice Department officials said "so what . . . voters have every right to bloc vote, or not vote at all." The angry whites blamed the Justice Department for the plurality/non-post election which they felt led to the black victories via a black bloc-vote.[59] Although the mayor felt that the Justice Department created a situation where "future elections may be decided on the basis of race," the mayor and council felt that it would not be fruitful to challenge the Justice Department's May 26 ruling, which simply called for the continuance of the policy already adopted by the council under pressure.[60]

The fate of W. A. Alford, the first Republican to hold office in the history of the county, in the 1974 Democratic primary provided evidence for those who argued for the importance of race in Peach County elections. Running for re-election in 1974, Alford was defeated by Edward Woodard, a white building contractor who was a Democrat and a newcomer to politics, by the huge margin of 1,390 (41 percent) to 1,994 (59 percent.)[61] With this, his second loss to a white candidate in as many elections, it appeared that Alford could only garner white support when his candidate was black.[62]

H. W. Berry et al. vs the Jury Commission

H. W. Berry, a FVSC professor affectionately known as "Mr. Civil Rights," was the chief plaintiff in a suit filed on May 27, 1971, in federal district court in Macon, Georgia. The suit charged that, due to a significant under-representation of blacks and women on the jury, it was unconstitutionally composed according to the 1970 census population figures.

After analyzing a list of jurors who had served between March

1974 and March 1976, it was revealed that of the 2,904 jurors, 30 percent were black and 44 percent were female. There were 306 grand jurors, of which 16 percent were black and 11.7 percent were female. Census figures showed that Peach County was 57 percent black and 53 percent female.[63]

Judge C. Cloud Morgan, after a May 31 hearing with plaintiffs and county officials, signed an order which found the trial and grand jury lists unconstitutionally composed in that black and female citizens were under-represented. The jury commissioners were ordered to develop a new list. The potential jurors were to be selected from the voter-registration list after questionnaires had been mailed out.[64]

On August 27, 1976, Judge Owens approved the new list submitted by the commission. The black plaintiffs appealed to the Fifth U.S. Circuit Court of Appeals, charging that blacks were still "under-represented and the new system was inadequate." The appeals court agreed with them on July 31, 1978; it ruled that the new system was "inadequate." Moreover, it ruled that Peach County "must take steps to produce a jury list in which the percentages of black jurors more nearly approaches the percentage of eligible blacks.[65] The plaintiffs eventually got their desires, and court resumed in February 1979 with a constitutionally composed list of voters.[66]

Berry et al. vs the Peach County
Board of Commissioners
The legal road to district county commission elections was also a long and circuitous one. After having been denied an injunction to stop the election in 1976, the black plaintiffs took their case to a panel of three U.S. district judges in Macon. On February 28, 1977, they ruled that the commission failed to comply with the preclearance provision of the Voting Rights Act of 1965 when it changed its method of election back in 1968. The judges called the violation a "technicality" and ruled that a new election was not necessary since the commission had not made an attempt to discriminate. After the U.S. Supreme Court failed to rule on their request to overturn the aforestated decision in March 1977, the matter was eventually arbitrated locally in Peach County. The black plaintiffs got their basic requests: Peach County commis-

sioners would be elected from four districts, and one seat would be elected at large. With two predominantly black districts, two predominantly white districts, and a predominantly black at-large seat, the results of the 1980 election fell perfectly in line with the predictions of the plaintiffs: two blacks were elected from the two predominantly black districts; two whites were elected from the two predominantly white districts; and a white candidate was elected at large (see Table 35).

Black Political Empowerment and Organizational Maintenance

As was noted in the preceding chapter, there are six mainte-nance functions that resource-poor organizations must address in order to attain or retain power: (1) economic development; (2) provision of services; (3) political mobilization; (4) politi-cal education; (5) resolution of conflict; and (6) management of fear.[67]

Both CEC and CASBC had comprehensive and widespread political-education programs. They held basic political-education seminars, invited civil rights celebrities such as Julian Bond, John Lewis, and Shirley Chisolm to speak, and canvassed the black neighborhoods to turn out the vote. With the aid of the Voter Education Project grants, they were able to sustain mod-erate registration rates.[68] However, the data on black turnout suggest that their efforts to mobilize their numbers were not successful.[69] Moreover, the relatively well-executed political-education plan was undermined by: (1) the lack of a program of economic development, (2) lack of service provision, and (3) in-tragroup conflict.

Like most black political organizations in the black belt, nei-ther CEC nor CASBC had a program of economic development. Thus, they were basically defenseless when, because of eco-nomic intimidation, black citizens refused to participate. Mem-bers of CEC and CASBC could not help but understand, since it had not been very long since the county schoolteachers and some FVSC faculty used that same excuse. Moreover, when there were cases of blacks being afraid of losing their social security or welfare benefits, intervening in their behalf was not an institutionalized procedure. While the fear of physical violence was practically nonexistent, fear of economic intimidation was rampant. The most glaring example of economic intimidation occurred during the election of 1972. With the black students at FVSC having recently obtained the right to vote in Fort Valley elections and with blacks running for all of the county and city offices, the threat of a massive increase in black elected officials was a real possibility. During the heat of the campaign, a rumor began to circulate that the Blue Bird Bus Company, the town's major employer, would relocate if there was a "black takeover." Some observers argue that this threat was enough to keep some blacks away from the polls and to keep a considerable number of blacks from voting for the black candidate.[70]

Black Class Antagonism
Class antagonism in Peach broke down primarily along "town-gown" lines, i.e., a substantial number of FVSC faculty and the native blacks of Peach tended to feel alienated from each other. This feeling of alienation kept local blacks from supporting "outsiders" who were primarily FVSC faculty. Although the founder of CEC was a FVSC professor and the faculty had been active in political affairs since 1965, from 1964 to 1982 no FVSC faculty person was elected to public office. Seven of the eight black elected officials in Peach were natives; the nonnative was a longtime resident.[71]

The inability of FVSC faculty to get elected has not yet created a substantial problem for those faculty members who are dedicated to the goal of black political empowerment. However, the marginally interested are discouraged since it appears that their chances of ever holding an office is small.

Recognizing the problem, CEC has formed a committee to try to find ways to eliminate the schism. The committee has been basically non-functional, however. Moreover, the situation is made worse by the residential segregation of the FVSC faculty— many of the longtime faculty members live in a modern residential area called "Ponderosa Estates." This increases the feeling of alienation that the townspeople feel with respect to the FVSC faculty.[72]

The relationship between the college and the town has not always been one of alienation. Before free public education was provided by the state for blacks, Peach's blacks went to high school on the campus of the college. During this time, the relationship between the "town" and the "gown" was an intimate one. The "Annual Ham and Egg Show," a farmers' fair sponsored by the local black county agent, was always held on the campus of FVSC. Together, the high school and the fair made the local black community feel a strong attachment to the school. When these two activities ended, the class difference between the two communities became more prominent.[73]

CEC and Organizational Transformation
Founded as an organization to further black interest via black elected officials, CEC usually supported the black candidates. From 1963 until 1978, members canvassed the community and tried to turn out the black vote. Under the leadership of Evelyn McCrary, however, the organization became nonpartisan. Beginning in 1980, it started to operate as a public service group whose goal was to increase overall citizen participation. It held a "meet the candidate forum" during the 1980 campaign to encourage more informed voting. Although this elaborate transition displeased many of CEC's original members who were no longer active, the new members basically felt that this new posture was good for the black community.

The Potential for Black Political Influence—1980

In April 1980, Rudolph Carson became the first black mayor of Fort Valley. After having served eight years on the city council, Carson ran on an eighteen-plank "unity and progress" platform for the mayor's office. Carson announced his decision to run for mayor in the following manner:

During the past two years, I have had the opportunity to assume many of the mayor's responsibilities. I was able to see and realized how important the role of mayor is in setting the pace for members of the council and also in creating an atmosphere, good or bad, for the entire city. Unfortunately I have begun to see far too many negative things happening in our community—too much discord and a spirit of disunity with some of the key elements of the city.[74]

Carson tried to keep the factor of race out of the election. He made no reference to race in either his political advertisements or in his published platform. The phrase "all our citizens" was perhaps Carson's most popular saying throughout the campaign. Even after the historic mayoral race ended with Carson victorious, he called his win "a people's victory." In a *Macon Telegraph* interview, Carson stated ". . . it was a people's victory for Fort Valley because that's who I represent. In my eight years on the council, I have demonstrated concern for the whole community. Race has not been a concern of my thinking. I have always tried to do my best for the entire citizenry of Fort Valley."[75]

Although some prominent white businessmen publicly supported Carson's candidacy, there can be no reasonable doubt that the majority of Carson's support came from the black community. Losing by a 6 percent margin of only 114 votes,[76] Lloyd L. Westmoreland, the defeated candidate, blamed his defeat on a low white turnout: "I was really disappointed because I felt that the white voters did not turn out as they should have. To a degree . . . it was racially *[sic]*, it [the election] was [a racially split vote], but just to a degree.[77]

A black presence in Peach County politics had been common ever since Claybon Edwards took his seat on the council in 1972. Nonetheless, Carson's 1980 victory marked the first time that blacks actually had the majority of votes on the two primary decision-making bodies of the city. There were three blacks and three whites serving on the city council, and the mayor would break ties; the utilities commission had two blacks and two whites, and the mayor would break ties there also (Tables 36 and 37). Moreover, blacks held two of the five county commission seats. Thus, within ten years the number of black elected officials soared from zero to eight in Peach County. Although they failed to capture any of the non-board county offices, e.g., probate judge, clerk of courts, etc., there was still a sense of political efficacy in Peach's black community.

Black Political Empowerment in Peach

The chief resource of Peach's organizations were human resources: the FVSC faculty, the public schoolteachers, and the Fort
Valley State students. The FVSC faculty broke their traditional
nonparticipatory mode when Professor Stallworth led the drive
to form CEC in 1963. W. S. M. Banks II ran for office in 1964,
and most of the remaining faculty soon became active in some
manner. The FVSC staff and students were more isolated from
economic intimidation than the black Peach schoolteachers.
Nonetheless, they participated just as heavily.

The FVSC students and staff brought a new aggressiveness to
the thrust for black political empowerment. They wanted to win
as many offices as possible. Professor H. W. Berry maximized the
use of lawsuits to make empowerment easier: the change from
majority to plurality city elections was crucial to the effort toward
empowerment.

The FVSC students provided a tremendous amount of volun-
teer help. They ran registration drives, canvassed neighborhoods
to get out the vote, and tried to educate the inactive part of the
black community regarding the importance of political participation. However, their greatest contribution was the "balance of
power" role that they played in the elections. Highly politicized
and lacking the constraints of the adults, the students provided
the solid support for black candidates that was crucial for any
prospective black victory.

The Peach leaders, using their two organizations and resources, brought Peach County blacks to the threshold of playing a political part in Fort Valley politics. Despite the measures
whites took to prevent them—noncompliance with the Voting
Rights Act, the purging of voting lists, bloc-voting, the firing and
harassment of teachers, and the attempt to integrate FVSC to neutralize the black college vote—blacks held the majority of official
political power in 1980.

Rudolph Carson assumed the mayoralty during a time of high
expectations on the part of the black community. Ever since
Claybon Edwards took his seat on the city council in 1972, basic
services to the black community, i.e., paved streets and roads,

garbage pick-up, lighting, etc., had been delivered. The black voters expected innovative leadership from Carson; they wanted a program to increase their overall standard of living.

Carson was encouraged to run for mayor by a very influential group of white business and professional men. Political observers in Peach felt that this was their last ploy to unseat Mayor Paul Reehling. Reehling was elected to his second term with heavy support from the black community. It is argued that the businessmen reasoned that a black candidate would take the majority of the black vote from Reehling. Once the black mayor assumed office, he could be defeated more easily than Reehling. Reehling decided not to run for mayor, but Carson's white business support remained intact.

"Mayor Carson": The People's Mayor

During his victory interviews, Carson constantly asserted that his victory was not a racial victory, i.e., not a black victory, but a "people's victory." Although some blacks were already somewhat skeptical of him since he had open white business support, they realized that his politically "colorless" rhetoric could be described as conciliatory in light of the hotly contested election.

Carson was determined to be a good mayor. During his first months in office, his schedule was so frantic that he had to be hospitalized for a week due to exhaustion. After settling down to a more reasonable pace, he provided good overall leadership.[78]

During his first term, he led an effort to get the city on the road to regaining its status as a Georgia "Certified City"; he began to bring the city in line with its affirmative action goals; he secured a $500,000 HUD community development block grant; and the Citizens' Advisory Council seemed to be keeping him in touch with the feelings of the citizens. Thus, at the end of his first year, the mayor had a reasonably good record of achievement.[79]

Mayor Carson agreed to a lengthy interview for the local paper. Local political observers feel that Carson committed political suicide during the interview. After citing some of his accomplishments and challenges, he proceeded to make three extremely unwise statements. He stated that: (1) the white community supported him more than the black community; (2) he did not want to see Fort Valley become a black town (at the same time, he expressed disbelief that the town was already 65 percent black according to the new census figures); and (3) he did not want to be known as a black mayor, but just as the mayor of Fort Valley. Moreover, since he was striving to be mayor for all the people, he would never attend a conference of black mayors.

Even among those who understood that the mayor was probably courting his white business support, many members of the black community felt the mayor's strong denial of any special racial identification with the black community was an embarrassment. Even though blacks had made gains during his term, many blacks found his lack of identity distasteful, even if it was for political reasons. After all, they reasoned, he owed his election to the black community.[80]

The Carson anniversary interview caused such a stir that it was cited as being the unofficial beginning of the 1982 campaign. His supporters argued that Carson had played into the hands of his opponents. Knowing that he had won by only 164 votes, a slight shift of votes in the black community could easily defeat Carson (not to mention the white defection that was predicted to occur). The mayor tried to explain his statements, but the die had been cast, and most observers felt that the mayor would lose black votes due to his gaffes during the infamous interview.[81]

Despite his public posturing as a "colorless" mayor, Carson would continue in the second year of his term to fight for issues of importance to the black community. In two crucial votes during his second year, the city council split along racial lines with Carson breaking the tie by siding with the black councilmen. Both of the proposals—making Martin Luther King's birthday a city holiday and voting a pay increase for city employees—were popular in the black community. Thus, it appeared that Carson's rhetoric differed from his actions.[82]

Race was acknowledged as a key issue in the election of 1982. With the councilmen voting along racial lines on major proposed legislation, it was apparent to all that race did make a difference. Massive registration drives increased the voting list by 37.7 percent, compared to the 1980 registration level. As of April 1, 1982, the registrar reported a total registration figure of 4,450—2,367 blacks, 2,077 whites, and six others.[83] With a community divided along racial lines, both sides knew that turnout was crucial.[84]

The April 7 election decreased the number of black elected officials: the mayor, two councilmen, and a utilities commissioner all lost their seats. With 75.9 percent of the registered voters casting their ballots, the racial election of 1982 was won by the whites.[85]

The major reason for the defeat was lower black voter turnout vis à vis the white turnout. With whites voting practically 100 percent white and blacks voting 90 percent black, the black turnout would have had to exceed the white turnout by at least 11 percent. However, the opposite happened: while the white turnout was 81 percent of the registered white vote, the black turnout was only 69 percent of the registered black voters; 65 percent of the non-voters were black.[86] The defeat left Fort Valley with only one black city councilman, one utilities commissioner, and two county commissioners. However, the defeated black candidates vowed to continue to work for the welfare of the city.[87]

The twenty-two-year period from 1960 to 1982 saw Peach County blacks gain a relatively large amount of political power, although much of it was lost in 1982. Nonetheless, the goal of black political empowerment is firmly entrenched in the minds of black Peach County citizens. The next election, for better or worse, is never more than two years away.

5. Black Political Empowerment in Clay County, Georgia, 1960 to 1982

Blacks have been organized and striving to attain political power in Clay County since the formation of the Clay County Improvement Association in 1960. Despite their efforts, they were totally unsuccessful in their attempts to elect blacks to any of the elective city or county offices during the period of this study. Their failure was due to multiple causes. This chapter is an explication of the process which led to this failure.

Three major features characterized the political climate of Clay during the pre-sixties era, the period before the arrival of the opportunity to act. These were: (1) a white population comprised primarily of southern traditionalists; (2) an established fear of white violence; and (3) accommodationist black leaders.

Clay County's whites believed strongly in the southern tradition of segregation. The county's weekly paper, during the decade of the fifties, provides a number of examples of pro-segregationist and antiblack views[1] in news articles that shed light on the social and political attitudes of the white minority in Clay. Following the *Brown Decision* in 1954, the Fort Gaines city council passed an ordinance forbidding the mixing of races.[2] During the 1950s Clay County had a chapter of the Ku Klux Klan whose meetings were announced in the local paper.[3] In 1957, the Clay County chapter of the States Right's Council of Georgia was organized to defend the segregation of public schools.[4] And the "Declaration of Constitutional Principles," i.e., "The Southern Manifesto," was editorially supported by the *News-Record*, the county's weekly newspaper.[5]

The relationship of blacks and whites in Clay County has been archetypical of black-white relations in the rural South. After blacks were freed from slavery, segregation was reinforced as an integral part of life—blacks had no political rights. Voting was a privilege granted to blacks considered to be good enough to be trusted with the franchise. Black voters before 1960 were usually landowners, ministers, or other individuals who were in the good graces of an influential white.[6] Although these blacks were leaders within the black community, they were basically accommodationist—they provided no political leadership for the black community at large.

These blacks did provide educational leadership, however. In 1889 the Chattahoochee River Baptist Association decided to build a school in Fort Gaines.[7] Black Clay Countians C. N. Gigger, Peter Carter, Moses Turner, and John Turner were influential in helping the church organization to make Fort Gaines the site of the Association's school, The Chattahoochee Institute. Fort Gaines was selected as the location for two main reasons: (1) the location of Fort Gaines, on the Alabama line, made it accessible to over a half million blacks in southwest Georgia and eastern Alabama; and (2) Fort Gaines did not have a black high school. Thus, Fort Gaines was an educational center for blacks in the area until the states of Alabama and Georgia decided to provide educational facilities for black students. Clay County got their first black high school in 1958.[8]

The Chattahoochee Institute depended heavily on financial contributions from local whites. During one fund-raising drive, the white community was asked to contribute one-half of the overall goal of the drive ($2,000). The school principal and the prominent black ministers were the liaison to the white community. They were required to cultivate a pleasant working relationship with the white business and government leaders. Thus, any attempts to mobilize the black community around racial concerns were considered to be against the best interests of the educational institution.[9]

The lack of assertive leadership on the part of the accommodationist leaders made the fear of violence an even more effective deterrent to black political assertiveness. Although milder forms of social control and repression were common everyday occurrences, the Grinnison Goolsby incident confirmed the reality that harsher forms of violence were in the realm of the possible.

The Grinnison Goolsby incident would have a lasting impact

on black-white relations in Clay County. Although the incident happened in neighboring Early County, blacks in the entire southwest Georgia area were affected. In 1916, a black man named Grinnison Goolsby killed a white man who had whipped his son. In retaliation, a group of white men burned several black churches and black masonic halls mainly in the Early County area. Moreover, many blacks were randomly killed during this rampage. Cornered in an upper chamber of a masonic lodge hall, Goolsby shot several white men before he was eventually shot and killed. Although Goolsby is still regarded as somewhat of a folk hero in the black community, the story of his fate is also a mild deterrent to political participation. Strong fears of a Goolsby recurrence existed at least until 1956, and would-be activists are still reminded that similar white violence could recur.[10]

Black Educators and the
Repression of Leadership

The white support for the establishment of the Chattahoochee Institute placed the principal in the position of attempting to maintain this financial support. By the time that a state-supported black school was established in 1958, the black principal was expected to act as a keeper of the peace, as liaison between the black and white communities.

The principal of Clay County's black schools tried to keep a line of communication open between the two communities. More than any other person, the black principal had both an intimate relationship with the black community and a close working relationship with the white community, and, during the pre-sixties era, there was no doubt that the black principal's job description called for political inactivity and active support of the status quo. The case of Harrison Lee is illustrative of the role that principals have usually played in Clay County.

In early 1953, a black high school teacher in a neighboring county circulated a letter expressing some very negative attitudes concerning blacks. His major thrust was that blacks were not ready for integration.[11] Although he lived in Alabama when the letter was circulated, he was hired the following year as the principal for the black high school in Clay County, Georgia.

Harrison Lee, the new principal, soon found himself in disfavor within the black community both because, knowing that he was a privileged person with the "angels,"[12] he boasted throughout the black community about his power, and because he continued to make speeches all over the South concerning blacks' lack of readiness for integration.[13] Lee instituted a practice of firing the black schoolteachers from Clay County. The terminated instructors had to commute to adjoining counties for employment. Moreover, Clay County residents graduating from college could not expect employment in Clay County. Although Clay County instructors had never been very active in political affairs, they represented a potential pool of leadership, and this principal's new practice removed even this potential. With most of the new teachers coming from outside of the county, the likelihood of their becoming politically active in Clay's affairs was extremely low.[14]

After the publishing of the principal's letter in a January 1956 edition of the *News-Record*,[15] sixty to seventy black men signed a petition asking for the immediate termination of the principal's contract. Citing immorality as the chief reason for the request, they also accused the principal of being a "white man's negro" and of holding certain views in order to "keep his job."[16] Although he had the support of the school superintendent, the principal soon left town, alleging that threats were made on his life.[17]

The Clay County board of education found a temporary principal for the rest of the 1956–57 school year, and a new principal was hired for 1958–59. Although he built a home in Clay County and took an active leadership role in the black community, his contract was not renewed for the 1960–61 school term. He was replaced by the present principal, who has kept a much lower political profile.

The 1960s and Political Organization

It was under these circumstances that a few local black activists tried to make some strides toward political empowerment in the county. The nonsupportive white community would not turn out to be the only obstacle to progress. The 1960s found the vast majority of Clay County blacks uneducated and impoverished; 96 percent of blacks over twenty-five had less than a high-school education; (5.3 years was the median number of school years completed by blacks over twenty-five). The median black family income was $1,212,[18] and only forty-one blacks were registered to vote.[19] Thus, Clay County did not appear to be the most fertile of soils in which to nurture the seeds of black political participation. Nonetheless, the 1960s would witness the birth of the county's first black political organization since the efforts to organize the NAACP foundered in the early forties.[20]

The new organization, the Clay County Improvement Association (CCIA), was the object of intense curiosity since it was the first major black organizational effort to do anything even tangentially political since 1956, when the group of black men demanded the dismissal of the principal. James Clark, a Hancock County native, was the driving force behind the formation of the CCIA. The organization's purpose was to serve as a citizen-education group for the black community. Blacks still had to pass literacy tests in order to become registered voters. Thus, the first phase of the CCIA's objective—registration—had two components: one was to aid the black Clay Countians in learning to read the Constitution, and the second component was to help them pass the literacy test, which consisted of approximately thirty-three questions.

Civil rights attorney C. B. King of Albany, Georgia, was hired to handle the legal aspects of chartering a nonprofit organization. Upon his filing the charter in the Clay County courthouse, curiosity began to mount as to the exact nature of this organization. Although its primary purpose was to promote black political participation, James Clark also wanted to use the organization to initiate a drive to secure a Headstart program for Clay County.[21]

Initially James Clark wanted the Chattahoochee River Baptist Association, an affiliation of approximately fifty black churches in southwest Georgia, to be the sponsoring agency for the Headstart program. The association flatly denied his request. Thus, Mr. Clark turned to the CCIA to act as the sponsoring agency, since it was a nonprofit organization. Moreover, he reasoned that the CCIA's sponsorship of such a worthwhile program would reflect favorably upon the organization.[22]

Thomas Delton, of Fort Valley, Georgia, and Alfred Dempsey

and Joe Thornton of Atlanta were the chief resource persons in the CCIA effort to bring Headstart to Clay. The CCIA proceedings were not transpiring unnoticed by the white community; the curious whites had their representatives in the early CCIA meetings. The "angel system" was thriving in 1960.[23]

The CCIA ran into two major problems in their efforts to secure the Headstart program for Clay County: a lack of matching funds, and the need for county officials to approve the program. The first problem led to the second, and the CCIA found themselves in a difficult situation.

Without funds of their own to meet the federal matching funds requirement and having been turned down by the church association, the CCIA felt that the county was the place to turn. But the county officials would not approve of the program unless the funds were handled through the county. The CCIA members consented to this stipulation. Thus, the Headstart funds came to Clay County without the CCIA receiving any credit for procuring the program, nor did they have any management responsibility for it.

Annexation: An Opportunity to Act

When an annexation issue surfaced in 1963, the CCIA missed the opportunity to politicize it. The residents of Rosehill, a predominantly black neighborhood of approximately three hundred people, requested that the city supply them with water and sewage service. This request was denied due to the city's low financial resources. When these services were provided a few years later, it ended the neighborhood's effort to be included within the city limits of Fort Gaines.[25] If the annexation attempt had been successful, blacks would have constituted a majority of the residents of Fort Gaines. More numbers would have been a valuable resource in their efforts toward empowerment. While the CCIA leaders recognized the political advantages of annexation, they did not know exactly how to push the issue more fervently.[26]

The Voting Rights Act of 1965 made things a bit easier for organizers in Clay County. With the banning of literacy tests, it was no longer necessary to spend hours coaching individuals regarding the best way to pass the exam. When CCIA was founded in 1960, less than 1 percent (41) of Clay's voters were black.[27] By 1966, blacks accounted for 20 percent (245) of the registered voters.[28] Most of this modest gain occurred after the passage of the Voting Rights Act. At this juncture, CCIA received assistance from the Student Non-Violent Coordinating Committee's Southwest Georgia Project. The Southwest Georgia Project was an effort by SNCC to mobilize voters in the largely black southwest section of Georgia.

The SNCC Southwest Georgia Project operated out of Albany, Georgia, the commercial hub of southwest Georgia. Funded from various sources, including Atlanta's Voter Education Project, the project sought to mobilize all of southwest Georgia, which primarily included the heavily black Second Congressional District and several predominantly black state-house districts.[29]

Randy Battle and Joe Pfister, two SNCC workers, were assigned to organize Clay County in 1966. They received a positive response from the blacks in the "Cotton Hill" section of the county. The first meetings were attended by small groups of fewer than ten people, but the crowds grew to fill the Midway Baptist Church to its capacity of about 150 people.[30]

The mobilization of SNCC workers did not make life for James Clark, the CCIA's founder, any easier. Although he had been the object of intense attention ever since he initiated plans to form a black non-profit organization, the harassment became more intense after it was discovered that he was the initial contact of the SNCC workers. When he opened an auto-repair shop shortly after the founding of CCIA, some of the local whites accused him of starting an NAACP and using the funds to launch a business enterprise. Moreover, the police began to park approximately a hundred yards beyond his auto repair shop. This harassment led to a *de facto* boycott since many of his customers would not take the risk involved in continuing to patronize Clark. The police watch was interpreted as a display of disfavor on the part of the white influentials in Clay. Clark's Garage survived the boycott, although it presented a great challenge to Mr. Clark's economic status and his political commitment.[31]

The SNCC workers soon discovered a factor which the CCIA had overlooked: basic survival needs were much more paramount in

Clay than the need to vote. The SNCC workers found that Clay blacks were interested in material benefits: jobs, welfare, unemployment compensation, and social security. Having initially planned to aid the voter-registration efforts of the CCIA, the SNCC workers had to revise their strategy: the attainment of material benefits became primary, while voter registration received secondary attention.[32] However, SNCC lacked the resources to provide services in a widespread fashion.[33]

The SNCC Southwest Georgia Project workers would take all interested workers to Albany for meetings concerning voter registration, welfare regulations, and the duties and responsibilities of elected officials. Moreover, they organized a youth group, the Clay County chapter of the Southwest Georgia Youth Club, which provided a social outlet for the youth of the rural area of Cotton Hill.[34]

Black Clay Countians who worked with the SNCC project felt that fear of economic intimidation and violence were the major barriers to black political participation.

We are now moving on the south side of the county, and on this side most of the land is owned by whites, and it is always harder to get black folk to do things when they are living on a white man's place. . . . We meet some people that still have the fear of the white man. Then we have to explain that nothing will happen to them. . . . There are so many people who refuse us because they are afraid. . . . They are afraid of Mr. So-and-So because they are living on his place, "and if I do something against Mr. So-and-So, he might throw me out."[35]

Although the project workers could offer assurances of safety, and though there was in reality small chance of intimidating or violent acts occurring, many of the would-be voters had heard too much evidence to the contrary. Moreover, neither CCIA nor SNCC were equipped to respond adequately to these reasons for nonparticipation, as they did not have the resources to protect Clay's black citizens from economic intimidation or violence.

Vote Dilution and Black Political Empowerment

In 1967, a piece of local legislation was introduced in the Georgia House that would change the method of electing the county commissioners in Clay. Previously they had been elected by districts; the new bill changed the method to at-large elections. The bill passed and the election method changed in 1968, although the change was not precleared as required by Section 5 of the Voting Rights Act of 1965. Thus, between 1968 and 1980, elections for county commissioners were held in violation of federal law. This practice went unchallenged for twelve years, despite the negative effect it had on the chances for black political empowerment.[36]

This change was apparently a well-calculated move made to dilute the strength of the new black voters. Since at least three of the four voting districts would have been predominantly black, ruling whites felt a real need to eliminate this political threat. Previously there had been no such need, since, prior to the enactment of the Voting Rights Act, only 10.4 percent of the eligible blacks were registered to vote in Clay.[37]

Walter Patmon, a retired staff worker for the Southwest Georgia Project, ran for coroner in 1968, despite the problems of fear and low black voter registration in Clay: blacks accounted for only 33 percent (610) of the total electorate.[38] Given the strong likelihood of racial bloc-voting, Patmon's candidacy stood practically no chance of victory. Patmon was determined to run nevertheless. Having worked with the Southwest Georgia Project, he felt confident about his abilities and his candidacy. To counter the anticipated ubiquitous charges of "lack of qualifications," he participated in an intense coroner training program with financial assistance from the Southwest Georgia Project. Nonetheless, that was the first charge levelled against him by local whites. Although Patmon lost his bid for coroner, he felt that another stride had been made toward black political empowerment in Clay County.[39]

With the help of SNCC Southwest Georgia Project workers, the quest for a political empowerment appeared to be making slow but steady progress. Although the project workers did not have the resources to overcome the fear of economic intimidation, they were a positive force in a county which needed support: (1) they raised consciousness through political education; (2) they sponsored the candidacy of Walter Patmon; (3) they were partially responsible for the 13 percent increase in black voter registration; and (4) they provided discount food items from a farm that they owned in Lee County, Georgia. Thus, when they decided to leave Clay, the residents of Cotton Hill were saddened.

The SNCC workers and the Southwest Georgia Project decided to focus their resources toward the development of Featherfield Farms, a tract of six thousand acres of black-owned land. For all practical purposes, the Southwest Georgia Project disbanded and became the New Communities Corporation.[40] Through the use of land for a variety of economic ventures, they hoped to bring economic security to blacks in Lee County as well as in southwest Georgia in general. Although Clay County would stand to benefit in the long run, the removal of the SNCC Southwest Georgia Project resources seriously retarded the momentum for black political power in Clay.[41]

When the SNCC workers left Clay County in 1969, CCIA was the only black group in the county whose goal was to affect county politics. Although SNCC diverted attention from the CCIA, the latter was still basically concentrating on civic education and providing registration. Thus, it is ironic that the first black candidate for office was primarily affiliated with the SNCC Southwest Georgia Project. Nonetheless, the CCIA ran candidates after SNCC left.

The demise of the dual school system came in 1970 when the federal government mandated that all dual school systems would have to be disbanded. A few blacks had attended predominantly white Clay County Elementary and High School, but no whites had attended the all-black Speight Elementary and High School. The federal desegregation order stipulated that all schools in Clay County would have to merge, i.e., a unitary school system would have to be constructed. The desegregation process went smoothly. There were no major disturbances. The whites accounted for 35 percent of the school population; unlike their elders in county government, the black students won the major offices in the student government.

Despite the lack of any major disturbances in the integration process, a group of white Clay County citizens decided to organize to attempt to establish a private school in Clay County. Although there were many planning meetings during the spring of 1970, Central Christian Academy, the would-be private school, never came to fruition. Most of the prospective students for Central Christian Academy went to the private school in bordering Abbeville, Alabama.[42]

The CCIA was very active in the minor problems that arose in the school system: one white bus driver insisted that her black students sit in the back of the bus; black students felt that hall monitors treated them unfairly; and most of the classes were segregated within the school.[43] The CCIA successfully remedied the problem of discriminatory hall monitors and the seating arrangement on buses, but the problem of segregated classes continued. There was a system of "freedom of choice" within the school: each student could choose their teachers for any subject. This resulted in two practically all-black classes and one practically all-white class in each subject being offered.[44]

The CCIA continued to encourage voter registration and participation, although it did not attempt to groom candidates for election. Thus, between 1968 and 1976, only three blacks offered themselves as candidates: Reverend J. S. Standford ran for justice of the peace in 1972; Jerry Alexander and Freddie Johnson ran for the county school superintendent and sheriff, respectively, in 1976. With blacks constituting only approximately 37 percent (810) of the total voters in 1976, all three of these candidates lost.[45]

Opportunity Knocks Twice:
The Re-Emergence of Annexation

In 1977, the annexation issue surfaced again. The city, with Justice Department approval, annexed two areas. The purpose of the annexation was to provide "a water line in the area for the industry that eventually failed to come." The new annexation brought thirty-three new white residents and twenty-two blacks. Of the white citizens, twenty-six or 79 percent were registered to vote; and only two or 9 percent of the twenty-two blacks were registered to vote. This gives a rough indication of the still-existing registration disparities between blacks and whites.[46]

The city officials made an effort to include the Rosehill Community in the annexation, but many of the influential blacks of that community fought the annexation, ultimately defeating the effort that would have given blacks a voting majority in Fort Gaines, the county seat of Clay County. The increased taxes that annexation would bring were the apparent cause for such a fervent organized effort against the annexation.[47]

The failure of the CCIA's leadership to recognize the merit of annexation in their quest for political empowerment illustrates both their lack of crucial political information and their refusal to sacrifice a personal interest for a group interest. They operated under the false assumption that Fort Gaines, the county seat, was predominantly white—according to the 1980 census, it was predominantly black. This assumption prevented blacks from seeking candidacies in the city.[48] At the same time, no one was aware that the elections for county commissioners were being held in violation of the Voting Rights Act. Due to low levels of registration, chances are that any black candidacy would have ended in defeat. Nonetheless, the point is that a lack of knowledge prevented useful political action.

The Rosehill residents were heavily influenced by CCIA members who argued that annexation would mean more taxation. To them, the personal cost of more taxation outweighed the group benefits that could be gained from black empowerment. Whereas this position may have reflected realistic practical considerations, it also reflected an unwillingness to make small personal sacrifices for the benefit of the group. As it happened, the increase in taxes would have been offset by reduced insurance premiums from having the protection of the city's fire department.[49]

The Formation of the NAACP
and the Strategy of Litigation

Frank Davenport, a black Clay County activist who spent a good deal of time in Atlanta, initiated an effort to start an NAACP chapter in early 1978. By early 1979, the fifty members necessary to start a chapter had been recruited. Many blacks in Clay County were afraid to join the NAACP; they viewed it as being basically a trouble-making organization and they wanted no part of it. Some even argued that the NAACP was the black counterpart of the

KKK. Thus, to get fifty people to apply for a charter was a challenge. Nonetheless, Davenport was successful.[50] Frank Davenport was elected president of the chapter. While speaking with Christopher Coates, an ACLU attorney based in Atlanta, the two men discovered that Clay County officials had changed their method of electing the county commissioners from districts to at large. A suit was filed on February 22, 1980, by the ACLU, charging that the act that changed the method of voting from districts to at-large was instituted without preclearance from the Justice Department and that, therefore, elections held for county commissioners were being held in violation of Section 5 of the Voting Rights Act. On June 23, 1980, District Judge J. Robert Elliot of Columbus, Georgia, signed an Interim Decree which reappointed the Clay County Board of Commissioners. Four of the five districts were predominantly black: one was 58 percent black; two were 66 percent black; and one was 77 percent black. Thus, it appeared that the chances were good that a black could be elected as a commissioner in the upcoming election.[51] Whereas blacks only accounted for 53 percent of the voters in the county at large, three of the new districts were "safe districts" for blacks by Justice Department standards; two were 66 percent black and one was 77 percent black.[52]

Four blacks qualified for the August Democratic primary in 1980: Freddie Johnson for sheriff; James Clark for county commissioner in District Two; Arnett Richardson for county commissioner in District Five; and Walter Patmon for county commissioner in District Three. When the polls closed, they showed Clark and Richardson leading by slim margins in their respective races. Moreover, the black candidate for sheriff placed second in a field of five, thereby forcing his opponent into a run-off. The attention now turned to the courthouse, where the absentee ballots were to be counted.[53]

The two white candidates won the absentee balloting. Of the 36 ballots cast in District Two, the white candidate received 28, or 77 percent of the absentee ballots, with the black candidate receiving the remainder (8, or 23 percent). The white candidate in District Five received 90 percent (47) of the absentee ballots.[54] The power to decide who could get absentee ballots was crucial in this election. Thus, after coming close, the black community was once again denied black representation in a policy-making role. Moreover, the black candidate for sheriff lost badly in the run-off. In all likelihood, the white community strongly supported the sole white candidate in the run-off after having split their vote in the primary.[55]

Officials of the ACLU were suspicious of the results, due to the extraordinary high number of absentee ballots. They brought a suit charging that persons were allowed to vote in the primary who were not legally qualified to vote in Clay County. During the trial which took place in October 1980, evidence was presented to prove the following: Clay residents who had long since left Clay County and were voting in other cities were also voting in Clay County; persons owning plots of land in Clay County who were not residents were voting; and absentee ballots were sent from the tax commissioner's office by the sheriff to many residents.[56] The allegations that irregularities existed was proven to be accurate. Nonetheless, the judge ruled that the irregularities were not sufficient to call for a new election.[57] He did order the tax commissioner to purge the voting list in order to make sure that the list contained only legitimate Clay County residents. The purge actually had a more injurious effect on the black voters than the white. A large number of blacks, including Frank Davenport, the NAACP president, were purged.[58]

The defeat of the black commission candidates left the black community embittered, and the decision of the judge rubbed salt on a fresh wound. For all practical purposes, the judge said, "what the election officials did was wrong—they cheated, but I will not punish them for it this time. The tax commissioner must purge the voting list and make sure that nothing of this nature happens again."[59] The election and the trial made the white community aware that the blacks were at least attempting to wage a battle for representation.

The white influentials, who basically controlled the politics of the county, had the first real challenge to their hegemony in 1980. Since 1970, however, the white decision makers had made a considerable number of black appointments to various boards. On paper, this gave the impression that blacks were sharing decision making in the county—in reality, the black members of the board were always in the minority. In some cases, they did not know of their appointment.[60] With the predominance of racial bloc-voting, the black members could always be out-voted. Moreover, the appointees were those blacks perceived by the white selectors as least likely to threaten the status quo.[61]

The election of 1980 left many black activists dejected, angered, and "battle weary." Although they felt that the 1980 election represented a strong showing, no black candidate ran for office in 1982. The road to black political empowerment in Clay County is likely to be a long and circuitous one. Nearly two decades after the passage of the Voting Rights Act, black political empowerment is still a dream.

Clay County: An Analysis of the Collective Action Components

Clay County blacks failed to gain political empowerment due to their lack of organizational development. The leadership lacked the vision and the resources necessary to overcome the barriers to organizational development. The purpose of this section is to illustrate how the weakness of the leadership, organization, and resources resulted in few substantive political gains for blacks in Clay County.

Leadership
Clay County's potential leaders—the landowners, schoolteachers, business persons, and ministers—were political accommodationists during the pre-sixties era. This group, with the exception of the teachers, is traditionally viewed as being economically independent. However, their economic independence is indeed marginal: the landowners, usually farmers, must depend upon the local banks to finance their crops. The ministers need some other form of employment to support themselves; and the small business persons must get their licenses from the local city officeholders. Thus, the group that traditionally provides the leadership is actually only a few steps removed from being vulnerable to the same type of economic intimidation more commonly aimed at their lower-status counterparts.

Clay County's black leadership grew more assertive beginning in the early sixties with the formation of the Clay County Improvement Association. However, the leadership pool was a shallow one: several of the economically independent blacks remained inactive, and the black ministers, save one, did not reside in the county. Despite the leadership problems, the Clay County Improvement Association represented the beginning of a new quest for political rights.

Organization
A major problem with the black leadership in Clay County was its inability to obtain popular support. None of the three organizations which were active during the period could claim widespread appeal. The Clay County Improvement Association was composed mainly of citizens who lived in the city of Fort Gaines; the sncc Georgia Project drew its membership from the Cotton Hill area of the county; and the naacp had the same basic membership as the ccia. Moreover, all of these groups—with the sncc group being the least guilty—appealed mainly to the already interested. The ccia and naacp did little to interest the hard-core nonparticipant.

The lack of popular support was largely a result of the lack of proper organizational development. Neither ccia, the naacp, nor the sncc Georgia Project executed a successful campaign to remove the four major barriers to the establishment of an organization in the rural black belt South: (1) economic intimidation, (2) fear, (3) black class antagonism, and (4) the angel system.

Economic Intimidation. The fear of losing their jobs kept practically all of the black schoolteachers, who were perceived by the black community as being the most capable of leadership, from participating in any political organizational effort. The teacher firings during the Lee administration were a constant reminder that their jobs were tenuous. The sncc Georgia Project also encountered problems resulting from economic intimidation. Like the ccia, the sncc project workers in Clay were mainly landowners. They found that trying to get sharecroppers to take part in any of the project affairs was practically impossible.

Economic intimidation played a salient role during the election and the trial of 1980. Sharecroppers were brought down in their employers' trucks to vote; sharecroppers are usually encouraged not to vote. Since there was so much attention on this election, many blacks were brought to the polls by their overseers. They were told to vote for the white candidates, and, more likely than not, they did. Since most blacks felt that the poll watchers and election officials had a system of "knowing who they vote for," many economically vulnerable blacks were afraid to vote for their chosen candidate.[62] Several activists made the point that the sharecroppers had good reason for this fear: The Clay County ballots were made like raffle tickets. One had to write one's name at the top of the Ballot next to the number of the ballot and on the ballot itself. Moreover, one's name and number were written on a separate sheet of paper.[63] Whether or not these were actually used to see how citizens voted, the existence of such a possibility made the system a potent deterrent for those who were fearful. On one occasion during the early sixties, the white superintendent approached several black teachers and authoritatively informed them that they had voted for his opponent. He was so accurate that the possibility of his having guessed was soon dismissed. Although the teachers were not threatened, the evidence was adequate to convince them and others that the "lottery ticket" ballot was a method of vote verification.[64]

The most damaging example of economic intimidation involved James Clark and Eddie Ricks. Ricks, a native Clay Countian who had recently returned from New York, became a plaintiff on behalf of James Clark who had recently been defeated in his bid for county commissioner. Mr. Clark, the owner and operator of an auto repair shop, felt that his business would suffer further damage if he continued to press the suit; his white and black patronage had declined after his involvement with the original suit. Many vulnerable blacks were afraid to be seen at his shop.[65]

Eddie Ricks became a plaintiff while he was laid off from the Columbia Peanut Mill. He was never called back to work; after the trial ended, he inquired about his job. He was told that things were slow and he would be called when things picked up. Meanwhile, other laid-off employees were reclaiming their jobs. Some of the white supervisors were overheard saying that "Eddie Ricks will never work here again because of what he did." Eddie Ricks was never called back to his job. Moreover, his wife was the object of job harassment also.[66]

Mrs. Ricks worked at the only factory in town, Carter's Manufacturers. When her husband became a plaintiff, she began to get erratic hours on her job, and she was eventually laid off. When she was approaching the eligibility deadline for unemployment benefits, she was called back but given only one or two days to work. After having been back on the job with drastically reduced hours for a week or so, she was laid off again and rehired in time to keep her from drawing unemployment benefits. This pattern continued until she finally quit—she eventually left town, and her husband soon followed her.[67]

Fear of Violence. The fear of white violence was not a major concern for most of the period between 1960 and 1982. Nonetheless, the possibility of violence was always in the background. During the early fifties the Grinnison Goolsby incident in neighboring Early County was still brought up as a reminder that whites in the area were capable of violence. Although Clay County had no physical racial violence within its borders, their neighboring counties earned such names as "Bad Baker" and "Terrible Terrell" from the civil rights workers in the area. The issue of violence was realistic enough that it could always be invoked when an individual did not especially want to participate.

Black Class Antagonism. Neither SNCC, CCIA, nor the NAACP addressed the problem of class antagonism in Clay's black community. Perhaps this was due to the extremely subtle form that such antagonism took in Clay. The classes or black social groups in Clay County were not especially antagonistic toward each other, although all the groups may have had their likes and dislikes concerning the others.

For the purposes of this analysis, there were three major black social groupings in Clay: the schoolteachers, the church members and officers, and the non-church members. Although there was a slight overlap at various points, they were quite distinct with respect to how they spent their time. The schoolteachers primarily socialized among themselves informally, and formally as well, through their social club, The Ebonaires. The primary social activities for church members and officers were church activities and the NAACP and the CCIA. The non-church members usually socialized among themselves at the local night spots.

These rather distinct groups of black citizens rarely crossed paths.[68]

The NAACP and the CCIA, primarily composed of church members and officers, had never attracted a substantial number of the other two groups. The teachers stayed away from these organizations primarily for reasons of job security, and the non-church members claimed that they had never been actively recruited and, hence, felt unwanted. Moreover, there was a feeling of betrayal on both sides: the CCIA-NAACP-church-member group felt that the non-church members should have a greater sense of responsibility with respect to their citizenship duties, while the non-church members felt that the organizations' members were pretentious and that political participation was futile. Both groups expected more leadership from the teachers, who, in turn, felt that the stakes were too high to jeopardize their relatively comfortable lifestyle when the likelihood of success was perceived to be minimal.

The Angel System. Although SNCC workers did not report any problems stemming from the angel system, it continues to be a nemesis for CCIA and the NAACP. The principal of the black high school has always been regarded by his fellow blacks as the carrier of news to the white community. Some CCIA members blame him for the loss of the Headstart Program during the sixties. Not only is the principal disliked for not working toward the goal of black political empowerment, he is held in even lower esteem by the black community for allegedly working against it.

Clay County activists were unsuccessful at overcoming the major barriers to organizational development. Nonetheless, the organizations indigenous to the county continued to exist despite the obstacles that hindered their effectiveness. Without the support of this basic foundation, Salamon's six necessary functions for organizational maintenance were not attainable.[69]

Fear Management and Economic Intimidation. The chief fear in Clay County during the period was the fear of economic intimidation. None of the three groups had a program to combat this fear. Thus, when black citizens decided not to participate due to fear of economic retaliation, there was little that could be said since their political organizations could not offer them any form of support. This state of affairs seriously hampered many of the efforts of groups organizing in Clay.

Provision of Services. The CCIA failed in their major attempt to provide a basic service to the black community when they failed to secure the Headstart programs. The NAACP did not use any of their small financial resources to provide some basic services. And, although the SNCC workers provided low-cost food and tried to increase the welfare rolls, their efforts were too localized and too shallow to have a widespread effect.

Education and Communication. The SNCC Southwest Georgia Project workers were the only group during this twenty-year span who focused on mass education and communication. They canvassed the various communities, trying to encourage blacks to participate and help to bring about change in their community. The CCIA and the NAACP would often have VEP representatives and other speakers come to their meetings to give politically informative speeches, but this did little for the absent and disinterested. In addition to failing to communicate with or politically educate the larger black community in Clay, CCIA lacked much of the political information that it should have had, as witnessed by its failure to capitalize on the annexation incident and the passage of the 1967 legislation changing the method of voting for the county commissioners from district to at-large elections.

Resolution of Conflict. None of the three groups in Clay put forth any appreciable effort to diminish the conflicts within the black community during the 1960–82 period. As stated earlier, the conflicts did not manifest themselves in any type of overt negative behavior. The three basic groups peacefully coexisted but made no gains toward black political empowerment. Although the NAACP and the CCIA viewed this situation as a problem, little effort was focused in the direction of alleviating it. During the SNCC period there was also a sectional cleavage: the blacks in the southern part of the county were CCIA members, whereas the blacks in the northern part of the county were SNCC Southwest Georgia Project members. There was very little interaction between these two groups.

Political Mobilization. The chief goal of the ccia at its inception was to increase the level of black registration. They distributed copies of the literacy test throughout the black community. At various times, they arranged for longer registration periods prior to elections. However, this activity falls short of being a mobilization. Although sncc was helpful in launching the candidacy of the first black candidate for public office, the sncc workers concentrated on provision of service rather than voter mobilization, since this was the request of the "Cotton Hill" residents. The naacp, during its brief history in the county, concentrated mainly on litigation. Table 38 indicates that black registration rose from 20 percent to 53 percent from 1966 to 1980. Nonetheless, the black registration rate lags 18 points behind that of the white community.

Resources. Clay County organizers were weak with respect to resources, material and immaterial. The first major weakness manifested itself in the lack of vision of the leadership. The leaders' goals were to get blacks registered, get blacks to the polls, and get blacks to office. The problem is that they did not have the resources to overcome the fear of violence or the fear of economic intimidation. Moreover, they could not provide services to show the effectiveness of political participation or to allay the fears which could have provided the foundation for mass popular support. With the existence of fear and economic intimidation and the lack of popular support, political education and mobilization were futile. Thus, in Clay County, black political empowerment has yet to be realized.

6. Hancock, Peach, and Clay: A Comparative Analysis

The predominantly black counties of Hancock, Peach, and Clay experienced varying degrees of black political empowerment during the period from 1960 to 1982. The beginning of the sixties found all three counties without any black elected officials and with only a few blacks voting. Yet, at the end of the period, there was a significant difference in their overall success at moving toward political empowerment: in Hancock, after 1974, blacks held all of the county slots with the exception of sheriff; from 1980 to 1982, Peach County blacks held the mayor's seat and controlled the city council and the utilities commission. Although this control was lost in the election of 1982, blacks are still represented on these bodies as well as on the county commission. And Clay's blacks failed to elect a black to any county or city office. Why did these counties have different rates of black political empowerment? The answer lies in the organizational effectiveness of the black political groups.

The removal of legal barriers to voting was a major victory for the post-World War II civil rights movement. But open enfranchisement was analogous to allowing a group to compete in an activity from which it had been previously barred. Because the group is suddenly free to participate does not mean that it has the skills or the resources to compete successfully. Moreover, even with enfranchisement, many barriers still exist. To the extent that a black community can organize itself and overcome these barriers, it can achieve some degree of political empowerment. Hancock's success at overcoming barriers to organizational development and other obstacles best explains their greater success at black political empowerment when compared to Peach and Clay.

Hancock and the Importance of Numbers

The Hancock elections in 1966 provide an excellent example of the importance of numbers. In 1966, 66 percent of the black population of Hancock was of voting age; blacks constituted 51 percent of the total electorate. Only 52 percent of the black voters were registered, while 100 percent of the whites were registered.[1] Thus, even with all of their group registered, Hancock whites did not equal the number of blacks registered at half strength.

The black vote turned out in full force and apparently heavily bloc-voted. They elected the first black officials in the county with a little over half of their potential registrants, a feat that would have been impossible anywhere else. While smaller black voting-age populations, lower level of registration and turnout, and lower rates of bloc-voting have been a nemesis for black empowerment efforts across the black belt South, they have been far less problematic in Hancock, even though all of their elections are at large. With such a large voting-age majority, blacks can register at a lower rate, vote at a lower rate, and bloc-vote at a lower rate, and a black candidate can still have a reasonable chance at winning. Hancock's overwhelmingly black population allows it to absorb losses from each of the aforementioned factors.

It is important to note here that, although numbers are important, they are only a potential resource; they alone do not bring about empowerment. However, HCDC was able to mobilize these potential voters. By 1980, blacks constituted 73 percent of the voters and had a 100 percent registration rate in Hancock.[2]

Peach County and the Importance of Election Methods

The political groups in Peach were not organized adequately to translate its narrow black voting-age majority into black political empowerment without the help of electoral methods. Part of even the moderate success of black candidates in Peach County can be largely attributed to the plurality standard used in their at-large non-post elections. However, it is important to note that effective organization was necessary to take advantage of the electoral methods.

Prior to 1964, candidates for the city council and utilities commission were elected on a plurality non-post basis. A candidate simply had to garner more votes in this at-large election and he was declared the winner. In violation of the Voting Rights Act of 1965, the method of election was changed from "plurality non-post" to "majority post" during the 1965 session of the Georgia legislature. This "majority post" method was instituted in 1966 and used for four elections, 1966 to 1972, in violation of the 1965 act; the Justice Department intervened before the 1974 municipal elections. To avoid litigation, the city returned to the plurality non-post method. From 1966 to 1972, ten blacks ran for political office. Two were winners, three were clear losers by any standard, and five were clear victims of the majority vote requirement. All five candidates won a plurality of the votes in the first election but failed to capture a majority in the run-off. Blacks were far more successful under the plurality non-post method. From 1974 to 1978, all of the black candidates who sought vacancies on the six-member city council and four-member utilities commission were successful. For this period, blacks held 50 percent of the positions on each of these governing boards.[3]

The four utilities commissioners served staggered terms. Every four years two seats would be up for grabs. With only one candidate running from 1974 to 1978, a single-shot black vote assured the black candidate of re-election.

The six councilmen of Fort Valley served four-year staggered terms. Hence, every two years, three councilmen were up for re-election. The winners were the three candidates with the highest number of votes. With blacks never having more than two candidates, black voters could single-shoot or double-shoot vote for their candidate. In 1980, Carson left his council seat to run for mayor. With his victory and his replacement by another black councilman, blacks had the controlling share of decision-making power.

The importance of election method was evident in county elections. Prior to 1980, elections for county commissioners were held at large with candidates running from posts. Only one black candidate, Peach County native David Carter, was a successful candidate under this plan. In 1977, he was chosen by the commission to replace a resigning white member. Thus, in 1978 he had the support of many in the white community. Black candidates who were considered threats had been unsuccessful.

As a result of *Berry vs Dole* (1980), Peach would have to change from a three-member board to a five-member board. Four of the members would be elected by districts, while the chairperson would be elected at large. Two of these seats would have a predominantly black constituency. In 1980, black candidates captured these two seats, while the predominantly black at-large seats and the predominantly white districts were won by whites.[4]

By 1980, the black political registration rate in Peach was only 57 percent of its potential strength. This spelled trouble for any black candidate in a two-person race. Rudolph Carson was the first black candidate to find himself in this predicament. In 1980, he was successful; in 1982 he was not.

Mayor Carson was elected at a time when blacks made up 52 percent of the voters in Fort Valley. Given that the black and white turnouts were equal, it is reasonable to argue that the white business support gave Carson the margin of victory. When blacks made up 53 percent of the voters in 1982 but turned out at 61 percent, while whites turned out at 80 percent, Carson lost. Observers argue that the same 1980 white support provided the margin of victory for the white candidate.

Clay County and the Importance of Organization

Much of Hancock's early electoral success (1966) can be attributed to its overwhelming black voting-age population, whereas Peach's later success (1974 to 1980) can be attributed to the methods of election after 1974. While Hancock had its numbers and Peach had its methods—Clay had neither. Prior to 1980, all elections for the city and county were held at-large, with a majority vote requirement. With the presence of strong white bloc-voting and a low black voting-age population, a black candidate's chances of winning were small. *Davenport vs Isler* (1980) gave Clay four predominantly black districts. Nonetheless, blacks lost three county commission races by thin margins. These losses highlight a crucial lesson: numbers and electoral methods are only potential resources in an empowerment effort; the numbers must be mobilized to vote. In 1966, Hancock blacks won offices with only half of their members registered to vote both because of their superior numbers and because they had the organization to turn out a mobilized group. Peach blacks could win during 1974–80, with lower black registration, due to their electoral methods and, again, because they had the organization to turn out the votes and take advantage of the methods. Clay blacks, even after having received more favorable electoral methods, did not have the organizational effectiveness necessary to mobilize their numbers. Black registration lagged behind white registration by eighteen points.[5]

The black political groups in these black belt Georgia counties were essentially challenging groups, vying with an establishment for power in the polity of county politics. The process of organizing to gain power and delivering the vote for black candidates is filled with hazards; nonetheless, deliverance of the black vote is the primary goal of all three organizations. Why has Hancock been more successful delivering the black vote than Peach and Clay? The answers lie in a comparative organizational analysis of Hancock, Peach, and Clay.

From Organization to Empowerment

Tilly argues that interests precede organization, and that organization orchestrates the mobilization which leads to collective action.[6] A focus on leadership, strategies, and resources reveals how the black political organizations in Hancock, Peach, and Clay attempted to facilitate black bloc-voting—the final step in the process of collective action.

Leadership
The leaders are the individuals who are responsible for articulating the interest, planning the strategy, and providing a sense of political efficacy to the rank and file. Thus, the role of leader is pivotal to the political empowerment process. Its influence can be seen clearly in Hancock, Peach, and Clay.[7]

Hancock had a good number of black landowners, educators, and ministers who provided leadership during the pre-1960s era. They preached the virtues of hard work, education, and political power. Moreover, they played an important role in maintaining a relatively mild political climate. Had the opportunity presented itself during this period, they probably would have been even stronger advocates of black political power.[8] After 1960, the leadership pool was even more extensive. Two public schoolteachers were among the first group to seek a political organization. They were later joined by ministers, businessmen, farmers, other schoolteachers, and SCLC organizers Carl Farris and John McCown (see Appendix).

Peach County's leadership pool prior to the 1960s was a shallow one; the relatively economically independent black businessmen were the leaders. With the exception of the black high school's principal and a professor at FVSC, the public schoolteachers and the college faculty were not involved in local politics. After 1960, the leadership pool expanded in Peach County. The traditionally economically independent were joined by the college faculty, college students, and the schoolteachers. It is noteworthy, however, that the leadership had a crucial cleavage; there existed a "town" leadership—local natives of Peach County—and a "gown" leadership—professors, students, and others who were not natives of Fort Valley (see Appendix).

The black leadership in Clay prior to the 1960s were accommodationist. They were landowners, educators, ministers, and businessmen; they were granted the "privilege" of voting. They solicited the support of white elites in providing for black education in the county. Thus, if there was a desire to develop a more assertive leadership posture, the white economic support placed the black leadership in a tenuous position. The era of the sixties did little to expand the leadership pool. Despite the brief intervention of SNCC, the leadership pool remained a shallow one. The small group of relatively economically independent blacks continued to provide the leadership. Black schoolteachers and ministers are conspicuous by their absence (see Appendix).

From these pools, the leadership of Hancock, Peach, and Clay would emerge. The wider and deeper the pool, the greater the chance of developing viable strategies and resources to carry them out. Hancock and Peach seem more advantaged because of the involvement of teachers; teachers provide the resources of efficacy and expertise, whereas the ministers perform the function of legitimating politics.

Forming the Organizational Base

In all three counties, the idea of organization came from a small group (or one individual in the case of Clay) and was introduced to the public. In Hancock, within a year, there were over 300 dues-paying members; 200 in Peach; and 125 in Clay County.[9] Salamon's barriers to organizational development (fear, violence, black class antagonism, and economic dependence) had little impact on this phase of organizational development. As the groups began to formulate mobilization strategies, however, these factors would increase in importance.

The leadership in each county understood that optimal levels of voting would be necessary to gain political power. A black voting-age majority was present in each case. The goal was to activate these potential voters. In each case, the leaders knew that political education was crucial to their goal. However, the strategies and the resources surrounding this political education process differed in response to the barriers of fear, violence, black class antagonism, and economic dependence.

Hancock County:
Strategies, Barriers, and Political Mobilization

The HCDC's founders reasoned that the pre-existing network of the black church could be utilized to spread the idea of a potential political organization. The church members were receptive and HCDC began to grow. The county's overwhelmingly black population and their pre-existing organization attracted the attention of SCLC. Carl Farris, a young black sociologist working with SCLC, was assigned the task of aiding the mobilization effort in Hancock. By 1966, 52 percent of Hancock's blacks were registered.

The attempt to provoke fear did not become a factor until the passage of the Voting Rights Act of 1965. On the night before the act became effective, the KKK burned two crosses in black neighborhoods. However, few blacks were intimidated. Hancock was one of the few counties across the South where blacks stood in line to register on the first day the act went into effect.

McCown came to Hancock in early 1966 because he saw the potential for black political empowerment. Although fear, violence, economic intimidation, and black class antagonism were not paramount issues upon his arrival, McCown's strategy for political empowerment attacked all of these issues.

The 1966 Elections: Fear and Economic Intimidation
The fervent political activity in the black community in Hancock seemed to create a need for white repression. Two events are the most outstanding examples of this repression: Reverend Edwards, an activist schoolteacher and minister, was forcibly removed from his home and warned to stop his activism; and, in an attempt to provoke fear, the KKK marched on downtown Sparta on the eve of the election. Neither of these events accomplished its goal: Reverend Edwards continued his political activism, and black Hancock voters turned out to elect all three of the candidates to office. In both cases, the creation of an institutionalized strategy for overcoming the provocation of fear was necessary.

The election of Robert Ingram, Sr., brought about the threat of economic intimidation. Ingram, the only black on a five-person board, was constantly dissenting to policies advocated by the other four members. His advocacy of issues of special importance to the black community is the alleged reason for the attempt to have him removed from the board. Because of a Georgia law prohibiting elected officials from holding state jobs, Ingram, Sr., was asked to either resign from his job or give up his seat on the school board. This created the opportunity for HCDC to either undermine their mobilization efforts or facilitate them: If they could somehow remove the threat of economic intimidation, they would facilitate participation; if they could not, participation would be threatened.

When the HCDC membership told Robert Ingram, Sr., to resign from his job and remain on the school board, promising to help him financially, a kind of "political participation insurance" became standard operating procedure. Although they had marginal resources, HCDC had recognized a case of economic intimidation and had made an attempt to remove a possibly debilitating barrier.

The HCDC's leadership felt that it needed a safeguard against fear. Although many blacks were not afraid to participate—enough to elect three blacks to office—it was reasonable to assume that some people were fearful. Moreover, as the thrust for empowerment grew, so did the repressive measures (threatening phone calls, telephone disconnections, harassment by Sparta police, etc.). When HCDC decided that they would have to protect themselves [10] and instituted the network of CB radios to keep in touch, help was never far away.

HCDC and Material Incentives

The HCDC provided strategies to eliminate fear and economic intimidation. Although the "political participation insurance" was not based on firm economic foundations, it served well until something more comprehensive could be offered. However, the absence of fear and economic intimidation does not guarantee participation. Their absence is necessary but not sufficient to facilitate mobilization. What would it take to facilitate widespread black voting in Hancock? McCown's answer was material incentives.

McCown was a strong advocate of instrumentalist politics. The importance of participation was premised on the notion that there was a reciprocal relationship between political inputs and political outputs. If you participated, you should get tangible rewards for your participation. The notion of *quid pro quo* was the core of his political education lesson. However, the most salient feature of the HCDC's political-education program was McCown's teaching by example.

Working as a member of HCDC, McCown provided crucial services for Hancock's black community from 1966 to 1968: he secured a Headstart program for Hancock County; he secured twenty-five FHA loans; and he placed one hundred eligible blacks on welfare. He never ceased to stress that his accomplishments were the result of knowledge gained through political participation. He stressed that even more gains could be made if blacks had the power to make public policy. Thus, blacks were encouraged to vote, not because of the duties of citizenship but for the hopes of a better life.

Blacks gained more offices in Hancock in 1968, and more benefits were forthcoming. In addition to the pride of having a black probate judge, a black clerk of the superior court, and a black-controlled commission, the presence of these officials produced important tangible benefits. The black officials of Hancock provided information, paid bills, and assisted with health care, financial procurement, and personal matters. These benefits did not require huge sums of money; the major resource utilized here was a willingness to help.

The political activism insurance did not alleviate the fundamental problems of economic intimidation. The root problem was that blacks did not provide jobs for themselves. McCown felt that blacks would never be completely free until they were economically independent. Thus, he sought to bring industries to Hancock and to develop black businesses. With the founding of ECCO in 1970, HCDC had an economic branch dedicated to the creation of a black economic infrastructure. Since there was somewhat of an incestuous relationship between ECCO and HCDC, economic development became associated with political participation.

The "Black Takeover," ECCO, and Black Political Empowerment

The 1968 elections gave blacks a controlling majority on the three-member county commission. When the newly elected black officials began to press for school desegregation, race relations reached an all-time low. The formation of ECCO marked the beginning of McCown's attempt to bring economic prosperity to the county without the assistance of the county's whites. After two years of trying to coalesce, McCown decided to go it alone and began to make a black town out of the largely abandoned Mayfield district of the county. These two events, the desegregation crisis and the establishment of ECCO, facilitated a sharp racial cleavage.

The black vote was already mobilized as a result of material incentives, fear management, and political participation insurance. The desegregation controversy and the controversy surrounding ECCO almost insured heavy racial bloc-voting in the black community. Between 1970 and 1974, ECCO brought over $10,000,000 into Hancock in an attempt (albeit unsuccessful) to eliminate poverty. Moreover, this period marked the real black takeover: between 1970 and 1974 all of Hancock's white officials, save the sheriff, lost their offices. Phase one of black political empowerment had been reached.

Peach County:
Strategies, Barriers, and Mobilization

Peach County's black political organizations—CEC and CASBC—relied primarily on political education as their main strategy to mobilize the black voters for black candidates. Their major obstacle was their appeal to solidarity when black class antagonism and economic intimidation were major depressants of black political empowerment though not necessarily depressants of black political participation.

Black Class Antagonism
The "town-gown insider-outsider" schism in Peach County was a major reason for the defeat of the CASBC candidates for county and city offices in 1972. Although the "one on one" contests were detrimental to black candidates' chances for victory because of low registration, the lack of enthusiastic support by CEC also had a chilling effect on their chances. Many local blacks refused to vote for the FVSC faculty members and other CASBC candidates. It is important that the mobilized black vote delivers in a bloc for the black candidate. Black class antagonism kept this from happening in Peach throughout the period of this study.[11]

Economic Intimidation
Neither CEC nor CASBC had the economic resources to deal successfully with the threat of economic intimidation. When many poor blacks could not be convinced that their public assistance or social security checks would not be cut off because of political participation, neither CEC nor CASBC provided any political participation insurance. Approximately four hundred of the potential voters gave this excuse for not voting during the 1972 mobilization effort.[12] This indicates that a significant number of unreg-

istered individuals were afraid of economic intimidation. These potential voters would remain nonparticipants due to a lack of resources.

The case of the Blue Bird Bus Company offers a counterpoint to many of the arguments concerning the efficacy of bringing industries to the black belt to eliminate poverty and dependence. It is alleged that the Blue Bird Bus Company used its power to depress black political empowerment. During the 1972 elections, the company's threat to relocate in the event of a black takeover had two effects: (1) some blacks simply chose not to vote; and (2) many blacks felt compelled to vote for the white candidates.[13] Thus, lower levels of voting and lower rates of black bloc-voting combined with the already debilitating effect of the low level of black registration. Tables 39 and 40 illustrate that black registration in Peach has usually been lower than the level of white registration in Fort Valley and the county at large. In the years when there were black majorities ('66, '72, '74, and '80), they were marginal majorities which never exceeded 52 percent.

Clay County:
Strategies, Barriers, and Mobilization

The CCIA was founded in 1960 with the express purpose of increasing black registration. Political mobilization would be hampered by economic intimidation, the lack of popular support, and factionalization in the black community. The CCIA did not have the necessary resources to combat the problem of economic intimidation; they did not provide the services or material incentives that could have led to popular support; and they did little to bridge the class and sectional differences. Thus, their efforts to mobilize black voters failed.

The association endorsed candidates for office, but there were no full-fledged, organized campaigns; there were no coordinated outreach programs to politically educate; there was no program of economic development. Members of CCIA would meet, discuss problems, "spread the word" about meetings, and hope that new faces would show up. There was not a comprehensive agenda for political empowerment—problems were handled in piecemeal fashion. The ccia bemoaned the fact that their membership was low and the enthusiasm that they created was minimal. Nonetheless, they continued to hold registration drives and conduct political education seminars that were primarily attended by the already interested.

The sncc Southwest Georgia Project had a good outreach program of political education and a small-scale program of service provision. However, their failure to provide a comprehensive strategy for political empowerment (including economic development) seriously hampered their ability to mobilize the community. During its brief two years in the county, the naacp has followed the same basic pattern set by ccia. However, the naacp did file the suit that gave Clay the more desirable district elections.

Hancock, Peach, and Clay: A Final Comparison

Hancock's black political empowerment was a result of five major factors: (1) Hancock's mild political climate was conducive to political activism; (2) initially their overwhelming numbers gave blacks the opportunity to gain political offices with only half of their eligible voters registered; (3) the leadership was able to secure the resources to combat fear of violence and economic intimidation; (4) they were able to provide material incentives which spurred optimal levels of black voting; and (5) the empowerment effort created a wide racial cleavage which facilitated high levels of black racial bloc-voting.

Peach's and Clay's black political organizations faced three major obstacles to black political empowerment: (1) they lacked the resources to combat fear of economic intimidation; (2) they failed to bridge class cleavages in the black community, which weakened the black bloc-vote; and (3) they lacked the resources to provide material incentives that might have led to higher levels of participation.

The black leadership in Hancock realized that practical issues came first. One cannot expect individuals to participate if they are afraid. Neither can one expect participation by resource-poor individuals to be motivated by lofty notions of civic duty. McCown and hcdc argued that organizations must combat economic intimidation through group solidarity and economic development. Moreover, material incentives must be provided for the would be participant. Hancock achieved black political empowerment because the organizers were able to garner the resources which were necessary for the implementation of this strategy.

Table 41 explicates a model of successful empowerment such as occurred in Hancock. A leadership group organized itself, removed the barriers to black political participation, and provided an incentive to participate. Hancock successfully removed the fear of violence and of economic intimidation, and provided services to gain popular support. Peach and Clay did not develop a strategy to combat fear and economic intimidation. Nor did they provide any important basic services. Thus, they failed to gain popular support.

The popular support of HCDC created an environment conducive to political education. Notions like "specific efficacy," "group consciousness," and self-help through politics seemed more reasonable to a population that was not afraid. Political education led to political mobilization and the attainment of the first phase of black political empowerment. Since the political organizations of Peach and Clay failed to eliminate fear, economic intimidation, and other basic barriers to citizen participation, their efforts to politically educate, mobilize, and empower the black community ranged from less successful, in the case of Peach, to complete failure, in the case of Clay.

Epilogue: The Impact of Black Elected Officials

It is a political puzzle that blacks control few of the predominantly black jurisdictions in the South,[1] and this work has focused primarily on analyzing the problems encountered by blacks in the southern black belt as they strive for political offices. But what happens in those cases where blacks have gained political offices? Do they make a difference?

The question is somewhat rhetorical, of course. Black elected officials do make a difference. The real question is how much of a difference do they make? One's assessment probably depends largely on one's expectations regarding the power of the ballot. For those who felt certain that black political power would bring about economic equality and a reordering of governmental priorities,[2] there is a great sense of disappointment at the actual outcome. On the other hand, for those who felt that blacks would not be able to make substantive changes within the existing structure due to their lack of political experience,[3] there is the perception that a great deal has been accomplished.[4] In sum, blacks in office have not brought about a socioeconomic revolution, but neither have they been completely ineffective in serving the needs of the black community.

Black political empowerment has had its most positive effects in providing black constituents with a more equitable share of benefits distributed by the public sector. David Coomb's study of Greene County concluded that "the new (black) administration in Greene County had created new jobs (predominantly in the public sector), acquired substantial outside resources, raised the level of living for blacks, and reached some type of accommodation with white leaders."[5] A similar study by Hugh Perry of

Greene County found a host of symbolic and material benefits: group pride, improved access to public officials, a decline in police brutality, more job training, a municipal water system, better medical services, studies for industrial growth, and increased federal low-income housing.[6] James Button's study of black political empowerment in Florida yielded similar results. The primary gains for blacks were in the area of symbolic benefits and improved basic services.[7]

However, all three studies also point out the limitations of the vote as a tool of black betterment. Button found the black officials in his counties were unable to provide private sector services like housing and employment.[8] Perry concluded that black political empowerment was effective in bringing about an equitable share of public sector resources but it had not been effective in providing private sector opportunities, weakening social barriers between blacks and whites, and scaling down unemployment.[9] The Coombs study notes that employment gains were short term due to their dependence on public sector funds and foundation monies.[10]

Black elected officials are usually operating in areas with low tax bases and increased demands for services; there is no doubt that many expectations are not met. Even under the best of circumstances, however, there are numerous constraints on the ability of elected officials to provide policies even when there exists an ardent desire to do so.[11] With respect to the merits of black political participation as a socioeconomic uplifting agent, Perry offers an accurate assessment when he states that: ". . . political participation is not a panacea that can automatically overcome the crippling effects of years of disadvantage, but neither is it a useless and unproductive activity. Its real impact is somewhere near the midpoint of these two extreme positions. Used wisely, political participation can make some differences."[12]

The theory of black political empowerment overestimated the power of elected officials in general and of black elected officials in particular. Nonetheless, the limitations of black political empowerment have had a substantial impact on the manner in which blacks are now strategizing for political and economic parity. This impact has manifested itself in two major ways: (1) the expansion of the concept of black political empowerment and

(2) the development of an economic empowerment movement within the black community.

The concept of black political empowerment was originally deeply rooted in the notion of blacks representing blacks. Given the lack of sensitivity of the typical white elected officials to black interests, it was argued that blacks would have to gain power and represent their own interest in order to effect change. The theory of black political empowerment emphasized *interests* even though most of the theoreticians felt that the realization of these interests was most probable with *blacks in office*. The black political empowerment theorists who were largely young black activists, felt that *the realization of black interests* and *having blacks in office* were inextricably tied—due to the segregated nature of American life and the lack of an incentive, only blacks had enough at stake to aggressively represent blacks. However, the Voting Rights Act provided whites with an incentive to advocate black interests.

The passage of the Voting Rights Act of 1965 invested southern blacks with the ballot; white politicians could no longer ignore black interests without the fear of suffering repercussions. Even the likes of George C. Wallace disavowed their past views and openly kissed black babies while pursuing black votes. Thus, there is a growing realization in the black community that blacks do not necessarily have to hold political office in order to exert political power. This expanded view of black political empowerment emphasizes substantive policy over symbolic representation—the objective is to affect public policy regardless of what color the decision makers are.

With the death of Booker T. Washington in 1915, the exclusive thrust toward economic development as the means of improving black life came to an end. The NAACP aggressively pursued political and social equality. With the passage of the Civil Rights Act of 1964 and the Voting Rights Act of 1965, blacks gained access to places of public accommodation and access to the ballot. Thus, political and social equality had arrived in the legal sense of the word, i.e., the U.S. government no longer sanctioned discrimination. However, the lack of economic power would severely limit the fruits of this political and social victory: economic intimidation would keep many blacks from voting; a lack of economic resources would seriously hamper the campaigns of black candidates; and lack of money would keep the large majority of blacks from patronizing many places of public accommodation. These factors, coupled with the constraints on black elected officials, have led many to the conclusion that politics alone will not solve the economic problems of black Americans.

This conviction has given new impetus to the black *economic* empowerment movement. Black leaders from all points on the political/ideological spectrum are calling for black Americans to develop the economic resources of their community. The new economic empowerment theorists argue that to the extent that black Americans can start to provide jobs for themselves, the gap in economic parity will be lessened. Black capitalists, entrepreneurs, and consumers must develop a group consciousness with respect to economic development; the black dollar has to stay in the black community longer than it presently does. Although there is a role for government in the black economic empowerment facilitation process, there is a growing consensus that the ultimate answer to black economic inequality must come from within the black community.

Almost two decades after the passage of the Voting Rights Act of 1965, the political potential of the black belt South is still dormant. Although it is obvious that political participation will not solve the root causes of inequality in our society, it can make a great deal of difference in the small towns and counties of the black belt South. It is clear that political power is worth having—it is also clear that it must be won through long and difficult struggles. As Frederick Douglass once said: "Power concedes nothing without a struggle, it never has, it never will." Until more people are ready to struggle, black political empowerment in the black belt South will continue to be a dream deferred.

Appendix: Tables 1-42

Table 1. Black Voter Registration in the Southern States,
1956–60

State	Estimated Percentage of Voting-Age Blacks Registered			Estimated Number of Black Registrants		
	1956	1958	1968	1956	1958	1960
AL	11	15	13.7	53,366	70,000	66,009
AR	36	33	37.3	69,677	64,023	72,604
FL	32	31	38.9	148,703	144,810	183,197
GA	27	26	29.3	163,389	161,958	180,000
LA	31	26	30.9	161,410	131,068	159,003
MS	5	5	5.2	20,000	20,000	22,000
NC	24	32	38.1	135,000	150,000	210,450
SC	27	15	15.6	99,890	57,978	58,122
TN	29	48	58.9	90,000	185,000	185,000
TX	37	39	34.9	214,000	226,818	226,818
VA	19	21	22.8	82,603	92,172	100,000
Average:	23.5	26.5	27.5	—	—	—
Total:	—	—	—	1,238,038	1,303,827	1,463,203

Source: David Garrow, *Protest at Selma: Martin Luther King, Jr., and the Voting Rights Act of 1965* (New Haven: Yale Univ. Press, 1978), 11.

Table 2. Black Voter Registration in the Southern States, 1960–65

State	Estimated Percentage of Voting-Age Blacks Registered		Estimated Number of Black Registrants		
	1962	*1964*	*1962*	*1964*	*1965*
AL	13.4	23.0	68,317	111,000	92,737
AR	34.0	49.3	68,970	95,000	77,714
FL	36.8	63.8	182,456	300,000	240,616
GA	26.7	44.0	175,573	270,000	167,663
LA	27.7	32.0	151,663	164,700	164,601
MS	5.3	6.7	23,920	28,500	28,500
NC	35.8	46.8	215,938	258,000	258,000
SC	22.9	38.7	90,901	144,000	138,544
TN	49.8	69.4	150,869	218,000	218,000
VA	24.0	45.7	110,113	200,000	143,904
Average:	29.4	43.1	—	—	—
Total:	—	—	1,480,720	2,164,200	1,907,279

Source: David Garrow, *Protest at Selma: Martin Luther King, Jr., and the Voting Rights Act of 1965* (New Haven: Yale Univ. Press, 1978), 19.

Table 3. Black Voter Registration in the Southern States,
1966–68

State	Estimated Percentage of Voting-Age Blacks Registered			Estimated Number of Black Registrants		
	1966	1967	1968	1966	1967	1968
AL	51.2	53.1	56.7	246,396	255,000	273,000
AR	59.7	62.8	67.5	115,000	121,000	130,000
FL	60.9	64.6	62.1	286,446	304,000	292,000
GA	47.2	54.5	56.1	289,545	334,000	344,000
LA	47.1	53.2	59.3	242,130	273,000	305,000
MS	32.9	45.1	59.4	139,000	199,000	251,000
NC	51.0	50.3	55.3	281,134	277,000	305,000
SC	51.4	50.8	50.8	190,609	189,000	189,000
TN	71.7	71.7	72.8	225,000	225,000	228,000
TX	61.6	61.6	83.1	400,000	400,000	540,000
VA	46.9	55.6	58.4	205,000	243,000	255,000
Average:	52.9	56.7	62.0	—	—	—
Total:	—	—	—	2,620,260	2,820,000	3,112,000

Source: David Garrow, *Protest at Selma: Martin Luther King, Jr., and the Voting Rights Act of 1965* (New Haven: Yale Univ. Press, 1978), 189.

Table 4. White and Black Registration in the South, 1964 and 1969

State	1964		1969	
	% White	*% Black*	*% White*	*% Black*
AL	69.2	19.3	94.6	61.3
AR	65.0	40.4	81.6	77.9
FL	74.8	51.2	94.2	67.0
GA	62.6	27.4	88.5	60.4
LA	80.5	31.6	87.1	60.8
MS	69.9	6.7	89.8	66.5
NC	96.8	46.8	78.4	53.7
SC	75.7	37.3	71.5	54.6
TN	72.9	69.5	92.0	92.1
TX	——	——	61.8	73.1
VA	61.1	38.3	78.7	59.8
Average:	72.9	36.85	83.5	66.1

Source: U.S. Department of Commerce, *Statistical Abstract of the United States, 1970* (Washington, D.C., 1970), 369.

Table 5. Black Elected Officials in
Southern States Covered by the Voting
Rights Act, July 1980

State	Number of Black Elected Officials
MS	387
LA	363
GA	249
NC	247
SC	238
AL	238
TX	196
VA	124
Total	2,042

Source: The U.S. Commission on Civil Rights, *The Voting Rights Act: Unfulfilled Goals* (Washington, D.C.: U.S. Government Printing Office, 1981), 27.

Table 6. Black Percentage of Population and of
Elected Officials, 1980

State	Number of Black Elected Officials	Black % of Total Officials	Black % of Population
AL	238	5.7	25.6
GA	249	3.7	26.8
LA	363	7.8	29.4
MS	387	7.3	35.2
NC	247	4.7	22.4
SC	238	7.4	30.4
TX	196	0.8	15.3
VA	124	4.1	18.9

Source: The U.S. Commission on Civil Rights, *The Voting Rights Act: Unfulfilled Goals* (Washington, D.C.: U.S. Government Printing Office, 1981), 31.

Table 7. Black Elected Officials as a Percentage of Total Officials in Southern States Covered by the Voting Rights Act, July 1980: Specific Categories

State	% Black Population	% House Members	% Senate Members	% Municipal Boards	% County Boards
AL	25.6	12.4	5.7	5.3	6.6
GA	26.8	11.7	3.6	5.2	3.4
LA	29.4	9.5	5.1	9.4	13.2
MS	35.2	12.3	3.3	10.4	6.6
NC	22.4	3.3	2.0	6.0	3.7
SC	30.4	11.3	0	6.7	11.7
TX	12.0	8.7	0	1.4	0.5
VA	18.9	4.0	2.5	5.2	6.8

Source: The U.S. Commission on Civil Rights, *The Voting Rights Act: Unfulfilled Goals* (Washington, D.C.: U.S. Government Printing Office, 1981), 32.

Table 8. Black Elected Officials in Black Majority Counties in the South (1980)

State	Number of Predominantly Black Counties	Number (and Percent) of Counties Without Black Officials	Number (and Percent) Without Blacks on Governing Boards	Number (and Percent) Without Black School Board Members	Number (and Percent) Without Black Law Enforcement Officials
AL	10	2 (20%)	5 (50%)	4 (40%)	3 (30%)
AR	1	0 (0%)	1 (100%)	0 (0%)	1 (100%)
FL	1	0 (0%)	1 (100%)	1 (100%)	1 (100%)
GA	20	7 (35%)	13 (65%)	12 (60%)	18 (90%)
LA	6	1 (17%)	2 (33%)	1 (17%)	2 (33%)
MS	22	3 (14%)	8 (36%)	1 (5%)	6 (27%)
NC	7	2 (29%)	5 (71%)	2 (29%)	7 (100%)
SC	12	2 (17%)	2 (17%)	9 (75%)	7 (58%)
TN	2	1 (50%)	1 (50%)	2 (100%)	2 (100%)
TX*					
VA	6	0 (0%)	0 (0%)	6 (100%)	4 (67%)
Total	87	18 (21%)	38 (44%)	38 (44%)	51 (59%)

*Texas does not have any predominantly black counties.

Sources: *Population Trends in Majority Black Counties in Eleven Southern States, 1900–1980* (Atlanta: The Voter Education Project, 1981); U.S. Commission on Civil Rights, *The Voting Rights Act: Unfulfilled Goals* (Washington, D.C.: U.S. Government Printing Office, 1981), Appendix D, Table D-1, 272–79; *The National Roster of Black Elected Officials, Vol. 10, 1980* (Washington, D.C.: Joint Center for Political Studies, 1981).

Table 9. Average Number of Black Elected Officials, 1972–82

County	Black Elected Officials	County	Black Elected Officials
1) Hancock	14.0	13) Baker	1.0
2) Peach	6.0	14) Burke	1.0
3) Macon	4.0	15) Terrell	1.0
4) Washington	4.0	16) Twiggs	0
5) Calhoun	2.0	17) Stewart	0
6) Greene	2.0	18) McIntosh	0
7) Talbot	2.0	19) Clay	0
8) Jefferson	1.0	20) Crawford	0
9) Marion	1.0	21) Taliaferro	0
10) Quitman	1.0	22) Warren	0
11) Dooly	1.0	23) Webster	0
12) Randolph	1.0		

Source: *The National Roster of Black Elected Officials* (Washington, D.C.: The Joint Center for Political Studies, 1972–82).

Table 10. Median Income of Blacks in Black Belt Georgia

County	Median Income	County	Median Income
1) Peach	$5,477	13) Taliaferro	$3,289
2) Marion	$4,420	14) Terrell	$3,282
3) McIntosh	$4,220	15) Baker	$3,250
4) Talbot	$3,899	16) Stewart	$3,201
5) Greene	$3,878	17) Webster	$3,000
6) Twiggs	$3,785	18) Quitman	$2,926
7) Jefferson	$3,709	19) Calhoun	$2,833
8) Hancock	$3,640	20) Burke	$2,800
9) Macon	$3,606	21) Dooly	$2,753
10) Warren	$3,535	22) Randolph	$2,529
11) Crawford	$3,401	23) Clay	$2,304
12) Washington	$3,361		

Source: *Census of Population* (1970), Income and Poverty Status in 1969 of the Negro Population, 1970 (GA), 565–76.

Table 11. Black High School Graduates*

County	Percentage High School Graduates*	County	Percentage High School Graduates*
1) Webster	3.9	13) Talbot	18.0
2) Twiggs	10.5	14) Crawford	19.5
3) Randolph	11.8	15) Terrell	21.1
4) Marion	13.1	16) Dooly	21.2
5) Taliaferro	13.1	17) Stewart	21.4
6) Washington	13.8	18) Baker	21.8
7) Burke	14.8	19) Clay	22.7
8) Quitman	16.5	20) Greene	24.5
9) Jefferson	17.0	21) Macon	27.3
10) Hancock	17.0	22) McIntosh	31.8
11) Calhoun	17.4	23) Peach	59.3
12) Warren	17.5		

* Of black population over 25 in 1970.

Source: *Census of Population* (1970), Educational and Family Characteristic for Counties, 1970, Table 125, 525–37.

Table 12. Black Families Living in Poverty

County	% Black Families in Poverty	County	% Black Families in Poverty
1) Peach	37.6	13) Warren	59.8
2) Greene	48.7	14) Crawford	63.4
3) McIntosh	49.9	15) Baker	64.4
4) Talbot	50.7	16) Stewart	64.5
5) Marion	51.4	17) Calhoun	66.0
6) Jefferson	53.2	18) Burke	66.8
7) Twiggs	53.3	19) Randolph	67.1
8) Hancock	54.0	20) Webster	68.1
9) Washington	55.5	21) Dooly	69.8
10) Macon	57.1	22) Quitman	70.8
11) Terrell	58.3	23) Clay	76.5
12) Taliaferro	58.4		

Source: *Census of Population* (1970), Income and Poverty Status in 1969 of the Negro Population, 1970 (GA), 565–76.

Table 13. Economically Independent Blacks*

County	Economically Independent Blacks as % of Labor Force	County	Economically Independent Blacks as % of Labor Force
1) Randolph	22.3	13) Washington	6.6
2) Peach	18.1	14) Terrell	6.1
3) Baker	15.7	15) Clay	5.8
4) Marion	14.0	16) Quitman	4.8
5) Burke	11.2	17) Taliaferro	4.8
6) Macon	11.2	18) Crawford	4.6
7) Dooly	10.8	19) Jefferson	4.5
8) Greene	10.0	20) Stewart	3.9
9) Webster	8.9	21) Calhoun	3.1
10) Hancock	7.6	22) Warren	2.9
11) McIntosh	7.3	23) Talbot	2.0
12) Twiggs	6.9		

*Black farmers and blacks who are self-employed, 16 years and older.

Source: *Census of Population* (1970), Employment Characteristics of the Negro Population, 1970 (GA), Table 126, 538–50.

Table 14. Blacks Employed in Agriculture

County	Percentage Blacks in Work Force*	County	Percentage Blacks in Work Force*
1) Randolph	28.4	13) Terrell	12.4
2) Calhoun	26.2	14) Washington	12.2
3) Clay	25.4	15) Stewart	10.4
4) Dooly	23.1	16) Peach	9.7
5) Baker	22.6	17) Jefferson	8.1
6) Quitman	22.4	18) Warren	6.2
7) Macon	22.0	19) Taliaferro	4.6
8) Webster	20.7	20) Talbot	4.1
9) Greene	17.9	21) Twiggs	3.7
10) Crawford	13.3	22) Hancock	3.3
11) Marion	13.1	23) McIntosh	1.6
12) Burke	12.8		

* Sixteen years and older.

Source: *Census of Population* (1970), Employment Characteristics of the Negro Population, 1970, Table 26, 538–50.

Table 15. Socioeconomic Variables

Median Income	0.2991[a] 0.165[b]	not significant
Median School Years	0.4029 0.056	slightly significant
Percent High School Graduates	0.2616 0.227	not significant

Table 16. Fear Variables

Economically Independent Blacks (%)	0.151[a] 0.48[b]	not significant
Blacks Employed in Agriculture (%)	−0.197 0.36	not significant
Blacks in Poverty (%)	−0.376 0.07	not significant

Table 17. Organizational Variables

Economically Independent Blacks	0.151[a] 0.48[b]	not significant
Size of the County	0.153[a] 0.48[b]	not significant

[a] Pearson's Product-Moment Correlation Coefficient
[b] p is less than .05

Table 18. Black Belt Georgia Counties by Area

County	Square Miles	County	Square Miles
1) Burke	822	13) Marion	365
2) Washington	674	14) Baker	365
3) Jefferson	532	15) Terrell	329
4) Hancock	478	16) Crawford	313
5) Stewart	463	17) Calhoun	289
6) Randolph	436	18) Warren	284
7) McIntosh	431	19) Clay	224
8) Greene	403	20) Webster	195
9) Macon	399	21) Taliaferro	190
10) Dooly	394	22) Quitman	170
11) Talbot	394	23) Peach	151
12) Twiggs	365		

Source: The Cooperative Extension Service, *The 1981 Georgia County Guide* (Tifton: College of Agriculture, Univ. of Georgia, 1981), 77–78.

Table 19. Georgia Counties with Black Majority Populations, 1976

County	Black Voting-Age Population	County	Black Voting-Age Population
1) Hancock	70.3	13) Randolph	52.8
2) Talbot	65.3	14) Baker	50.9
3) Stewart	60.5	15) Calhoun	50.8
4) Taliaferro	59.4	16) Jefferson	50.3
5) Clay	57.3	17) Washington	50.1
6) Macon	56.8	18) Marion	49.8
7) Peach	55.9	19) Crawford	49.5
8) Burke	55.1	20) Terrell	49.5
9) Quitman	54.9	21) Greene	48.2
10) Warren	54.5	22) McIntosh	48.2
11) Webster	53.2	23) Dooly	45.7
12) Twiggs	53.0		

Source: The Voter Education Project, 1976.

Table 20. Outside Assistance, 1965–82

County	Outside Assistance	County	Outside Assistance
1) Baker	SNCC, VEP	13) Peach	VEP
2) Burke	VEP	14) Quitman	VEP
3) Calhoun	SNCC, VEP	15) Randolph	SNCC, VEP
4) Clay	SNCC, VEP	16) Stewart	VEP
5) Crawford	VEP	17) Talbot	VEP
6) Dooly	VEP	18) Taliaferro	VEP
7) Greene	VEP	19) Terrell	VEP, Federal Examiners on 3/23/67
8) Hancock	SCLC, VEP, NUL, GCHR, and the Justice Dept.	20) Twiggs	VEP
9) Jefferson	VEP	21) Warren	VEP
10) McIntosh	VEP	22) Washington	VEP
11) Macon	VEP	23) Webster	VEP
12) Marion	VEP		

Source: The Voter Education Project Grant File; The U.S. Commission on Civil Rights, *The Voting Rights Act: Unfulfilled Goals* (Washington, D.C.: US Government Printing Office, 1981); and Larry Dobbs (Director of Project 23), Interview, Nov. 1980, Atlanta, Ga.

Table 21. Elected Officials in Hancock County, by Race, 1964–74

Offices	Years					
	1964	1966	1968	1970	1972	1974
County Commission	W	B	B	B	B	B
	W	W	B	B	B	B
	W	W	W	B	B	B
Probate Judge	W	W	B	B	B	B
Tax Commissioner	W	W	W	W	W	B
Clerk of Court	W	W	B	B	B	B
School Board	W	B	B	B	B	B
	W	W	B	B	B	B
	W	W	W	B	B	B
	W	W	W	W	B	B
	W	W	W	W	W	B
Superintendent	W	W	W	W	W	W
Justice of the Peace	W	W	W	B	B	B
Coroner	W	W	W	B	B	B
Sheriff	W	W	W	W	W	W
Hospital	W	W	W	B	B	B
	W	W	W	W	B	B
	W	W	W	W	B	B

Source: Edith Ingram, Probate Judge, Hancock County, Ga, 10 Dec. 1980.

Table 22. Hancock County's Black Voting-Age Population, 1960–80

Year	Black Population	% of Black Population over 21
1960	75.0%	67.0%
1970	73.8%	66.9%
1980	78.2%	73.3%

Source: *U.S. Census of Population* (1960), Volume I, Part 12, Georgia, "Characteristics of Population, For Counties: 1960," Table 28; *U.S. Census of Population* (1970), Volume I, Part 12, Georgia. "Characteristics of Population, For Counties: 1970," Table 35; Raymond Brown, *A Statistical Comparison: Registration Rates for Georgia by Race 1966–1980* (Atlanta: The Southern Regional Council, 1982), 3.

Table 23. Hancock County's Black Elected Officials: Services Provided, 1964–68

Service	Number of Beneficiaries
Securing FHA Loans	25
Placing eligible blacks on welfare	100
Job hunting	50
Credit searches	50
Political participation insurance	8
Wood	30
Food	75
Temporary housing	25
Bail money	30

Source: Personal interviews with Probate Judge Edith Ingram, 10 Dec. 1980, and Clerk of Court Leroy S. Wiley, 12 Dec. 1980.

Table 24. Hancock Election Returns for Probate Judge and County Commissioner, 1968

Candidates, Probate Judge:	Primary	General Election
Edith Ingram	1,870	1,934
Helen Miller	1,603	1,532
Candidates, County Commissioner:		General Election
John McCown		1,919
J. P. Stanton, Jr.		1,514

Source: 1968 Election Returns, Office of the Probate Judge, Hancock County, Ga.

Table 25. Hancock County's Black Elected Officials: Services Provided, 1966–80

Services	Beneficiaries
Payment of Bills (Writing checks, paying bills, balancing check books, etc.)	500
Assistance With Personal Matters (Writing and answering letters, buying groceries, arbitrating quarrels)	600
Assistance With Financial Procurement (Welfare recertification, Social Security recertification)	300
Assistance With Health Care Delivery (Making doctors' appointments, taking patients to doctors' visits)	300
Information (Providing advice and information concerning nongovernmental matters)	500

Source: Probate Judge Edith Ingram; Clerk of Court Leroy S. Wiley; and Tax Commissioner Sam Warren.

Table 26. Partial Listing of Financial Contributions to the
Eastern Central Committee for Opportunity, 1970–74

Source	Amount
Office of Economic Opportunity	$ 581,000
Department of Commerce	$ 68,550
The Ford Foundation	$ 850,000
Other Sources	$ 8,648,250
Total	$10,147,800

Source: "ECCO: An Experimental Empire," *Macon Telegraph,* 11 June 1974, p. 1.

Table 27. The Eastern Central Committee for Opportunity:
Services Provided, 1970–76

Service	Beneficiaries
Employment	50 Hancock Countians (45 blacks, 5 whites)
Keeping the hospital open (with a $175,000 donation)	Hancock community in general
Small business loans	5 black entrepreneurs
Housing Project (300 low rent units)	300 low-income blacks plus family members

Source: "Hancock Hospital Near Financial Collapse," *Macon Telegraph,* 6 Dec. 1974, p. 1.

Table 28. Hancock's Registered Voters by Race, 1966, 1968, 1974 and 1980

Year	Total Voting-Age Population (VAP)	% Black of VAP	% White of VAP	Number of Registered Voters	% Black Registered Voters	% White Registered Voters	Difference (%)
1966	4,965	66.4	33.6	3,367	50.7	49.3	1.4
1968	5,303	67.5	32.5	4,633	60.0	40.0	20.0
1974	5,235	66.9	33.1	4,918	68.2	31.8	36.4
1980	6,101	73.3	26.7	6,572	72.7	27.3	45.4

Source: Raymond Brown, *A Statistical Comparison: Registration Rates For Georgia by Race, 1966–1980* (Atlanta: The Southern Regional Council, 1982), p. 3; Voter Education Project, *Voter Registration in the South* (Atlanta: The Voter Education Project, 1968); data from a 1974 Voter Education Project pamphlet.

Table 29. Hancock's Registration Rates by Race, 1966, 1968, 1974, and 1980

Year	Voting-Age Population	Number Black	Number White	Registered Blacks	Registered Whites	Black Registration Rate (%)	White Registration Rate (%)	Difference (%)
1966	4,965	3,297	1,668	1,707	1,660	51.8	99.5	47.4
1968	5,303	3,576	1,727	2,781	1,852	77.8	100+	22.2
1974	5,235	3,506	1,729	3,316	1,602	95.8	92.7	3.1
1980	6,101	4,472	1,629	4,778*	1,794*	100+*	100+*	0

*This overage is due to a lack of purging of the invalid names from the voter-registration lists. Nonetheless, these figures are the most reliable available.

Source: *Raymond Brown, A Statistical Comparison: Registration Rates For Georgia By Race 1966–1980* (Atlanta: The Southern Regional Council, 1982), p. 3; *Voter Registration in the South*. Atlanta: The Voter Education Project, 1968; 1974 Data from a Voter Education Project pamphlet.

Table 30. Black Population of Fort Valley and Peach County,
1930–80

Census	Fort Valley			Peach County		
	Total	Black	% Black	Total	Black	% Black
1930	4,560	2,408	53	10,268	6,565	64
1940	4,953	2,665	54	10,378	6,366	61
1950	6,820	4,217	62	11,705	7,173	61
1960	8,310	5,083	61	13,846	8,130	59
1970	9,251	5,913	64	15,990	9,080	57
1980	9,000	5,198	66	19,151	9,767	51

Source: *Fifteenth Census of The United States: 1930 Population,* P-2, 433; *Sixteenth Census of The United States: 1940 Population,* Georgia 11, P-2, 11–78, 48; *Census of Population:* 1950, Georgia P-2, 11–22; *Census of Population:* 1960, Georgia 1, P-12, 12–24; *Census of Population:* 1970, Georgia, 1, P-12, 12–113; "Peach County's Population is Up as Fort Valley's Black Population Increases," 23 April 1981, p. 9.

Table 31. Fort Valley Municipal Democratic Primary Election
Returns, 18 March 1964

Office	Candidates	Race	Total Votes
City Council:	W. S. M. Banks	B	680
	J. W. Anthoine	W	523
	Clinton Hutto	W	1,034
	N. W. Jordan, Jr.	W	1,211
	J. C. Nutt, Jr.	W	630
	David Parker	W	692
	G. C. "Dud" Poole	W	695
	A. J. "Fat" Preston	W	414
Utilities Commission:	A. J. Edwards	B	645
	Jack R. Hunicutt	W	1,279
	Olen B. Reid, Jr.	W	1,167
	"Bill" Wilson	W	983

Source: *Leader Tribune,* 26 March, 1964.

Table 32. Fort Valley Municipal Election Returns, 1 April 1970

Office	Candidate	Race	Total Votes
City Council:	Claybon Edwards	B	1,172*
	J. W. Poole	W	1,149
City Council:	Willie D. Sneed	B	783
	L. B. Knight	W	1,014**
	Carolyn C. Burnett	W	523
Utilities Commission:	Hattie Banks	B	911**
	Olen B. Reid, Jr.	W	670
	Sol Vining	W	723

*Winner
**Run-off Required
Source: Certificate of Results, 1 April 1970, General Election for Fort Valley, Office of the Chief Registrar, City Hall, Fort Valley, Ga.

Table 33. Fort Valley Municipal Election Returns, 1972

Office	Candidate	Race	Votes
City Council:	Rudolph Carson	B	1,625
	J. W. Poole	W	546
	Dud Poole	W	469
	William Terrell	W	369
Utilities Commission:	Roosevelt Arnold	B	1,535
	Ed Matthews	W	1,379

Source: Certificate of Result, 1972 Municipal Election, Office of the Registrar, City Hall, Fort Valley, Ga.

Table 34. Returns for City Council and Utilities Commission, Municipal Run-Off, 1972

Office	Candidate	Race	Machine Total	Absentee Ballots	Total
Councilman	Clinton Dixon	B	1,509	48	1,557
	Ed Dent	W	1,411	275	1,986*
Councilman	William Arnold	B	1,544	39	1,583
	N. W. Jordon	W	1,368	275	1,643*
Utilities Commission:	Claude Lawson	B	1,500	42	1,542
	J. Hunnicutt	W	1,378	278	1,656*

*Winners
Source: Certificate of Results, 1972 Municipal Run-offs, Office of the Registrar, City Hall, Fort Valley, Ga.

Table 35. Returns for County Commission, Peach County, Georgia, 1980, Posts 1–5

	Race	Totals
Post #1 *		
Peavy	W	963
Unopposed	——	——
Post #2 *		
Banks	B	282
Carter	B	397
Hilson	B	114
Post #3 *		
Blount	B	245
Rumph	B	314
Post #4 *		
Brown	W	1,269
Unopposed	——	——
Post #5 *		
Doles	W	2,048
Jones	W	1,983

* District Elections
** At-Large Elections
Source: Official Report, the 1982 Election, August 5, 1976, Office of The Registrar, City Hall, Fort Valley, Ga.

Table 36. Fort Valley City Council Members by Race, 1970–82

1970	1972	1974	1976	1978	1980	1982
B	B	B	B	B	B	B
W	B	B	B	B	B	B
W	B	B	B	B	B	W
W	W	W	W	W	W	W
W	W	W	W	W	W	W
W	W	W	W	W	W	W

Table 37. Fort Valley Utilities Commissioners by Race, 1970–82

1970	1972	1974	1976	1978	1980	1982
W	B	B	B	B	B	B
W	W	B	B	B	B	B
W	W	W	W	W	W	W
W	W	W	W	W	W	W

Source: Official Returns for the City of Fort Valley, 1970–82, Office of the Chief Registrar, City Hall, Fort Valley, Ga.

Table 38. Clay County's Registration Rates by Race

Years	% Black of Registered Voters	Black Registration Rate (%)	White Registration Rate (%)	Difference (%)
1966	20	21	95	74
1968	33	42	100+	58+
1974	37	66	100+	34+
1980	53	80	98	18

Source: Raymond Brown, *A Statistical Comparison: Registration Rates for Georgia by Race* (Atlanta: The Southern Regional Council, 1982); The Voter Education Project, *Voter Registration in the South* (Atlanta: The Voter Education Project, 1968 and 1974).

Table 39. Voter Registration in Peach County by Race

Years	Totals	Black	% Black	White	% White
1944	3,300	1,200	33	2,100	67
1964	4,696	1,398	30	2,298	70
1966	3,941	1,025	26	2,916	74
1968	5,093	1,887	37	3,206	63
1974	5,694	2,180	38	3,514	62
1976	9,218	4,378	47.5	4,840	52.5
1980	8,322	3,578	43	4,744	57

Source: Interview with Bernard Young, Former Ordinary of Peach County by Professor Donnie Bellamy, September 11, 1978; *Leader Tribune*, 27 Feb. 1964; *H. W. Berry et al. vs James M. Cooper et al.*, Civil Action Number 763,862. United States Court of Appeals, Fifth Circuit, July 31, 1978, 5764; Raymond Brown. *A Statistical Comparison: Registration Rates for Georgia, 1966–1980* (Atlanta: The Southern Regional Council, 1982); The Voter Education Project, *Voter Registration in The South* (Atlanta: The Voter Education Project, 1968).

Table 40. Voter Registration in Fort Valley by Race

Years	Totals	Black	% Black	White	% White
1964	2,648	950	36	1,698	64
1972*	3,102	1,606	52	1,496	48
1974	4,187	2,128	51	2,059	49
1976	3,452	1,601	46	1,851	54
1978	2,402	1,125	47	1,277	53
1980	3,230	1,673	52	1,552	48

*Actual voters in the April 1972 election. In the 1980 registration figures, five were listed as "Other."

Source: City of Fort Valley's Registration Lists, City Hall, Fort Valley.

Table 41. Model for Successful Political Empowerment (A–E)

(A) A *leadership* group must *organize* itself with a strategy to achieve political empowerment. The achievement of the following goals is crucial:

  1) Fear must be eradicated as a cause of non-participation
  2) Economic intimidation must be removed as a cause of non-participation
  3) The organization must provide some important basic services

(B) *Popular Support* from the black community is the result of successful goal attainment. The popular support creates an environment conducive to successful political education

(C) *Political Education*

  1) The leaders must attack apathy by creating a sense of "specific efficacy." ("This county is predominantly black, you can exert power and influence here if you participate in the political process")
  2) The leaders must break down anything divisive in the black community. Black class antagonism must be replaced with a sense of "group consciousness" which lays the foundation for racial bloc-voting
  3) Leaders must explain how county government works; this allows the organizer to show how one's life can be made better by better public policy. This strategy makes material incentives apparent

(D) *Political Mobilization* is the logical outcome of an intense political education program. Political mobilization includes:

  1) Grooming candidates for office
  2) Working for full registration
  3) Working for 100% turnout
  4) Encouraging racial bloc-voting among blacks

(E) *Black Political Empowerment*
  Successful political mobilization leads to black elected officials

Table 42. Black Leaders in Hancock, Peach, and Clay Counties after 1960

Names	Occupations
Hancock County:	
1) Rev. Robert E. Edwards	Minister
2) John McCown	Full-time activist
3) Carl Farris	Sociologist, organizer
4) Kathryn Ingram	Housewife
5) Edith Ingram	Public schoolteacher
6) Robert Ingram, Sr.	Hospital employee
7) Robert Ingram, Jr.	Factory worker
8) E. R. Warren	Public schoolteacher
9) James McMullen	Public schoolteacher
10) Melvin Wopples	Public schoolteacher
11) Roosevelt Warren	Attorney
12) Johnny Warren	Public schoolteacher
Peach County:	
1) Houston Stallworth	Professor
2) W. S. M. Banks	Professor
3) Isaac Crumbly	Professor
4) Rev. Webb	Minister
5) Clinton Dixon	Professor
6) Claybon Edwards	Mortician
7) Rudolph Carson	Insurance agent
8) H. W. Berry	Professor
9) Evelyn McCrary	Public schoolteacher
10) Donnie Bellamy	Professor
11) Thomas Dortch	College student

Table 42. (*Continued*)

Names	Occupations
12) H. E. Bryant	Principal
13) Marvin Crafter	College student
14) Robert Church	County agricultural agent (retired)
Clay County:	
1) Frank Davenport	Plumber
2) Mamie Kendrick	Nurse
3) Lola Fair	Housewife
4) Walter Patmon	Retired
5) James Clark	Auto mechanic
6) Gene Mallard	Logger
7) Richard Bankston	Farmer
8) Rev. J. S. Stanford	Minister
9) James Smith	Plumber

Notes

Preface

1. For a brief essay detailing the widespread support for the notion of the ballot as the prime tool of black upward mobility, see David J. Garrow, *Protest at Selma: Martin Luther King, Jr., and the Voting Rights Act of 1965* (New Haven: Yale Univ. Press, 1978), 238–40.

Chapter One

1. Frances Fox Piven and Richard Cloward, *Poor People's Movements* (New York: Vintage, 1979), 184.

2. Lerone Bennett, *Before the Mayflower: A History of Black America* (Chicago: Johnson Publishing Company, 1982), 192.

3. Mervyn M. Dymnally, *The Black Politician: His Struggle for Power* (Belmont, Mass.: Duxbury Press, 1971), 15.

4. Ibid.

5. Norman W. Hodges, *Black History* (New York: Simon and Schuster, 1974), 43.

6. Ibid.

7. Ibid, 42–43.

8. Ibid, 43.

9. Ibid.

10. Bennett, *Mayflower*, 441–42.

11. Hodges, *Black History*, 58.

12. Richard Bardolph, *The Civil Rights Record: Black Americans and the Law, 1849–1870* (New York: Thomas J. Crowell, 1970), 3.

13. The Declaration of Independence as cited in ibid.

14. Bardolph, *Record*, 3.

15. John Locke, *Of Civil Government* (New York: Dutton, 1943), 3.

16. Robert Dahl, *Democracy in the United States: Promise and Performance* (Chicago: Rand McNally, 1976), 19.

17. The United States Constitution in Peter Woll, ed., *American Government: Readings and Cases* (Boston: Little, Brown, 1978), 570–90.

18. Bardolph, *Record,* 12.

19. Ibid.

20. Ibid, 15.

21. Ibid, 13.

22. Ibid, 18.

23. Hodges, *Black History,* 58.

24. Hugh Hawkins, ed., *The Abolitionists: Means, Ends, and Motivations* (Lexington, Mass.: Heath, 1968), vii.

25. Bardolph, *Record,* 4.

26. Hawkins, *Abolitionists,* 5.

27. Ibid, 10–14.

28. Ibid, 52–56.

29. Henrietta Buckmaster, *Let My People Go: The Story of the Underground Railroad and the Growth of the Abolitionist Movement* (Boston: Beacon Press, 1941), 106–26.

30. Ibid, 83–98.

31. Ibid, 1–3.

32. Ibid, 132.

33. Steve Lawson, *Black Ballots: Voting Rights in the South, 1944–1969* (New York: Columbia Univ. Press, 1976), 1.

34. Ibid, 2.

35. Bardolph, *Record,* 45–58.

36. E. L. Thornborough, ed., *Black Reconstructionists* (Englewood Cliffs, N.J.: Prentice-Hall, 1972), 2.

37. Ibid, 1.

38. For an in-depth analysis of black reconstruction in South Carolina, see Thomas Holt, *Black Over White: Negro Political Leadership in South Carolina During Reconstruction* (Urbana: Univ. of Illinois Press, 1977).

39. For an excellent essay on the Dunning School and revisionist debate on Reconstruction, see Harold Rabinowitz, ed., Introduction to *Southern Black Leaders of the Reconstruction Era* (Urbana: Univ. of Illinois Press, 1977), xi–xxiv.

40. Thornborough, *Black Reconstructionists,* 2.

41. Robert C. Goldston, *The Negro Revolution* (New York: Macmillan, 1969), 119.

42. Dymally, *Black Politician,* 16.

43. Ibid.

44. Hodges, *Black History,* 128.

45. Lawson, *Black Ballots,* 5–6.

46. Ibid.

47. Ibid, 59.

48. Ibid, 61.

49. Ibid, 62.

50. Harold Dye and Harmon Zeigler, *The Irony of Democracy* (Monterey, Calif.: Cole, 1984), 380–82.

51. Hodges, *Black History,* 129.

52. Bardolph, *Record,* 62–63.

53. Ibid, 62–72.

54. Rayford Logan, *The Negro in American Life and Thought: The Nadir, 1877–1901* (New York: Dial Press, 1954), 83.

55. Logan suggests that the Washington address "consoled the consciences of the judges of the Supreme Court" who later made this doctrine legal. Thus, he suggests that Washington influenced the court in this landmark ruling.

56. Booker T. Washington, *Up from Slavery* (Garden City, N.Y.: Doubleday, 1949), 218–25.

57. Washington stressed economic development, i.e., black economic independence, for the black community. While blacks now have the basic political and social rights, that is, the right to vote and equal access to places of public accommodations, the lack of economic independence and financial well-being in general weaken efforts toward black political empowerment.

58. Lawson, *Black Ballots,* 7–8.

59. Ibid, 11.

60. Ibid, 12.

61. W. E. B. Du Bois, *The Souls of Black Folk* (Chicago: A. C. McClurg and Company, 1903), 45–54.

62. Bardolph, *Record,* 114.

63. Robert Brisbane, *Black Activism: Racial Revolution in the United States, 1954–1970* (Valley Forge, Penn.: Judson Press, 1974), 20.

64. Piven and Cloward, *Movements,* 192.

65. Lawson, *Black Ballots,* 17.

66. Ibid, 18.

67. Ibid, 19.

68. Ibid, 22–25.

69. Ibid, 28.

70. Ibid, 23–54.

71. David Garrow, *Protest at Selma,* 8.

72. Bardolph, *Record,* 270–78.

73. See *Brown vs Board of Education of Topeka,* 349 US 294 (1955) in Woll, *American Government,* 162–164.

74. For a good description and analysis of white southern resistance to *Brown vs Board,* see Francis Wilhoit, *The Politics of Massive Resistance* (New York: George Braziller, 1973).

75. Donald R. Matthews and James W. Protho, *Negroes and the New Southern Politics* (New York: Harcourt, Brace, and World, 1966), 12.

76. Stephen B. Oates, *Let the Trumpet Sound: The Life of Martin Luther King, Jr.* (New York: Harper and Row, 1982), 55–112.

77. Piven and Cloward, *Movements,* 217–218.

78. Charles V. Hamilton, *The Bench and the Ballot: Southern Federal Judges and Black Voters* (New York: Oxford Univ. Press, 1973), 44.

79. Ibid, 42–43.

80. Ibid, 43–44.

81. Brisbane, *Black Activism,* 44–53.

82. Ibid, 51.

83. Oates, *Trumpet,* 162.

84. Ibid, 51.

85. Ibid, 165–66.

86. Quoted in Piven and Cloward, *Movements,* 226–27.

87. Ibid, 227.

88. Pat Watters and Reese Cleghorn, *Climbing Jacob's Ladder: The Arrival of Negroes in Southern Politics* (New York: Harcourt, Brace, and World, 1967), 223–24.

89. Louis Lomax, "The Kennedys Move in on Dixie," *Harper's Magazine* (May 1962), 27–33.

90. Ibid, 32.

91. The Voter Education Project, *A Brief History of the Voter Education Project* (Atlanta: The Voter Education Project, 1979), 2.

92. Lomax, "Kennedys," 28.

93. Brisbane, *Black Activism,* 58.

94. Garrow, *Protest,* 19.

95. Stokely Carmichael and Charles V. Hamilton, *Black Power: The Politics of Liberation in America* (New York: Random House, 1966), 46.

96. Garrow, *Protest,* 21.

97. John Herber, "Dr. King and 770 Others Seized in Alabama Protest," *New York Times,* 2 Feb. 1965, p. 1.

98. Martin Luther King, Jr., "Civil Rights No. 1- The Right to Vote," *New York Times Magazine,* 14 March 1965, pp. 26–27 and 94–95.

99. Garrow, *Protest,* 2.

100. "Transcript of Johnson's Address on Voting Rights to Joint Session of Congress," *New York Times,* 16 March 1965, p. 30.

101. Hamilton, *Bench and Ballot,* 235.

102. Bardolph, *Record,* 420–25.

Chapter Two

1. These newly enfranchised black voters have been given the credit for Carter's almost complete sweep of the South in 1976. A majority of whites voted for Ford, but the overwhelming support of black voters enabled Carter to carry all of the states of the old confederacy except Virginia. See Michael B. Preston, *The New Black Politics* (New York: Longman, 1982), 27.

2. The U.S. Commission on Civil Rights. *The Voting Rights Act: Unfulfilled Goals* (Washington, D.C.: U.S. Government Printing Office, 1981), 27.

3. Sidney Verba and Norman Nie, *Participation in America* (New York: Harper and Row, 1972), 13.

4. Matthews and Protho, *Negroes and the New Southern Politics*, 12.

5. Watters and Cleghorn, *Jacob's Ladder,* 324.

6. Raymond Wolfinger and Steven Rosentone, *Who Votes* (New Haven: Yale Univ. Press, 1980), 102.

7. F. Glenn Abney, "Factors Related to Negro Voter Turnout in Mississippi," *Journal of Politics* (Nov. 1975), 563–68.

8. Gerald Wright, "Black Voting Turnout and Education in the 1968 Presidential Election," *Journal of Politics* (Nov. 1974), 1057–63.

9. Verba and Nie, *Participation,* 157–60.

10. Lester W. Milbrath, *Political Participation* (Washington, D.C.: Univ. Press of America, 1977), 56.

11. Carmichael and Hamilton, *Black Power,* 46.

12. Lester Salamon and Stephen Van Evera, "Fear, Apathy, and Discrimination: A Test of Three Explanations of Political Participation," *American Political Science Review* (Dec. 1973), 1298–1300.

13. Ibid, 1296–1324.

14. David Garrow, "Black Voting in South Carolina, 1970–1976," *Review of Black Political Economy* 10 (Fall 1978), 60–78.

15. James Carlson, "Black Political Participation in the South: An Examination of Contextual Effects" (Ph.D. diss., Kent State Univ., Aug. 1975), 97.

16. Paul Stekler, "Black Politics in the New South" (Ph.D. diss., Harvard Univ., Oct. 1982), 58.

17. Brian Sherman, *Half a Foot in the Door* (Atlanta: Direct Research Service, 1982), 26.

18. Richard A. Hudlin and K. Brimah, *Barriers to Effective Participation in Electoral Politics* (Atlanta: The Voter Education Project, 1982), passim.

19. Laughlin McDonald, *Voting Rights in the South* (Atlanta: ACLU Southern Regional Office, 1982), 39.

20. Stekler, "Politics," 58.

21. There are two major studies that do not support the view that election method has an impact on black proportional representation: Susan MacManus, "City Election Procedure and Minority Representation: Are They Related?" *Social Science Quarterly* (June 1978), 158–161; and Leonard Cole, "Electing Blacks to Municipal Office: Structural and Social Determinants," *Urban Affairs Quarterly* (Sept. 1974), 17–39. Since there are several methodological problems with these studies, their conclusions are questionable. For a methodological critique of these studies, see Stekler, "Politics," 92–95.

22. Lee Sloan, "Good Government and the Politics of Race," *Social Problems* (Fall 1969), 161–75.

23. Clinton Jones, "The Impact of Local Election Systems on Black Political Representation," *Urban Affairs Quarterly* (March 1976), 345.

24. Albert Karnig, "Black Representation on City Councils: The Impact of District Elections and Socioeconomic Factors," *Urban Affairs Quarterly* (Dec. 1976), 235–36.

25. Stekler, "Politics," 96.

26. Theodore Robinson and Thomas Dye, "Reformism and Black Representation on City Councils," *Social Science Quarterly* (June 1978), 138–39.

27. Delbert Taebel, "Minority Representation on City Council: The Impact of Structure on Blacks and Hispanics," *Social Science Quarterly* (June 1978), 142–61.

28. Stekler, "Politics," 134.

29. John Dittmer, *Black Georgia During the Progressive Era, 1910–1920* (Athens: Univ. of Georgia Press, 1977), 3.

30. See Table 8.

31. Salamon and Van Evera, "Fear, Apathy," 1296–1300.

32. Raymond Brown, *The State of Voting Rights in Georgia in 1982* (Atlanta: The Southern Regional Council, 1982), pp. 48–53; and *The Georgia County Government 1980 Yearbook* (Atlanta: The Association of County Commissioners, 1980).

33. Michael Lipsky, "Protest as a Political Resource," *American Political Science Review* (Dec. 1968), 1146.

34. See Charles Tilly, *From Mobilization to Revolution* (Reading, Mass.: Addison-Wesley Publishing Company, 1978); William A. Gamson, *The Strategy of Social Protest* (Homewood, Ill.: Dorsey Press, 1975); Mancur Olson, *The Logic of Collective Action* (New York: Cambridge Univ. Press, 1975); and Jo Freeman, *Social Movements of the Sixties and Seventies* (New York: Longman, 1983).

35. Piven and Cloward, *Poor People's Movements.* See the chapter on the civil rights movement.

36. Charles Tilly, *Mobilization,* 84.

37. Lester Salamon, "Protest, Politics, and Modernization in the American South: Mississippi as a Developing Society" (Ph.D. diss., Harvard Univ., Nov. 1972).

38. See Table 9.

Chapter Three

1. John Rozier, *Black Boss: Black Political Revolution in a Georgia County* (Athens: Univ. of Georgia Press, 1982), inside cover.

2. An "opportunity structure" is the interactions between outside support and societal events which may facilitate or repress successful collective action towards the realization of interests. This concept is developed by Charles Tilly. See *From Mobilization to Revolution.*

3. A low level of racial antagonism is an aspect of a positive political climate which is conducive to black political participation. See Nicholas Danigelis, "Black Political Participation in the United States: Some Recent Evidence," *American Sociological Review* (Oct. 1978), 756–71.

4. Peter Range, "Black Boss," *Esquire* (Jan. 1973), 26.

5. Abigail Thernstrom, "The Odd Evolution of the Voting Rights Act," *The Public Interest* (Spring 1979), 65.

6. See the Committee on the Judiciary, *Hearings on The Extension of The Voting Rights Act,* Statement and Testimony of James W. Loewen to the Subcommittee on Civil Rights and Constitutional Rights, 19 May 1981, pp. 255–78.

7. Ibid, p. 264.

8. Robert Ingram, Sr. (first black school board member in Hancock County), Interview, Hancock County, 14 Dec. 1980.

9. Range, "Black Boss," 26.

10. Getrena Nelson (former Hancock County schoolteacher), Interview, Hancock County, 10 Dec. 1980; Probate Judge Edith Ingram (Hancock activist), Interview, Hancock County, 10 Dec. 1980. The Tuskegee lynching records for 1882–1950 indicate that there were four lynchings in Hancock County. See "Tuskegee Lynching Records, 1882–1950," Drawer 12 (Georgia File), Tuskegee Archives, Tuskegee Univ., Tuskegee, Al.

11. Rozier argues that this reputation was unfounded since Hancock's mulatto population (2.6%) in 1860 was far below Georgia's (8%) and the nation's (13.2%).

12. E. M. Banks, *Land Tenure in Georgia* (New York: Columbia Univ. Press, 1905), 64, 69, 89, 120, 138, 140.

13. David Norton, "Hancock Resigned to Negro Leadership," *Atlanta Constitution*, 22 Sept. 1968, p. 7A.

14. Rozier, *Black Boss*, 6–8.

15. Nelson interview.

16. Rozier, *Black Boss*, 13–14.

17. Ibid, 6–7.

18. Ibid, 7–8.

19. Johnny Warren (Hancock County Democratic Club activist), Interview, Hancock County, 12 Dec. 1980.

20. Nelson interview.

21. Ibid.

22. E. R. Warren (high school principal and one of the founders of the Hancock County Democratic Club), Interview, Hancock County, 17 Dec. 1980.

23. Robert Ingram, Sr., interview.

24. Robert Brisbane, *Black Activism*, 44.

25. E. R. Warren interview.

26. Ibid.

27. Salamon and Van Evera, "Fear, Apathy, and Discrimination," 1304.

28. E. R. Warren interview.

29. Ibid.

30. Ibid.

31. Robert Ingram, Sr., interview.

32. E. R. Warren interview.

33. Robert Ingram, Sr., interview.

34. Robert Ingram, Jr. (former ECCO worker), Interview, Hancock County, 12 Dec. 1980.

35. "Old John's A Bad Nigger," *People's Crusader,* 24 May 1974, p. 1.

36. Ibid.

37. Kathryn Ingram (former ECCO worker), Interview, Hancock County, 14 Dec. 1980.

38. Raymond Brown, *A Statistical Comparison: Registration Rates for Georgia by Race 1966–1980* (Atlanta: The Voter Education Project, 1982), 3.

39. Getrena Nelson interview.

40. "U.S. Officials Hail Election of Negroes," *Atlanta Constitution,* 12 Nov. 1966, p. 3.

41. Ann McCown (widow of John McCown), Interview, Hancock County, 15 Dec. 1980.

42. Robert Ingram, Sr., interview.

43. Ibid.

44. Ibid.

45. Judge Ingram interview.

46. Robert Ingram, Sr., interview.

47. Ibid.

48. Ibid.

49. Robert Ingram, Jr., interview.

50. Ibid.

51. Ibid.

52. Judge Ingram interview.

53. Kathryn Ingram interview.

54. Ibid.

55. Ibid.

56. Judge Ingram interview.

57. Ibid.

58. Ibid.

59. Ann McCown interview.

60. Kathryn Ingram interview.

61. Ibid.

62. Ibid.

63. Ibid.

64. Judge Ingram interview.

65. "Negroes Take Over in Hancock Voting," *Atlanta Constitution,* 8 Nov. 1968, p. 1.

66. Judge Ingram interview.

67. Ibid.

68. Norton, "Hancock Resigned to Negro Leadership."

69. Judge Ingram interview.

70. Ibid.

71. Judge Ingram interview.

72. Ibid. The superintendent of schools denied these charges. He said that Hancock Central had the same teacher-student ratio as that of Sparta High. See "Hancock Schools Seek Protest Ban," *Macon Telegraph,* 15 Sept. 1969, p. 1.

73. Phil Gailey, "Strong Winds of Change Blow in Hancock," *Atlanta Constitution,* 18 Sept. 1969, p. 1.

74. Judge Ingram interview.

75. Gailey, "Strong Winds of Change Blow in Hancock."

76. Ibid.

77. Ibid.

78. Ibid.

79. Phil Gailey, "Race Troubled Sparta Facing a School Crisis," *Atlanta Constitution,* 9 Sept. 1970, p. 1A.

80. Ibid.

81. Ibid.

82. Robert Ingram, Sr., interview.

83. Jim Rankin and Jeff Nesmith, "McCown Left Council Reeling," *Atlanta Constitution*, 4 July 1974, p. 1A.

84. Ibid.

85. Phil Gailey, "Blacks, Whites Work Together," *Atlanta Constitution*, 4 Jan. 1970, p. 1A.

86. Judge Ingram interview.

87. Ibid.

88. Gailey, "Blacks, Whites, Work Together."

89. Range, "Black Boss," 11–13.

90. Ibid.

91. Judge Ingram interview.

92. Rozier, *Black Boss*, 86–88.

93. Judge Ingram interview.

94. Ibid.

95. Ibid.

96. Phil Gailey, "Hancock Gun Race is Ended," *Atlanta Constitution*, 2 Oct. 1972, p. 1A.

97. Thomas A. Johnson, "Blacks in Georgia Let Minority Share Power," *New York Times*, 8 Sept. 1971, p. 6A.

98. Judge Ingram interview.

99. Phil Gailey, "Blacks in Hancock to Build Town with $7 Million Grant," *Atlanta Constitution*, 27 Jan. 1972, p. 1A.

100. Phil Gailey, "New Town Planners Say Publicity Has Hurt," *Atlanta Constitution*, 1 Feb. 1972, p. 1A.

101. Ibid.

102. Ibid.

103. Ibid.

104. Gailey, "Hancock Gun Race is Ended."

105. Jason Berry, "Poverty Group's Tax Troubles," *Washington Star*, 9 May 1977, p. 1.

106. Jeff Nesmith, "OEO to Pay County Chiefs in Hancock?" *Atlanta Constitution*, 10 April 1974, p. 1A.

107. Ibid.

108. Jeff Nesmith, "Nightclub Getting Hancock Poverty Funds," *Atlanta Constitution*, 18 April 1974, p. 1A.

109. Jeff Nesmith, "ECCO Audit Pressed in Hancock," *Atlanta Constitution*, 22 April 1974, p. 1A.

110. Berry, "Poverty Group's Tax Troubles."

111. Sally McCash, Ann Jones, and Bill Boyd, "A House Divided," *Macon Telegraph*, 9–12 June 1974, p. 1A.

112. Jim Rankin and Jeff Nesmith, "McCown Empire Prospers Hancock Stays Poor," *Atlanta Constitution*, 30 June 1974, p. 1A.

113. Nesmith, "ECCO Audit Pressed for in Hancock."

114. Bob Fort, "OEO Hancock Audit Shows Errors: Nunn," *Atlanta Constitution,* 24 July 1974, p. 1A.

115. Ibid.

116. Ibid.

117. Ibid.

118. Bill Montgomery, "Guilty Pleas End Legacy of McCown Run Hancock," *Atlanta Constitution,* 31 Jan. 1978, p. 1A.

119. Judge Ingram interview.

120. Ibid.

121. Ibid.

122. Jim Auchmutey, "The Struggle in Hancock," *Atlanta Constitution,* 18 Sept. 1983, p. 1A.

123. The major reason given for this lack of political activity is fear of losing one's job. See U.S. Commission on Civil Rights, *Hearings,* Jackson, Miss., February 16–20, 1965 (Washington, D.C.: U.S. Government Printing Office, 1965).

124. E. R. Warren interview.

125. "Georgia Election Results."

126. Keith Schneider, "An Arch of Misery," *Boston Globe,* 18 Sept. 1983, p. 1E.

127. Piven and Cloward, *Movements,* Ch. 2.

Chapter Four

1. Brailsford R. Brazeal, *Studies of Negro Voting in Eight Georgia Counties and One of South Carolina.* Unpublished study for the Southern Regional Council (Atlanta, Ga.: 6 June 1960), 44–46.

2. Cited in *H. W. Berry et al. vs James M. Cooper et al.* Civil Action Number 76.3862, United States Court of Appeals, Fifth Circuit, July 31, 1978, 5764.

3. Brazeal, *Negro Voting,* 44–46.

4. Ibid.

5. Ibid.

6. "Negro Doctor Quit Area Rather Than Go to Jail," *New York Times,* 27 March 1958, p. 28, C-7.

7. Brazeal, *Negro Voting,* 44–46.

8. *Census of Population Income and Poverty Status in 1959 of the Negro Population,* 1960, Georgia.

9. George Luce *et al.,* To the Mayor and Council of the City of Fort Valley, Memo Date, 12 Aug. 1963, Minutes of the Mayor and City Council of the City of Fort Valley, 15 Aug. 1963, City Hall, Fort Valley, Georgia.

10. George E. Luce (signer of 1963 petition and member of the bi-racial committee), Interview, 15 Oct. 1978. Interview conducted by Professor Donnie Bellamy of the Fort Valley State College, Fort Valley, Ga.

11. Luce interview.

12. "Negro Qualifies to Run for Council Post in Fort Valley," *Leader-Tribune*, 6 Feb. 1964, p. 1.

13. W. S. M. Banks II (Peach's first black candidate), Interview, 10 April 1981, p. 1.

14. City of Fort Valley's Voter List, Office of the Registrar, City Hall, Fort Valley, Ga.

15. *Leader-Tribune*, 28 March 1974, p. 1.

16. Due to the legacy of the one-party South, small towns usually do not have any Republican opposition. Thus, Peach officials probably decided to save time and money by forgoing the primaries.

17. *Leader-Tribune*, 28 March 1974, p. 1.

18. Certificate of Results, 1 April 1968, General Election for the City of Fort Valley, Office of the Registrar, City Hall, Fort Valley, Ga.

19. Certificate of Results, 10 April 1968, Run-off Election for the City of Fort Valley, Office of the Registrar, City Hall, Fort Valley, Ga.

20. Ibid.

21. *Ulysses Marshall et al. vs David T. Sammons et al.* "Motion for Preliminary Injunction," Civil Action Number 2542, Middle District Court of Georgia, 17 April 1970, p. 2.

22. Although there are fewer blacks in poverty in Peach (37.6%) than there are in the other black belt Georgia counties, almost two-fifths of the black population live in poverty.

23. 15 April 1970, Run-off Results.

24. *Edwards vs Sammons,* "Injunction."

25. *Edwards et al. vs Sammons et al.,* "Ruling, Number 30,061, United States Court of Appeals for the Fifth Circuit," 2 Feb. 1971, p. 9.

26. Ibid; Claybon Edwards (city councilman), Interview, 11 April 1981, Fort Valley, Ga.

27. *Berry et al. vs Doles et al.,* "Request for Admission," Civil Action No. 76, 130-MAC, p. 4.

28. Certificate of Results, 1968 General Elections; 1970 Democratic Primary; and 1970 General Election, Office of the Registrar, City Hall, Fort Valley, Ga.

29. Isaac and Dorothy Crumbly (CASBC members), Interview, 9 April 1981, Fort Valley, Ga.

30. "An Open Letter to Students at Fort Valley State College," *Peach County Enterprise,* 2 Nov. 1972, p. 4.

31. "Voter Registration Drive Elected White in Peach," *Macon Telegraph,* 20 Nov. 1972, p. 6.

32. Crumbly interview.

33. Ibid. Although the city eliminated the primaries after 1964, the county continued to hold them.

34. Ibid., Donnie Bellamy (FVSC professor), Interview, 5 April 1981, Fort Valley, Ga.

35. "Voter Registration Drive Elected Whites in Peach."

36. Ibid.

37. See the Committee on the Judiciary, *Hearings on the Extension of the Voting Rights Act.*

38. "U.S. Challenges Ft. Valley's Run-off," *Macon Telegraph*, 10 July 1973, pp. 1 and 5A; *Wilbur K. Avera vs W. Lee Burr et al.*, Civil Action Number 2832, "Complaint," U.S. District Court, Middle District of Georgia, Macon, Ga., p. 4.

39. Civil Action 76-139, MDC.

40. "Bias Charged at Fort Valley," *Macon Telegraph*, 12 July 1973, p. 2.

41. "Justice Department Suit Unfounded, Mayor Claims," *Macon News*, 10 July 1973, p. 1.

42. Ibid.

43. Crumbly interview.

44. Evelyn McCrary, (CEC president 1980), Interview, 29 May 1981, Fort Valley, Ga.

45. Ibid.

46. Ibid. "Peach County School System Told to Rehire Four Teachers," *Peach County Enterprise*, 14 Feb. 1974, p. 1.

47. Ibid.

48. Ibid.

49. *Avera vs Burge.*

50. Ibid.

51. Donnie Bellamy, "Whites Sue for Desegregation in Georgia: The Fort Valley State Case," *The Journal of Negro History* (Fall 1979), 320.

52. Ibid., 321.

53. Ibid., 322–23.

54. "Fort Valley Not Alone in Racial Imbalance," *Atlanta Constitution*, Opinion Editorial Page, 24 March 1974.

55. Crumbly interview.

56. Ibid.

57. "Candidates Ready for 'Confused' Elections," *Macon Telegraph and News*, 28 March 1974, p. 4.

58. "Fort Valley Won't Appeal Court Ruling," *Macon Telegraph and News*, 26 May 1974, p. 1.

59. "Whites Confront Federal Officials," *Macon Telegraph and News*, 4 April 1974, p. 1.

60. "Paul Reehling's Letter to the Editor," *Peach County Enterprise*, 11 April 1974, p. 4.

61. Certificate of Results, 1974 County Elections, Office of the Registrar, City Hall, Fort Valley, Ga.

62. Bellamy interview.

63. *Berry vs Dole*, Civil Action No. 760-139, MAC, 19 Nov. 1979.

64. "Federal Suit Disrupts Criminal Court in Peach," *Leader-Tribune*, 10 June 1976, p. 1.

65. "Peach Jury Plan Inadequate," *Macon Telegraph*, 27 Aug. 1978, p. 7B.

66. H. W. Berry (FVSC professor of education), Interview, 24 April 1981, Fort Valley, Ga.

67. Lester Salamon, "Modernization in the American South: Mississippi As A Developing Society," (Ph.D. diss., Harvard Univ., 1975), 407–566.

68. For the years '72, '74, '76, and '78, Fort Valley blacks represented 49% of the registered voters. For years '74 and '76, Peach County blacks averaged 57% of the registered voters.

69. For the crucial 1972 election, *Macon Telegraph* calculated a 90% white turnout and a 60% black turnout.

70. Christopher Coates (ACLU attorney), Interview, May 1981, Atlanta, Ga.

71. Bellamy interview.

72. Ibid.

73. Robert Church (city councilman), Interview, 12 April 1981, Fort Valley, Ga.

74. "Carson Joins The Mayor's Race," *Leader-Tribune*, 28 Feb. 1980, p. 1.

75. "Carson Elected Fort Valley's First Black Mayor," *Macon Telegraph*, 3 April 1980, p. 2.

76. Ibid.

77. Ibid.

78. Ibid.

79. "The Mayor Complete's First Year—A Look Back," *Leader-Tribune*, 30 April 1981, p. 3.

80. Ibid.

81. Personal correspondence from Professor Donnie Bellamy to Mayor Rudolph Carson, 1 May 1981. (Copy in author's files; used by permission.)

82. "Mayor-Elect Promise to work for Harmony," *Macon Telegraph*, 9 April 1982, pp. 1A, 10A; "Voter Turnout May Be Heaviest Yet," *Leader-Tribune*, 1 April 1982.

83. *Leader-Tribune*, 1 April 1982, p. 1.

84. "Black Turnout is Crucial," *Macon Courier*, 31 March 1982, p. 1.

85. "Fort Valley Vote Unseats 4 Black Elected Officials," *Macon News,* 8 April 1982, p. 1.

86. List of Voters, 1982 Municipal Elections, Office of the Chief Registrar, City Hall, Fort Valley, Georgia.

87. "Fort Valley Vote Unseats 4 Black Elected Officials."

Chapter Five

1. This point can be validated by checking practically any edition of the *News-Record,* the county paper, from 1900 to 1965.

2. Minutes of the Fort Gaines City Council, 24 May 1954.

3. "KKK Meeting Set for Monday Night," *News-Record,* 15 Nov. 1956, p. 1.

4. "County to Form State's Rights Chapter," *News-Record,* 26 Jan. 1956, p. 4.

5. "Declaration of Constitutional Principles," *News-Record,* 15 March 1956, p. 4. (This document is more commonly known as the Southern Manifesto.)

6. The Official List of Colored Voters, Various Years, 1936–1960. Clay County Voters List; James Clark (Clay County Improvement Association founder), Interview, 5 Feb. 1981, Fort Gaines, Ga.

7. "Chattahoochee Institute," *News-Record,* undated (copy in author's file).

8. "A Greater Chattahoochee Institute is Dawning Upon Fort Gaines and Vicinity," *News-Record* (copy in author's file).

9. Ibid.

10. Brazeal, *Negro Voting.*

11. Clark interview. Some local blacks assert that one of his letters was published in the *Albany Herald.* I could not verify this, however, since a three-year span was given in which the letter could have been published.

12. An "angel system" exists where there is a power group and a group or groups without power; a member of the group without power acts as an informant to a "guardian angel" within the power group. This informant is rewarded with favors by the power group since he provides the information necessary to combat any attempt of the powerless group to gain power.

13. "Lee to Speak in Mississippi on Segregation Text," *News-Record,* 26 Jan. 1958, p. 1.

14. John Smith (CCIA member), Interview, 16 Feb. 1981, Fort Gaines, Ga.

15. "Lee to Speak on Segregation Text."

16. "Lee Case Dropped By Sheriff; No Arrest," *News-Record,* 16 Feb. 1956, p. 1.

17. Ibid.

18. *Census of Population* (1960), Social Characteristics.

19. Clay County's List of Colored Voters, 1960, Office of the Clerk, Clay County Courthouse, Fort Gaines, Ga.

20. Richard Bankston (CCIA member), Interview, 4 Feb. 1981, Fort Gaines, Ga.

21. Clark interview.

22. Ibid.

23. Ibid.

24. Ibid.

25. Ibid.

26. Ibid.

27. Clay County's List of Colored Voters, 1960.

28. Raymond Brown, *A Statistical Comparison: Registration Rates for Georgia By Race 1966–1980* (Atlanta: The Southern Regional Council, 1982), 2.

29. Randy Battle and Joe Pfister (SNCC Southwest Georgia Project workers), Interview, 7 Aug. 1981, Albany, Ga.

30. Ibid.

31. Clark interview.

32. Battle and Pfister interview.

33. Ibid.

34. "Recreation in the Cotton Hill Community," *Southwest Georgia Project Newsletter,* II, no. 9, 1 Aug. 1968, p. 3, col. 2.

35. "The Voter Education Project, Clay County, Georgia," *The People's Voice,"* 5 July 1968, p. 4.

36. Christopher Coates (ACLU attorney), Interview, 10 May 1981, Atlanta, Ga.

37. "ACLU Suit Results in Voting Districts in Clay County, Georgia," ACLU Press Release, 24 June 1980, p. 2.

38. The Voter Education Project, *Voter Registration In The South* (Atlanta: Voter Education Project, 1968).

39. Walter Patmon (Southwest Georgia Project worker), Interview, 10 Feb. 1981, Fort Gaines, Ga.

40. Charles Sherrod (coordinator for SNCC Southwest Georgia Project), Interview, 20 Aug. 1981, Albany, Ga.

41. Lola Fair (Southwest Georgia Project staff worker), Interview, 2 Sept. 1981, Fort Gaines, Ga.

42. "Private School is Being Formed in Clay County," *News-Record,* 20 Feb. 1970, p. 4.

43. Bankston interview.

44. Ibid.

45. James Clark makes this estimate based on 1974 vep figures. Since no registration drives were held prior to the 1976 election, he assumes that the same figures are relatively valid. See *Voter Registration in Georgia, 1974* (Atlanta: Voter Education Project, 1974).

46. Personal correspondence to Joseph A. Sappey, U.S. Department of Justice from George A. Bell, Clay County Attorney, 24 June 1977.

47. Rev. J. S. Standford (ccia president), Interview, 18 Feb. 1981, Fort Gaines, Ga.

48. Ibid.

49. Clark interview.

50. Frank Davenport and J. S. Standford interviews.

51. "ACLU Suit Results in Voting Districts."

52. The Justice Department refers to political jurisdictions as "safe districts" when they are 65% black.

53. "Racial Bloc Voting Keeps Election Results Lily-White," *Atlanta Constitution,* 8 Dec. 1980, p. 13A; and Arnett Richardson (1980 Clay County Commission candidate), Interview, 20 March 1981, Fort Gaines, Ga.

54. Official results of District 2 and District 5 County Commission Returns, 5 Aug. 1980, Office of the Probate Judge, Clay County Courthouse, Fort Gaines, Ga.

55. Official results of the Democratic Primary and Run-off, August 5th and 26th, 1980, Office of the Probate Judge, Clay County Courthouse, Fort Gaines, Ga.

56. "Primary Election Results for Clay County Commissioners Challenged," *ACLU Press Release,* 13 Aug. 1980, p. 2.

57. "Judge Rules Vote Stands," *News-Record,* 2 Oct. 1980, p. 1; "Judge Denies New Election, Orders Clay Voters List Purged," *Albany Herald,* 29 Sept. 1980, p. 2A.

58. Davenport Interview; 1980 List of Purged Voters.

59. "Judge Rules Vote Stands."

60. Relton Fair was appointed to the board of registrars and received pay for serving although he was never informed about the time of meetings and, thus, never attended one. See Personal Correspondence to Richard Matthews from Christopher Coates, 25 April 1980, ACLU Files under Clay County.

61. Clark interview.

62. Ibid.

63. Stanford, Bankston, and Fair interviews.

64. Bankston interview.

65. Clark interview.
66. Eddie Ricks (plaintiff in *NAACP vs Clay County*), Interview, 23 Feb. 1981, Fort Gaines, Ga.
67. Ibid.
68. James Daniels (Clay County teacher), Interview, 12 March 1981, Fort Valley, Ga.
69. Lester Salamon, "Modernization in the American South: Mississippi As a Developing Society," (Ph.D. diss., Harvard Univ., 1972) 407–566.

Chapter Six

1. Brown, *A Statistical Comparison,* 3.
2. Ibid.
3. Election Returns for the City of Fort Valley (1966–1978), Office of the Registrar, City Hall, Fort Valley, Ga.
4. Official Report, The 1982 Election, 5 Aug. 1976, Office of the Registrar, City Hall, Fort Valley, Ga.
5. Brown, *A Statistical Comparison,* 2.
6. Tilly, *From Mobilization To Revolution,* chapter 3.
7. An initial list of leaders' names was obtained from the Voter Education Project. Each person on this list was asked to name other leaders of the community. The names of those individuals mentioned most often appear on the tables.
8. E. R. Warren interview.
9. Robert Ingram, Sr., interview; Donnie Bellamy interview; James Clark interview.
10. Ingram, Sr., interview.
11. Dorothy Crumbly interview.
12. Ibid.
13. Bellamy interview.

Epilogue

1. Paul Stekler, "Black Politics in The New South," (Ph.D. diss., Harvard Univ., 1982), 66.
2. For an analysis based on this perspective see Mack A. Jones, "Black Political Empowerment in Atlanta: Myth and Reality," *Annals* (Sept. 1978), 90–117; Harrell E. Rodgers, Jr., "Civil Rights and The Myth of Popular Sovereignty," *Journal of Black Studies* (Sept. 1981), 51–70; and

William E. Nelson, Jr. and Phillip Meranto, *Electing Black Mayors* (Columbus: Ohio Univ. Press, 1977), ch. 10.

3. Hanes Walton, Jr., *Black Politics* (Philadelphia: J. B. Lippincott, 1972), 196–202.

4. See Leonard A. Cole, *Blacks in Power* (Princeton, N.J.: The Russell Sage Foundation, 1976), 137–154, and James Button, "Southern Black Elected Officials: The Impact of Socioeconomic Change," *The Review of Black Political Economy* (Fall 1982), 29–45.

5. David Coombs et al., "Black Political Control in Greene County," *Rural Sociology* (Summer 1980), 204.

6. Hugh Perry, "The Socioeconomic Impact of Black Political Empowerment in a Rural Southern Locality," *Rural Sociology* (Summer 1980), 215–19.

7. Button, 44.

8. Ibid.

9. Perry, 219–20.

10. Coombs, 404.

11. For good analyses of the constraints and obstacles to effective black leadership see Kenneth S. Colburn, *Southern Black Mayors: Local Problems and Federal Response* (Washington: The Joint Center for Political Studies, 1974); William E. Nelson, Jr., "Black Mayors as Urban Managers," *Annals* (Sept. 1978), 53–57; Herrington J. Byrce, "Problems of Governing American Cities: The Case of Medium and Large Cities With Black Mayors," *Focus* (Aug. 1974), A1; and Herrington Byrce, "Black Mayors of Medium and Large Cities: How Much Statutory Power Do They Have?" *Focus* (Oct. 1974), A8.

12. Perry, 220–21.

Bibliography

Books

Bardolph, Richard. *The Civil Rights Record.* New York: Thomas J. Crowell Company, 1970.

Bennett, Lerone. *Before the Mayflower.* Chicago: Johnson Publishing Company, 1982.

Brisbane, Robert. *Black Activism.* Valley Forge, Penn.: Judson Press, 1974.

Brown, Raymond. *A Statistical Comparison: Registration Rates for Georgia by Race, 1966–1980.* Atlanta: Southern Regional Council, 1982.

————. *The State of Voting Rights in Georgia in 1982.* Atlanta: Southern Regional Council, 1982.

Buckmaster, Henrietta. *Let My People Go.* Boston: Beacon Press, 1941.

Carmichael, Stokely, and Charles V. Hamilton, *Black Power.* New York: Random House, 1966.

Colburn, Kenneth S. *Southern Black Mayors.* Washington: Joint Center for Political Studies, 1974.

Cole, Leonard A. *Blacks in Power.* Princeton, N.J.: Russell Sage Foundation, 1976.

Dahl, Robert. *Democracy in the United States: Promise and Performance.* Chicago: Rand McNally, 1976.

Dittmer, John. *Black Georgia During the Progressive Era 1910–1920.* Urbana: Univ. of Illinois Press, 1977.

Du Bois, W. E. B. *The Souls of Black Folk.* Chicago: A. C. McClurg and Company, 1903.

Dye, Harold, and Harman Zeigler. *The Irony of Democracy.* Monterey, Calif.: Cole Publishing Company, 1984.

Dymnally, Mervyn M. *The Black Politician.* Belmont, Mass.: Duxbury Press, 1971.

Freeman, Jo. *Social Movement of the Sixties and Seventies.* New York: Vintage Books, 1983.

Gamson, William A. *The Strategy of Social Protest*. Homewood, Ill.: Dorsey Press, 1975.

Garrow, David. *Protest At Selma: Martin Luther King, Jr., and the Voting Rights Act of 1965*. New Haven: Yale Univ. Press, 1978.

Goldston, Robert C. *The Negro Revolution*. New York: Macmillan, 1969.

Hamilton, Charles V. *The Bench and the Ballot*. New York: Oxford Univ. Press, 1973.

Hawkins, Hugh, ed. *The Abolitionists: Means, Ends and Motivations*. Lexington, Mass.: D.C. Heath and Company, 1968.

Hodges, Norman. *Black History*. New York: Simon and Schuster, 1974.

Holt, Thomas. *Black Over White*. Urbana: Univ. of Illinois Press, 1977.

Hudlin, Richard A., and King F. Brimah. *Barriers to Effective Participation in Electoral Politics*. Atlanta: The Voter Education Project, 1982.

Lawson, Steve. *Black Ballots*. New York: Columbia Univ. Press, 1976.

———. *In Pursuit of Power: Southern Blacks and Electoral Politics, 1965–1982*. New York: Columbia Univ. Press, 1985.

Locke, John. *Of Civil Government*. New York: Dutton Press, 1943.

Logan, Rayford. *The Negro in American Life and Thought: The Nadir, 1877–1901*. New York: Dial Press, 1954.

Matthews, Donald R., and James W. Protho. *Negroes and the New Southern Politics*. New York: Harcourt, Brace, and World, 1966.

McDonald, Laughlin. *Voting Rights in the South*. Atlanta: Southern Regional Office, 1982.

Milbrath, Lester. *Political Participation*. Washington, D.C.: University Press of America, 1977.

Oates, Stephen. *Let the Trumpet Sound: The Life of Martin Luther King, Jr.* New York: Harper and Row, 1982.

Olson, Mancur. *The Logic of Collective Action*. New York: Cambridge Univ. Press, 1975.

Piven, Frances Fox, and Richard Cloward. *Poor People's Movements*. New York: Vintage Books, 1979.

Preston, Michael B. *The New Black Politics*. New York: Longman, 1982.

Rozier, John. *Black Boss*. Athens: Univ. of Georgia Press, 1982.

Sherman, Brian. *Half a Foot in the Door*. Atlanta: Direct Research Service, 1982.

Thornborough, E. L., ed. *Black Reconstructionists*. Englewood Cliffs, N.J.: Prentice-Hall, 1972.

Tilly, Charles. *From Mobilization to Revolution*. Reading, Mass.: Addison-Wesley Publishing Company, 1978.

Verba, Sidney, and Norman Nie. *Participation in America*. New York: Harper and Row, 1972.

The Voter Education Project. *A Brief History of the Voter Education Project*. Atlanta: Voter Education Project, 1979.

Walton, Hanes Jr. *Black Politics*. Philadelphia: J. B. Lippincott, 1972.
Washington, Booker T. *Up from Slavery*. Garden City, N.Y.: Doubleday, 1949.
Watters, Pat, and Reese Cleghorn. *Climbing Jacob's Ladder*. New York: Harcourt, Brace, and World, 1967.
Wilhoit, Francis. *The Politics of Massive Resistance*. New York: George Braziller, 1973.
Wolfinger, Raymond, and Steven Rosentone. *Who Votes*. New Haven: Yale Univ. Press, 1980.
Woll, Peter, ed. *American Government: Readings and Cases*. Boston: Little, Brown and Company, 1978.

Journal Articles

Abney, F. Glenn. "Factors Related to Negro Voter Turnout in Mississippi." *Journal of Politics* (Nov. 1974), 1057–63.
Cole, Leonard. "Electing Blacks to Municipal Office: Structural and Social Determinants." *Urban Affairs Quarterly* (Sept. 1974), 17–39.
Danigelis, Nicholas. "A Theory of Black Political Participation in the United States." *Social Forces* (Sept. 1977), 31–47.
Garrow, David. "Black Voting in South Carolina, 1970–1976." *Review of Black Political Economy* 10 (Fall 1978), 60–78.
Jones, Clinton. "The Impact of Local Election Systems on Black Political Representation." *Urban Affairs Quarterly* (March 1976), 345–56.
Karnig, Albert, "Black Representation on City Councils: The Impact of District Elections and Socioeconomic Factors." *Urban Affairs Quarterly* (Dec. 1976), 223–42.
King, Martin Luther, Jr. "Civil Right No. 1—The Right to Vote." *New York Times Magazine* (14 March 1965), 26–27, 94–95.
Lipsky, Michael. "Protest as a Political Resource." *American Political Science Review* (Dec. 1968), 1144–58.
Lomax, Louis. "The Kennedys Move in on Dixie." *Harper's Magazine* (May 1962), 27–33.
MacManus, Susan. "City Council Election Procedures and Minority Representation." *Social Science Quarterly* (June 1978), 153–61.
Range, Peter. "Black Boss." *Esquire* (Jan. 1973), 26.
Robinson, Theodore, and Thomas Dye. "Reformism and Black Representation on City Councils." *Social Science Quarterly* (June 1978).
Salamon, Lester, and Stephen Van Evera. "Fear, Apathy, and Discrimination: A Test of Three Explanations of Political Participation." *American Political Science Review* (Dec. 1973), 1288–1306.

Sloan, Lee. "'Good Government' and the Politics of Race." *Social Problems* (Fall 1969), 161–75.

Taebel, Delbert. "Minority Representation on City Councils: The Impact of Structure on Blacks and Hispanics." *Social Science Quarterly* (June 1978), 142–61.

Thernstrom, Abigail. "The Odd Evolution of the Voting Rights Act." *Public Interest* (Spring 1979), 49–76.

Wright, Gerald. "Black Voting Turnout and Education in the 1968 Presidential Election." *Journal of Politics* (Nov. 1974), 563–68.

Newspaper Articles

"ACLU Suit Results in Voting Districts in Clay County, Georgia." ACLU Press Release, 24 June 1980.

Auchmutey, Jim. "The Struggle in Hancock." *Atlanta Constitution*, 18 Sept. 1983.

Berry, Jerry. "Poverty Group's Tax Troubles." *Atlanta Constitution*, 9 May 1977.

"Bias Charged at Fort Valley." *Macon Telegraph*, 12 July 1973.

"Black Turnout Is Crucial." *Macon Courier*, 31 March 1982.

"Candidates Ready for 'Confused' Election." *Macon Telegraph and News*, 28 March 1979.

"Carson Elected Fort Valley's First Black Mayor." *Leader-Tribune*, 3 April 1980.

"Carson Joins the Mayor's Race." *Leader-Tribune*, 28 Feb. 1980.

"Chattahoochee Institute." *News-Record*, undated.

"County to Form State's Rights Chapter January 26." *News-Record*, 15 March 1956.

"Declaration of Constitutional Principles." *News-Record*, 15 March 1956.

"ECCO: An Experimental Empire." *Macon Telegraph*, 11 July 1974.

"Federal Suit Disrupts Criminal Court in Peach." *Leader-Tribune*, 10 June 1976.

Fort, Bob. "OEO Hancock Audit Shows Errors: Says Nunn." *Atlanta Journal and Constitution*, 24 March 1974.

"Fort Valley Vote Unseats 4 Black Elected Officials." *Macon News*, 8 April 1982.

"Fort Valley Won't Appeal Court Ruling." *Macon Telegraph and News*, 26 May 1974.

"A Greater Chattahoochee Institute Is Dawning Upon Fort Gaines and Vicinity." *News-Record*, undated.

Gailey, Phil. "Blacks in Hancock to Build Town with $7 Million in Grant." *Atlanta Constitution*, 27 Jan. 1972.

———. "Blacks, Whites Work Together." *Atlanta Constitution*, 4 Jan. 1970.

———. "Hancock Gun Race Is Ended." *Atlanta Constitution*, 2 Oct. 1972.

———. "New Town Planners Say Publicity Has Hurt." *Atlanta Constitution*, 1 Feb. 1972.

———. "Race-Troubled Sparta Facing a School Crisis." *Atlanta Constitution*, 9 Sept. 1970.

———. "Strong Winds of Change Blow in Hancock." *Atlanta Constitution*, 18 Sept. 1969.

"Hancock Hospital Near Financial Collapse." *Macon Telegraph*, 6 Dec. 1974.

Herbers, John. "Dr. King and 770 Others Seized in Alabama Protests." *New York Times*, 2 Feb. 1965.

Johnson, Thomas A. "Blacks in Georgia Let Minority Share Power." *New York Times*, 8 Sept. 1971.

"Judge Denies New Election, Orders Clay's Voters List Purged." *Albany Herald*, 29 Sept. 1980.

"Judge Rules Vote Stands." *News-Record*, 2 Oct. 1980.

"Justice Department Suit Unfounded, Mayor Claims." *Macon News*, 10 July 1973.

"KKK Meeting Set for Monday Night." *News-Record*, 15 Nov. 1956.

"Lee Case Dropped by Sheriff; No Arrest." *News-Record*, 16 Feb. 1956.

"Lee to Speak in Mississippi on Segregation Text." *News-Record*, 26 Jan. 1958.

"The Mayor Completes First Year—A Look Back." *Leader-Tribune*, 20 April 1981

Montgomery, Bill. "Guilty Pleas End Legacy of McCown-Run Hancock." *Atlanta Constitution*, 31 Jan. 1974.

"Negro Doctor Quits Area Rather Than Go to Jail." *New York Times*, 27 March 1958.

"Negro Qualifies to Run for Council Post in Fort Valley." *Leader-Tribune*, 6 Feb. 1964.

"Negroes Take Over in Hancock Voting." *Atlanta Constitution*, 8 Nov. 1968, p. 1.

Nesmith, Jeff. "Nightclub Getting Hancock Poverty Funds?" *Atlanta Constitution*, 18 April 1974.

———. "OEO Audit Pressed For in Hancock." *Atlanta Constitution*, 22 Sept. 1968.

———. "OEO to Pay County Chiefs in Hancock?" *Atlanta Constitution*, 10 April 1974.

Norton, David, "Hancock Resigned to Negro Leadership." *Atlanta Constitution*, 22 Sept. 1968.

"Old John's A Bad Nigger." *People's Crusader*, 24 May 1974.

"An Open Letter to Students at Fort Valley State College." *Peach County Enterprise*, 2 Nov. 1972.

"Paul Reehling's Letter to the Editors." *Peach County Enterprise*, 11 April 1974.

"Peach Jury Plan Inadequate." *Macon Telegraph*, 27 Aug. 1978.

"Primary Election Results for Clay Commissioners Challenged." ACLU Press Release, 13 Aug. 1980.

"Private School Is Being Formed in Clay County." *News-Record*, 26 Feb. 1970.

"Racial Bloc Voting Keeps Election Results Lily-White." *Atlanta Constitution*, 8 Dec. 1980.

Rankin, Jim, and Jeff Nesmith. "McCown Empire Prospers But Hancock Stays Poor." *Atlanta Constitution*, 30 June 1974.

Rankin, Jim, and Jeff Nesmith. "McCown Left Council Reeling." *Atlanta Constitution*, 4 July 1974.

"Recreation in the Cotton Hill Community." *Southwest Georgia Project Newsletter*, 1 Aug. 1968.

Schneider, Keith. "An Arch of Misery." *Boston Globe*, 18 Sept. 1983.

"U.S. Officials Hail Election of Negroes." *Atlanta Constitution*, 12 Nov. 1966.

"The Voter Education Project, Clay County Georgia." *People's Voice*, 5 July 1968.

"Voter Registration Drive Elected Whites in Peach." *Macon Telegraph*, 20 Nov. 1972.

"Voter Turnout May Be Heaviest Yet." *Leader-Tribune*, 1 April 1982.

"Whites Confront Federal Officials." *Macon Telegraph and News*, 4 April 1974.

Unpublished Papers

Brazeal, Bailsford R. "Studies of Negroes Voting in Eight Georgia Counties and One of South Carolina." Unpublished study for the Southern Regional Council, 1960.

Carlson, James. "Black Political Participation in The South: An Examination of Contextual Effects." Ph.D. diss., Kent State Univ., 1976.

Salamon, Lester. "Modernization in the American South: Mississippi as a Developing Society." Ph.D. diss., Harvard Univ., 1971.

Stekler, Paul. "Black Politics in the New South: An Investigation of Change at Various Levels." Ph.D. diss., Harvard Univ., 1982.

Public Documents

Department of Commerce, Bureau of the Census. *U.S. Census of Population* (1960), Vol. I, Part 12, Georgia.

——. *U.S. Census of Population* (1970), Vol. I, Part 12, Georgia.

Election Returns for Clay County, Georgia, 1960–1982. Office of the Probate Judge, Clay County, Georgia.

Election Returns for Fort Valley, Georgia, 1960–1982. City Hall, Fort Valley, Georgia.

Election Returns for Peach County, Georgia, 1960–1982. Office of the Registrar, Peach County Courthouse, Fort Valley, Georgia.

Election Returns for Hancock County, Georgia, 1960–1982. Office of the Probate Judge, Hancock County, Georgia.

The U.S. Commission on Civil Rights. *The Voting Rights Act–Unfulfilled Goals.* Washington, D.C.: 1981.

The Committee on the Judiciary. *Hearings on the Extension of the Voting Rights Act.* Washington, D.C.: 1981.

Interviews

Banks, W. S. M. II, first black candidate in Peach County, Fort Valley, Ga., 10 April 1981.

Bankston, Richard, CCIA member, Fort Gaines, Ga., 4 Feb. 1981.

Battle, Randy, and Joe Pfister, SNCC Southwest Georgia Project workers, Albany, Ga., 8 Aug. 1981.

Bellamy, Donnie, FVSC professor, Fort Valley, Ga., 5 April 1981.

Berry, H. W., FVSC professor, Fort Valley, Ga., 24 April 1981.

Carson, Rudolph, mayor, Fort Valley, Ga., 12 April 1981.

Church, Robert, city councilman, Fort Valley, Ga., 12 April 1981.

Clark, James, CCIA founder, Fort Gaines, Ga., 5 Feb. 1981.

Coates, Christopher, ACLU attorney, Atlanta, Ga., May 1981.

Crumbly, Dorothy, CASBC member, Fort Valley, Ga., 9 April 1981.

Crumbly, Isaac, CASBC member, Fort Valley, Ga., 9 April 1981.

Daniels, James, Clay County schoolteacher, Fort Valley, Ga., 12 March 1981.

Edwards, Claybon, city councilman, Fort Valley, Ga., 11 April 1981.

Fair, Lola, Southwest Georgia Project staff worker, Fort Gaines, Ga., 3 Sept. 1981.

Ingram, Edith, probate judge, Hancock County, Ga., 10 Dec. 1980.

Ingram, Kathryn, former ECCO worker, Hancock County, Ga., 14 Dec. 1980.

Ingram, Robert, Sr., HCDC founder and first black school board member, Hancock County, Ga., 14 Dec. 1980.

Ingram, Robert, Jr., former ECCO worker, Hancock County, Ga., 12 Dec. 1980.

Kendrick, Mamie, Southwest Georgia Project, Fort Gaines, Ga., 1 Feb. 1981.

McCown, Ann, widow of John McCown, Hancock County, Ga., 15 Dec. 1980.

McCrary, Evelyn, CEC president (1980), Fort Valley, Ga., 29 May 1981.

Nelson, Getrena, former Hancock County schoolteacher, Hancock County, Ga., 10 Dec. 1980.

Patmon, Walter, Southwest Georgia Project worker, Fort Gaines, Ga., 10 Feb. 1981.

Richardson, Arnett, county commission candidate (1980), Fort Gaines, Ga., 20 March 1981.

Ricks, Eddie, plaintiff in *NAACP vs Clay County*, Fort Gaines, Ga., 23 Feb. 1981.

Sherrod, Charles, coordinator of the SNCC Southwest Georgia Project, Albany, Ga., 20 Aug. 1981.

Smith, John, CCIA member, Fort Gaines, Ga., 16 Feb. 1981.

Standford, J. S., Rev., CCIA president, Fort Gaines, Ga., 19 Feb. 1981.

Warren, E. R., HCDC founder and high school principal, Hancock County, Ga., 17 Dec. 1980.

Warren, Johnny, HCDC activist, Hancock County, Ga., 12 Dec. 1980.

Warren, Sam, tax commissioner, Hancock County, Ga., 13 Dec. 1980.

Wiley, Leroy, clerk of Superior Court, Hancock County, Ga., 12 Dec. 1980.

Court Cases

Avera vs Burr (1972), Middle District of Georgia, Civil Action #2832.

Berry vs Cooper (1978), U.S. Circuit Court of Appeals, Civil Action #76.3862.

Berry vs Dole (1970), Middle District Court of Georgia, Civil Action #2542.

Marshal vs Sammons (1970), Middle District Court of Georgia, Civil Action #2542.

Index